I0427090

ANEMIA

By

B. A. Floyd

This book is a work of fiction. Places, events, and situations in this story are purely fictional. Any resemblance to actual persons, living or dead, is coincidental.

© 2002 by B. A. Floyd. All rights reserved.

No part of this book may be reproduced, stored in a retrieval system, or transmitted by any means, electronic, mechanical, photocopying, recording, or otherwise, without written permission from the author.

ISBN: 1-4033-6084-7 (e-book)
ISBN: 1-4033-6085-5 (Paperback)
ISBN: 1-4033-6086-3 (Rocket Book)

This book is printed on acid free paper.

1st Books - rev. 08/29/02

Chapter One

As Dr. Bishop made the long drive to their country retreat, he felt somewhat relieved. Just the smell of the air made him feel alive. It would be a new start for the whole family. "Why didn't I do this sooner?" he thought as the road curved gently ahead of him. The vivid colors of the trees and the blue sky were a masterpiece that only God could paint. Everything was so peaceful and calm. He glanced at his sleeping wife and child. In his heart he knew he had made the right decision. Mary had retired early from her teaching position to spend more time with their son Troy, who was suffering with sickle cell anemia. Like most kids his age, he had more energy than his battling system could handle. In the rear view mirror, Ben could see Troy still holding his toy space shuttle. After a school field trip to the space museum all Troy thought about was astronomy and becoming an astronaut.

Ben couldn't stop the feeling of nostalgia as he slowly drove through the small town where he grew to manhood. He passed his old high school where he first met Mary when she was just a shy newcomer. He remembered how hard she had tried to fit in with the rest of the kids. How times change! He chuckled as he thought of the outspoken, confident woman she had become. As he passed the church his family had attended, he was suddenly struck by the thought that he would need all that faith and conviction to continue his research and find a real cure for the strange plague that was sweeping the population. In his heart, he also hoped he could find a way to save his son. Ben sent up a silent plea that it would be so. Time was short for Troy now.

Ben reached the edge of town and stopped at the gas station where the attendant, Horace, warmly greeted him. "If this don't beat all, Ben and Mary Bishop, how you folks doin'? How long has it been Doc? And this little tadpole gotta be junior!" Troy waved hello and climbed out of the jeep to join his parents as they began to stretch after the long drive. Ben grabbed Troy in an affectionate bear hug, lifting him effortlessly off the ground. "Horace, this is Troy. Say hello to Mr. Horace, son." Troy took Horace's big outstretched hand in his and dutifully said, "Pleased to meet you, sir." A huge smile covered Horace's face as he rubbed the top of Troy's head and remarked to Mary about the fine job she had done raising her son. Mary blushed at the easy praise and felt how good it was to be home where people liked to tell you when you have done well. She reached into her dress pocket and pulled out some coins for Troy. "Son, go inside and see if they have your favorite soda." Troy dashed off to the small country store and the treasures such places always hold for a young boy with a big imagination. Horace cleared his throat and said "Now Ben, I didn't want to say anythang in front of the boy, but ya'll just be careful up there. There's been some strange tales about eerie blue lights at night, weird sounds, and animals actin' peculiar. Now you didn't hear this from me, but there's also some feds snoopin' around up there lookin' for aliens!" Ben and Mary looked at Horace in disbelief and then at one another as if to ask, "Do you believe this?" Troy came bounding out of the store before either could get a word out. "Sweetheart," Mary said as she nudged Ben with an elbow, "we still have a ways to go." She opened the door for Troy, who was struggling with his drink and the door at the same time. He managed a quick swallow of his soda while Mary opened the door for him. Excitedly waving, he shouted "Bye Mr. Horace! Can I come back soon and see the rest of your stuff and talk about the aliens?" Horace turned red-faced as he stammered back to Troy, "Sure thang tadpole!" Ben watched Horace as he lifted a tire from the rack and started to roll it back to the garage. "Now how do you suppose that boy heard about aliens?" Ben asked. Horace huffed as he began rolling the tire, "Musta been that dang Billy, he's a good kid but I'll be durned if he can keep his trap shut for more than five minutes at a time!" Ben laughed and patted Horace's back. "Don't worry old man, Troy already has outer space on the brain, now he has one more reason to be excited about our new home." Ben reached for his wallet and was about to hand Horace a credit card when the old man shook his head and told Ben, "Don't worry about payin' me now, I don't take them durn thangs no how. I'll just put it on your tab, okay?" Ben smiled feeling again how wonderful it was to trust your neighbor. "Well thanks Horace, I'll be back down tomorrow for supplies." As Ben closed the driver side door, Horace called out "Ya'll be real careful and stay out them woods after dark!" Troy pulled himself up by the back of his mother's seat to get closer as his dad pulled onto the highway. "Mom, what's a tadpole?" Mary turned to her son, smiling "Ask your dad, sweetie." Troy smiled in agreement. "Hey Pop!" Ben laughed and poked at Mary's ribs as he began explaining the life cycle of the frog.

The rest of the drive home was relaxing. Mary had nodded off again and Troy started a new round of twenty questions, this time about every cow, horse, and pond they passed. He finally gave in to the Sandman, but only after Ben had promised to set up his telescope when they got home. As far as Ben was concerned, all he needed now was one of his world-famous oldies but goodies tapes as he cruised down the sun-dappled road. "I've got just the one!" he thought to himself as he slid the tape from his personal collection. "Heatwave," he bragged, "now we can do this!" The music filled the jeep and Ben growled out "Always and forever". Mary opened her eyes and looked up at him. She rested her head on his shoulder, smiling. Ben reached over and turned down the volume, "Sorry I woke you honey. I guess you're thinking I should have taken that Motown contract. I see you smiling, am I right?" Mary lifted one brow and in her sexiest voice told Ben, "Baby, I was thinking how glad I am that you kept your day job and turned Motown down flat!" Ben bellowed in disbelief, "Oh, keep the day job, huh? Let me pull over and tell you something!" He laughed the laugh that meant Mary was in for more than teasing as he carefully brought the jeep to a halt at a turnout along the road. Mary softly kissed him on the cheek, caressing his face as if she really meant it, "Baby, I'm sorry." They embraced and their laughter filled the air. The view across the green meadow was soothing as waves of daisies swayed with the breeze. In the distance, they could see their home completing the backdrop of the lush valley. A small, sleepy voice broke the spell. "Are we there yet?"

As the Bishops approached the house, Mary sighed in satisfaction that the trip was over. Ben stopped the jeep in front of the porch and looked around, lost in the beauty that surrounded them. They slowly began opening their doors and stepping out into the evening sunlight. Mary walked around to Ben's side and took his hand in hers. No words could express what she was feeling, but it showed in her eyes as she looked lovingly at the man who would help her through the ordeal ahead. For a moment she was taken back to the time when they were told of Troy's condition and how devastated they were. Afraid to have more children and blaming herself, she had the hardest time coping with the situation. Ben had given her his quiet strength and made her believe that everything would turn out right for their little family. She hoped they could pull a rabbit out of the hat now. The sound of laughter brought Mary back to the present and she smiled at her son's abandon as he ran around the porch exploring their new home. She laughed as she caught Troy in her arms and hugged him tight. She heard his little tummy rumble and let him go. She looked at her two favorite guys and said, "If you boys want some dinner, I suggest you get busy with the luggage." Ben looked at Troy with a twinkle in his eye, "You heard your mother, son. We better get started if we want to eat." Mary grabbed some smaller bags from the front and went inside. Troy and Ben began pulling the heavy bags from the back. Little Troy struggled with the luggage as if to prove he was becoming a big strong man like his dad. Ben smiled at his son's effort, but the pain in his eyes betrayed him. Watching Troy tire so easily reminded him of the fragility of his boy. He carried the rest of the luggage inside and swooped Troy off the porch where he was sitting and catching his breath. He tossed Troy into the air as only a father can. "That's my little man," he praised as he held Troy in a big bear hug. "How about we go set up that telescope, son?" Troy scrambled out of Ben's arms, excited about the idea. "Come on dad!" he shouted and ran inside. Ben followed shaking his head, amazed by the recuperative powers of children.

Troy was already at the stairs with his telescope case when Ben came inside. Ben sent Troy upstairs as he grabbed the case and followed. Mary called to them when she heard their footsteps on the stairs, "Dinner will be ready in about fifteen minutes." Ben and Troy both shouted "Alright!" as they continued their climb. In Troy's room, Ben began setting up the telescope as Troy looked out the window at the woods behind the house. "I'm gonna have so much fun here, dad." Ben smiled as he heard the joy in his son's voice. "You sure are sport, I spent most of my time in these woods as a boy and it was the most fun I ever had." Troy sighed as Ben brought the telescope over to the center window and sat it down. "Dad, will I ever be able to explore space?" Ben hugged his son to his chest as his eyes misted over, he struggled to clear his throat, "Son, one day you will be the best astronaut in the world." Troy broke free from his dad and began focusing his telescope, knowing in his heart that his dad was right. Someday he would reach the stars, no matter what his disease wanted.

The smell of dinner wafted upstairs and Mary called out "Dinner is served!" Ben lifted Troy into flight position, "Let's get your medication and wash up, ok sport?" and flew him into the bathroom. Troy started to imitate his dad as they washed their hands and then followed him down to the dining room. Mary had everything ready and the boys dug right in. Troy even ate all of his vegetables. Holding his empty plate, Troy pleaded, "Mom can I have some dessert now?" Mary smiled and put a slice of warm apple pie on Troy's plate, "Would you like some vanilla ice cream too?" she asked. "Uh-huh!" Troy answered with his eyes shining. Ben laughed and said "Son, this place seems to have improved your appetite already, but are you sure you can handle all that after everything you've already eaten?" Troy laughed and went to work on his mom's great homemade apple pie. After a few bites of the pie and ice cream, the look on Troy's face sent Ben and Mary into a round of laughter. Troy smiled and said, "What's so funny you guys?" This brought even more waves of laughter from his parents. "Oh honey, we're just so happy to see you enjoying your dessert!" Mary chuckled to Troy, wiping the tears from her eyes. "But now it's time to go upstairs and wash up for bed." "But maaaa," Troy started to whine. "Son, it's been a long day and you need to call it a night." Ben said. "But Dad, I wanted to use my telescope tonight." "Troy there is plenty of time for that tomorrow night and all the nights ahead, we're going to be here all summer." Mary put her hands on her hips and gave Troy her patented "try-me" look. Ben looked at Troy and said, "Son, you heard your mother, you best get going." "You better give your mama her goodnight kiss before you really get in trouble," Mary smiled and said to her son. Troy, pouting and knowing there's no getting mom to change her mind, went over and barely kissed Mary on the cheek. "Now I know you can do better than that." Mary said as she took Troy's face in her hands and kissed his little cheeks on both sides, as mothers love to do. "Ah maaa..." Troy moaned trying to wipe off her kisses, as sons will sometimes do. "You two!" Ben laughed "Honey, if Troy doesn't want those kisses I will be glad to take them for him." He looked at Mary and raised his eyebrows in that signal she recognized all too well. Ben wanted some loving too. "I'm outta here, you guys are gonna get mushy!" Troy giggled and ran upstairs. Mary began to collect the dishes from the table. Ben rose, kissing her on the cheek and remarking about the meal, "Honey, that was wonderful, can I help with anything?" "No, I think I can handle it. Go ahead and relax, with all of the driving you did today you must be exhausted. Besides, I have a little surprise for you." She winked before going back into the kitchen. Ben smiled as he got his pipe from over the fireplace and walked out onto the front porch. As he lit his pipe, Ben could see the sun setting in the purple horizon. The screen door squeaked as Mary came out with two filled wine glasses and handed him one. "It's beautiful out here," she whispered. Gently placing his arm around her waist, Ben tapped his glass to Mary's and toasted to a long and wonderful life together. Their eyes met as they embraced, knowing in their hearts this might be the last time they would have with their son. Just then Troy burst between the two of them, pointing to the edge of the woods surrounding their home. He whispered, "Look, Mom and Dad, it's a family of deer, just like us! See the baby deer! Mom, see it, see it!" They both looked down at their small intruder and were delighted by his excitement. The deer soon left the clearing. Mary gave Troy the "you're not off the hook" look saying, "Young man, I thought you were supposed to be in bed." Thinking fast Troy said, "I forgot to say good night to dad." Easing closer to his dad, he searched his eyes for support. Ben knelt with outstretched arms as he hugged his son. He whispered, "Good night tiger. You better get upstairs now, before we're both in hot water," as he playfully swatted Troy off to bed. Troy ran back upstairs and hopped onto his bed and bounced off the other side to his telescope. He hoped to see the aliens he overheard Mr. Horace talking about at the gas station. He just knew if he could find them they would take him on great adventures beyond the stars. As Troy adjusted his telescope, an owl flew into his line of vision with a spooky, "whoo, whoo!" Startled, Troy fell backwards over his suitcase and landed with a loud thump. Mary's radar picked up the noise and she yelled up to her son, "Troy Donovan Bishop! Get your little butt in bed and leave that telescope alone!" As Troy scrambled to get into bed he wondered how she knew what he was doing. Through his window he could see the bright stars in the sky and started to count them as he drifted to sleep.

Downstairs Ben and Mary stood silently in the bright moonlight. Ben remembered the surprise she had spoken of earlier and asked, "Am I still going to get the surprise you promised?" Mary took his empty glass and said, "Why don't you get the fireplace lit and I'll be right back," blowing him a kiss as she left. Ben rushed in behind her and lit the fireplace. He looked around and saw what he needed. He grabbed some pillows off the couch and arranged them neatly by the fire. Still not content, he walked over to the stereo and dusted off an old Spinners LP. He grinned, "The icing on the cake!" Soon the room was filled with his other favorite song, "It takes a fool." Suddenly the lights went out. He turned to see Mary by the fireplace in a sheer nightgown. "Surprise!" Ben gazed in amazement as the light of the fire revealed Mary's lovely figure. As he slowly moved closer he took her in his arms, kissing her passionately, caressing her ever so gently to absorb the soft warmth of her body. The music seemed to take control as they slowly began to dance. Ben looked deep into his wife's eyes as they indulged in this bliss with one another. Mary smiled saying, "Seems like you still have that magic touch." Ben could only stare at the woman that was the love of his life. His thoughts drifted like pages of a book flashing back to their younger days; the walks in the park, his proposal and the birth of their son. God, how he loved her! He finally said "Darling, I just want you to know how much I love you. All these years I've let my work consume me and you alone carried the burden of caring for Troy. I know I can't turn back time; I just want us to be a family again." Mary smiled as a tear rolled down her cheek. She softly touched Ben's lips with her fingers. "Shhh, I couldn't ask for a more wonderful husband and father, so don't you go blaming yourself for anything. Now for your real surprise!" she whispered kissing him as she pulled him down with her to the pillows.

Chapter Two

The warm breeze of the summer night blew through the curtains in Troy's window. Suddenly a brilliant light followed by a high-pitched sound of rushing air awakened Troy. He struggled out of bed and over to his window in time to see a jubilation of lights circling over the forest. Troy was overcome with wonder and curiosity. He grabbed his shoes and headed quietly downstairs to sneak past his snuggling parents. He silently slipped out the back door into the night air and dashed into the forest. As Troy rambled deeper into the forest he saw a faint glow in the distance. To his amazement the animals of the forest were headed towards the glow as well. Soon Troy came to the place where a strange craft had settled in a clearing on the forest floor. He was immediately drawn to the gathering of woodland creatures, the spacecraft, and the beings emerging from within. The sight held Troy spellbound. Magnificent beings were regally descending from the craft. Troy's mouth dropped open as he looked upon their countenance. They seemed to be of African descent just as he was, but their blackness was deeper than Troy had ever seen. Their skin was so rich and warm, as if lit from inside with a glow rivaled only by the stars in the night sky. It was clear to Troy that they had been here before. The animals seemed totally relaxed and even playful in their presence. As the beings moved about, Troy realized that they did not walk so much as they floated. It seemed as though they called the very air beneath their feet to carry them wherever they wished. Troy heard a young voice from within the spacecraft calling to one of the beings that was clearly the "leader" of this group. The voice was so melodic and full of pure light that Troy couldn't imagine that there was ever any pain or suffering endured by its owner. His galloping heart seemed to stop for an eternity as she skipped lightly from the craft into the clearing and embraced the young deer that only a few hours ago was in front of Troy's house. As the beings turned to watch the young girl with her deer, Troy could see the faces of each one. These were his people. He knew that they were different, but his heart and soul told him that he was a part of their wondrous lineage. A wonderful peace enveloped him as the warmth of belonging and identity seeped into his young mind. He knew without a doubt he would be safe in their midst and even welcome. Time had stopped for Troy as he observed the activity in the clearing. The adults were collecting samples of the local flora and recording data into handheld instruments. The girl floated to the being that must be her mother and began to discuss the findings from this mission. Even though she was still very young, it was apparent to all that she would assume her mother's position once she was grown. Troy's gaze was drawn to the small figure again and again. He was confused by the feelings he had for the young visitor. If only he could speak to her or see her more clearly. The girl's spell over Troy was broken as the cruel snap of a poacher's snare echoed throughout the clearing. Troy could see the small deer struggling in pain against the trap and quickly losing the fight. As the deer fell to the ground, Troy forgot himself and rushed to the small animal that was panting its last breath. Startled animals bolted from the clearing as Troy struggled to free the frightened and bleeding animal from its pain. All of a sudden Troy heard a voice in his mind telling the small shocked animal, "I am here little one, my Zoë, there will be no more pain." Troy slowly turned. He recognized those beautiful gossamer tones as the girl's sweet voice. She was so close to him he could feel the energy radiating all around her. A life force as old as time itself was at work here in the close moonlit darkness. Troy, overtaken with the beauty and surreal quality of the girl, fell back away from the deer. The glow from her ebon skin enfolded Troy in a waking dream.

The others had silently levitated around the girl and he heard the name "Zenani" in his mind as her mother called her. She had given Zenani permission to save the young animal. Troy watched as she bent toward the tiny deer. He saw her reach out her hand. The velvet darkness of her skin and the gentle touch of her hand as she caressed the dying animal struck Troy in his heart. Never had he experienced this bond with another, especially a girl. He could feel her sadness and the depth of her love for the deer. As Zenani lifted her head, Troy saw that she was crying for her friend. Her tears were clear crystal blue just like the light now coming from both of her small hands. His eyes were riveted to her face and the blue tears coursing freely down her soft cheeks. In the small space of a second her eyes fluttered open and the long lush lashes parted to reveal the most unusually wondrous eyes. They were pure black in the irises and the pupil was surrounded by a paler black instead of white like human eyes. In these eyes Troy saw all the wonders of the universe and the certain cycle of time unending. She placed her small palms together as if in prayer. A warmth washed over Troy that calmed all his fears. As she parted her hands he could see a small star in her left palm. It pulsed with every beat of her heart and grew ever brighter until the small deer was bathed in a circle of blue light. Zenani placed her left hand upon the dying deer's chest and a pure blinding surge of light pierced the night mist. A faint "thump-thump" was heard that grew stronger as she gently stroked the animal's neck. The small deer opened its eyes and looked at Zenani as if to say "thank you". Suddenly Zenani's head jolted back and the baby deer rose as if taking its first steps. It then stumbled to its waiting parents at the woods edge. The glow that had surrounded Zenani began to fade. Though still kneeling, her body had never actually touched the ground. Her head slowly came forward and Troy was in the presence of a true princess. The sheer beauty and life force surrounding her was simply overwhelming. In the distance Troy saw the other beings floating serenely around Zenani for the first time since the whole miracle had occurred. He hadn't realized they had been there all along, so taken by Zenani and her powers that all around him had paled in comparison. The spectacle of the others and the enormity of what he had just witnessed finally hit Troy like a hard blow to the stomach and his body responded in an adrenaline rush to escape. In his fear and confusion he ran straight into Kasha, the being he had correctly assumed was Zenani's mother when he had first seen them together. He was transformed by the contact with Kasha's strange flowing outer garment. His vision was changed and he was traveling through the brief past of his young life. His birth, the love in his parents eyes as they held him for the first time, his illness and the recurring hospitalizations. The pain and suffering he had endured and the grim reality that he would never be free of this disease that held him fast in its cruel embrace. The good times were there too. The loving parents who had given up their dreams and goals to spend time with him, this wonderful, magical forest and the meeting with Zenani. Troy was in a time warp of some sort but still he knew where he was and that the beings, including Zenani, had surrounded him and enclosed him in their healing blue light. He overheard their conversation in his mind as his past replayed before his closed eyes. Kasha felt all that he had experienced in his young life and her heart was moved that one as young as her daughter had been made to suffer so. In her world children were spared the pain and suffering that could stunt their spiritual and psychic abilities until these natural gifts were fully cultivated. This was how it must have been for the Ancient Ones who had come before and escaped this planet during the first plague. Her deep respect and devotion for the elders was greatly increased as she realized the total devastation they had endured to save their progeny and ensure survival. Troy heard Kasha speak. "This young one must be healed, his blood is rich with the gift but it also makes him ill." He felt a small hand in his and realized Zenani had touched him. He sensed their souls joining. Troy was suffused with a peace beyond understanding as Zenani searched his soul. "Mother, he has suffered far more than any child could endure." Zenani's voice was trembling with emotion as she released Troy's hand. "I know my child. There are many of our kind still here on this planet that share the gift. For some reason it makes them weaker instead of giving them the gifts that we are blessed with. We must report to your father, Balimar, that the unspoken ones exist and are suffering for their birthright." "But mother he will die soon, I felt it." Zenani cried as sparkling blue tears streamed down her cheeks once more this night. At the mention of Balimar's name, Troy was struck with a new vision. A man, large and regally clothed in flowing garments that shimmered with the luminescence of a blue deeper than black, appeared before Troy's eyes. The magnificence of the man was plain in the arch of his brow, the curve of his lips, and the rise of his cheekbones. His skin was like the night sky absent of starlight. Kasha's voice dispelled the image and drew him back to the scene around him. "My daughter, weep no longer. He will not perish. His fate was long ago drawn in the sands of time and written in the very stars above. I will give him our light so that he may retain the gift and live on in good health as he should." A smile spread on Zenani's small face as she asked her mother if she could give Troy her light. "I can't see that it would hurt, but daughter you must never do this again without your father or I giving you permission first. Remember, you must only give him enough to heal him and enable him to live with the gift, no more." "Yes mother." Troy could feel Zenani reaching for him in the soft darkness. As her hand found his, he felt the small star in her palm pulsing against the flesh inside his hand. For a moment he was filled with fear, worried about what would happen next. No one knew he was out here. Why didn't he leave when he first saw these beings? His mind was whirling with thoughts when suddenly the blue light filled him to overflowing. The visions before his eyes confused him for he had never heard of the Ancient Ones or this group of beings. He could see their whole history unfold before him and he was stunned to realize that they were here first. The kings of the world almost brought them to extinction, but they escaped and regrouped in the stars above to form a new world where the rulers could never reach them again. Now they had returned through some portal to monitor the plague and its possible return to this planet. They had been returning on a schedule of every twenty Earth years because the portal only opened in those time increments. Troy was inundated with too much information that he could not understand and his mind was working overtime to piece it all together. Just then, he felt a warm flooding sensation in his body as Zenani cast the light around him just as she had done for the baby deer. Instantly Troy knew he would no longer suffer from the disease that had ravaged him for as long as he could remember. He felt strength he had never known and the peace of his soul was one that few humans would ever attain. He felt like he had been reborn and everything would be new to him from this night forward. Kasha's voice brought Troy back to the present and he was once more in the clearing surrounded by Zenani and the others. Kasha looked at him and said to her companions "Prepare him now, he must remember nothing of this night. Return him to his home."

The early morning light filtered gently through Troy's bedroom window. As the last traces of sleep left him wakeful yet still half dozing, Troy tried to hold on to the wispy edges of a dream that was so real. He slowly rose from his rumpled bed and went to his window. The woods were shrouded in a clinging veil of mist that seemed to hide what his dreams had revealed. If only he could remember! Troy's stomach growled loudly as breakfast smells from the kitchen wafted upstairs. Mary entered his room and was surprised to see him up so early. "Dear, are you feeling alright this morning?" she asked. Troy smiled as he looked at her, "Mom, I feel great!" "You were up kind of late last night and all the traveling we've done must have had an effect, son. You know it's important that you get your rest." Mary was puzzled and a little worried. Proper rest along with good nutrition and his medication combined with supplements was their only defense now. It was hard to get a young active boy to slow down. As she took out her stethoscope and prepared to take his vitals, Mary noticed a change in Troy. She couldn't put her finger on it, but somehow he had a healthy glow to his skin this morning and he wasn't acting like himself. He was staring out his window at the forest below. He seemed to be in deep thought. Mary came up behind him and gave him a good morning hug. "Troy, let's take your vitals and see how you are this morning." "Mom, I told you I feel great. Really." He turned back to the window with a wistful look in his eyes. "I'm better now. I won't be sick anymore, I promise." "Son, I hope that's true. Your dad is working hard to make that a reality, but we still have to monitor your health and do all the things necessary to maintain these good feelings." "Mom, you'll see. I am better. Something is different now. I don't know how or why but I'm okay." Mary looked at her son and decided to let him have this moment of optimism. If he felt fine this morning then that was enough for her. One day at a time, she told herself. A positive outlook was also important for Troy. It looked as if this move was already proving to be the right medicine for her son. When she finished with his vitals and the routine questions about how he felt, Mary told Troy to wash up for breakfast. On her way downstairs, Mary stopped at the bathroom door and saw Ben in the middle of his morning grooming. She stared for a moment at the back of his head and thought of the wonderful night they had shared. Ben saw her in the mirror with a dreamy look in her eyes and a smile spread across her face. "Hey baby, you look like heaven this morning, care to clue me in?" "You ought to know, dear. You were at the scene of the crime last night." she laughed and hugged him from behind. "Well sugar, if last night was a crime then I'm a career criminal." Ben smiled and gave her a long good morning kiss. As they parted, Mary told him about her visit to Troy's room and his upbeat mood this morning. "I took his vitals, and checked him from head to toe and he was fine. He looks better today than ever. I also drew a small sample of his blood for you to test later on this morning, okay?" Ben took Mary's hand and assured her he would take a look at their son too and get on that sample right after breakfast. Just then Troy stuck his head between his parents and excitedly asked his mom, "Is that French toast I smell?" Ben and Mary both laughed. "Yes son, you better hurry and come on down before your dad or it'll all be gone." Mary headed down stairs as Troy joined his dad in front of the mirror. "Dad move over and let me wash my hands, I got to get to breakfast before you!" Ben laughed and rubbed his son on the head. "Alright son." Ben also noticed the glow about his son as Mary had earlier. "Little man, you're looking good this morning. I guess this place really agrees with you." "Yeah dad, I feel better than I've felt in a long time." They finished up in the bathroom and Ben gave Troy his daily medication. Troy took his medicine but told Ben that he really wouldn't need it anymore. He dashed out the door and ran downstairs to the enticing smell of breakfast. Mary, setting the table and moving from the refrigerator to the stove, asked Troy to take out the trash. The smell of breakfast was calling so he wasn't about to argue. As Troy stepped into the brisk morning air and was about to place the trash in the can, he heard a rustle in the bushes. It was

Zoë, the baby deer. Neither made a move as they stared. Gingerly the deer walked up to Troy. Troy slowly reached out his hand in friendship and the baby deer welcomed the greeting by licking his hand. Both became overjoyed with their newfound friendship. As Troy knelt to hug his bubbly friend, the baby deer licked his face and began to bounce around him like a playful puppy. Hearing laughter outside, Mary looked out the window. "Will you take a look at that?" she sighed as Ben stood at her side. Troy sat on the cool grass rubbing his head blankly, staring into the sky trying to think of a name for his new pal and whispered, "Zenani?" The baby deer's licking brought him out of the clouds. Where had he heard that name before? "I'll just call you Zoë." Troy heard his mother call and hugged his pal good-bye. "Got to go now, see you later Zoë." He ran to where his mother was waiting on the steps. They watched as Zoë darted back into the woods. "Looks like you have a new friend," she said as Troy trotted past. "Yeah, that's Zoë."

Inside, Ben was reviewing some documents and listening to the news on the radio as they joined him for breakfast. It didn't take long before Troy had cleaned his plate and requested seconds. After finishing his second helping Troy excused himself to go wash up. Mary shook her head in disbelief at the clean plate and began to clear the table. "Ben I can't believe that boy ate all that food," she remarked. Ben, lost in his paperwork, looked up surprised as Mary raised her voice. "Benjamin!" snapped Mary as she playfully threw the wet dish towel, breaking his trance. Ben laughed, wiping the soap from his forehead. "Sorry baby, what were you saying?" Pushing his papers away, Mary arranged herself on Ben's lap. Pleased now that she had his attention, she said, "About Troy honey, you know how finicky he eats, always picking at his food and then this morning he's a human garbage disposal, don't you find that odd?" Ben squeezed her closer, "Now mother, our little boy is just growing.'' Mary huffed, springing up not satisfied with his answer. "Just growing! Some hotshot doctor you turned out to be! Don't forget to check his blood sample," Mary blurted, returning to her sink. Ben sipped his coffee in thought. He too had noticed how well Troy looked. He didn't seem to have the usual recurring morning discomforts, either. He had already started testing the sample before breakfast. It should be ready now. As he pondered, he could hear the radio in the background rambling different issues. "In world news today, fighting continued on the borders of India and Pakistan after each country last month conducted nuclear tests. World leaders fear that tensions will escalate in the region. Scientists continue to track fall-out levels in surrounding countries. Continued flooding in Asia and China has left thousands homeless as authorities comb flood areas in search of survivors. To top the news, the CDC finally announced the outbreak of a skin cancer researchers earlier had suspected to be a strain of the HIV virus. Reports indicate a worldwide death toll in the millions linked to this unknown disease, mainly affecting Caucasians and the elderly. Convalescent homes throughout the US confirm that the strange disease is attacking the elderly in alarming numbers. Similar to the HIV virus of the last decade, it destroys the immune system, causing blotching and body sores with soaring fevers and death resulting within months of contraction. Citizens are urged to seek medical attention immediately if sun blotches appear. Scientists have linked the possible cause of the disease to the apparent high pollution rates and the critical breakdown of the ozone allowing harmful levels of UV rays to penetrate the atmosphere. As cases of the outbreak continue to climb with no cure available, researchers fear this disease could reach plague proportions by years end. Doctors and scientists are recommending that citizens avoid as much direct sunlight as possible and strongly encourage the use of high protection sunscreen. This has been world news today." After the brief news flash, Mary asked, "Ben isn't that outbreak similar to the studies you've been working on?" The look on Ben's face told it all and Mary sensed that he was clearly disturbed as he mumbled, "They should have alerted the public years ago, the fools!'' The suspense was too much for Mary, as she demanded an explanation. "Ben, are they the same?" The intensity in Ben's eyes flickered, "Yes they are, and as a matter of fact they are identical. When I first found the strain it mainly occurred in elderly whites, then clinics across the country were swamped with cases ranging from the elderly to infants. Why the medical community didn't release this information earlier has me stumped. When I first addressed the medical review board with my findings I was shocked by their allegations that my findings were unfounded and racially motivated. They laughed and insinuated that I was the "Malcolm X'' of the medical profession. But in the cases I studied, their pigmentation didn't produce the antibody necessary to fight this virus. I don't know honey, this plague can make AIDS look like the common cold." Mary stared in disbelief. "Is that the reason why you left? I thought...'' "No sweetheart, you and Troy are all that I have in this world and nothing will ever keep us apart." He took Mary in his arms and tried to calm her. "Here, let me show you some of my findings." He took her hand and led her to his computer. Ben masterfully stroked his keyboard unlocking his research. "In the beginning of Troy's illness, my work focused around the sickle cell trait within our blood that caused Troy to develop sickle cell disease. With all the problems our son was having, I concentrated on the sickle cells themselves and how they operate in both carriers and those who are actually afflicted with sickle cell disease. We know about all the options to treat our son, but there is no cure. The interesting thing is that sickle cell trait and the resulting disease are only prevalent in peoples of an

African ancestry and also in the people of the Middle East, India, and the Mediterranean. What do all these people have in common?" "Well, Ben, that's rather obvious. We all have greater pigmentation to our skin than most people. So what are you saying?" "That was the reason that the Board reacted to my findings as being racially motivated. Then all of a sudden this offer to privately fund my research with three times the previous budget, Mary I don't know exactly what they're after, but I know I'm the only hope they have. These findings are only the tip of the iceberg. Somewhere I struck a nerve with these people. There were government officials present when they offered me this researcher's dream come true. I know that the sickle cell is the key to curing this epidemic, but I haven't found how to extract the antibody or apply it. Mary was stunned at what her husband had revealed. "Honey the possible implications scare me more than you can imagine." Ben understood exactly what Mary meant. His worried face betrayed his charged emotions. "Honey, when cases were first appearing, we all thought it was part of the AIDS epidemic but it quickly revealed itself as a super infective agent that attacked the blood regardless of gender or race. It seemed to be introduced through the skin and the majority of cases were in the white community." Mary stared past Ben as a look of horror came over her face. "All the cases I've heard of on the news..." Ben crossed the space between them to hold Mary in his arms. He took her face in his hands and said, "All those dark spots you see on an elderly person's hands...those are early stages of the plague. All the skin cancers and the hype to use sunscreen...they knew even then that it would evolve over time as the ozone disappeared and possibly become the strain that is killing all these people now. Its not just light-skinned people who will perish, eventually all people will be afflicted. It will just take longer for some than others." Mary pulled back from Ben with tears now streaming down her face, but he refused to release her. "If you knew this how come you didn't...." her voice broke as she looked her husband in the eye. "Didn't what, Mary? Get on TV and announce the plague of all time? Start global panic when there was nothing anyone could do anyway? You know better than that! This information is classified around the world as Top Secret. Researchers who are involved are under the closest scrutiny and are sworn to secrecy. Any release of this information would result in an immediate charge of treason and would be treated as a breach of national security. I've just put this whole family at risk by telling you." Ben, upset that he had involved his family in all this madness, began to pace the floor. "Mary, this is why I had to get you and Troy out here where we can figure out what to do and just be a family. There is a lot going on that could destroy all that we have. I need you in my corner." Mary wiped her eyes and held Ben's hands. "I don't care for all this cloak and dagger business and I wish you had told me sooner, but I can see that you couldn't risk your family that way. I'm here with you and I always will be. All we can do is take this one day at a time. Let's work on Troy's cure. If we can help the rest of the world, well then that's great, but my world is you and our son. I want us to enjoy this time as much as we can under these circumstances. It's like the whole world has gone mad! But why the attacks on your work?" Though relieved of his secret, the serious nature of his work still showed on Ben's face. "Fear, I guess. Even at the top levels of government they've been building underground and sea facilities for years. There's rumor of future space stations in the event that we may have to abandon Earth all together. So much is based on the rapid decline of the ozone and at the rate we're going the future doesn't look bright." Mary sighed in disgust, "Ben, after the way you and other black scientists have been treated, how can you sit here and say we?" Ben lowered his head from the weight of his dark secret. "I know baby. If history were to repeat itself, they wouldn't hesitate to commit genocide to save themselves." Mary paced the floor in deep thought, snapping her fingers as if it was coming to her. "So where's the silver lining of this dark cloud and what does this have to do with your research of black people?" Ben seemed to come out of his blue funk as he stroked the keyboard revealing his files. "These are slides of the degenerative cancer cells of the victims, notice how the cells are consuming the red blood cells in the bloodstream." Mary watched in astonishment, "They seem to multiply after they destroy the red cells!" Ben continued to click as the slides began to bear the truth. "I know, this is what causes the rapid deterioration of the immune system and certain death of a patient within weeks." He continued to demonstrate, "On the next slides, I introduced some of our blood cells and cells of other black people that were carriers." Mary watched intensely as the cells merged together. "Nothing is happening." Ben just nodded in agreement, "That's right, they appear to be immune to the cancer cells and as these time lapse photos show, if the cancer cells can't feed they begin to die." The whole story finally took a toll on Mary as she pulled her chair next to Ben. "Which explains why most blacks aren't affected by the plague. Well, that's a relief." Ben pointed at the screen, "That's what made me curious of the affects the disease would have on our son, as if he didn't have enough problems. What I saw next was shocking!" Mary now observed with motherly concern, "Ben, I don't understand, what's happening?" Ben tried to comfort her as he held her hand. "I was also amazed. Compared to the cancer that consumed the normal blood cells, Troy's sickle cells are attacking the cancer, unlike ours that allowed them to remain dormant until death. His seem to sense their presence, then go on some kind of seek and destroy mission. But in their natural state, without medicine, they are a death sentence for Troy and kids like him." Mary leaned closer to the screen staring in disbelief,

"Ben it's a miracle, but are you sure?" Ben rubbed his chin and prepared to confirm his findings. "I'm sure of one thing, that these cells don't like each other. Watch as I freeze the frames, notice how the sickle cells surround the cancer then seem to diffuse a whitish membrane substance that eats away at the cancer. The substance released is the antibody and I'm sure it's the key to combating the plague." Mary stood suddenly as if she was convinced, "Alright, so let's give blood transfusions of the sickle cell patients to the victims of the plague." Ben looked oddly at Mary as he stretched his arms, "Well, first of all it's not that simple, transfusions such as these would surely kill the kids giving them. That's why I have to find a way to extract the antibody or how it's produced in the first place. It only seems to manifest in this manner when confronted by the cancer. So, for now it's back to the drawing board," Ben clicked a key and the screen faded to black.

Just then laughter floated in through the open kitchen window. Ben and Mary were surprised to see Troy in the back yard with the baby deer. "Honey, can you believe that?" Mary said, with a smile spreading across her face. "He's at it again, those two are really a pair!" Ben laughed in reply. "Well I hate to break it up, but we need to get going, the day is wasting!" Mary pushed Ben towards the back door. "Go get nature boy and let's hit the road." As Ben stepped on the porch he could hear the sound of playful laughter surrounding him. He stopped and let the moment sink in. It had been a long time since he had seen Troy so happy. The spell was broken when the baby deer sensed Ben's presence. He swiftly darted back into the woods with a lingering look at Troy as his only concession. Ben walked over to Troy and placed his hands on the boy's small shoulders. Neither said a word as they watched Zoë gracefully leap out of sight. As Troy turned to face his father, Ben could see the joy shining in his son's eyes. "Well young man, it seems as if you've got a special friend

24

in that little deer." Troy grabbed Ben's hand, "Yeah, Dad. That's Zoë." Ben smiled, "Zoë, is it? Well that's all right. Come on son, your mom is ready to go into town and you know she doesn't like to be kept waiting." Troy looked at his father with a serious demeanor. "Dad, you ever have a dream that you could fly?" Ben noticed the change in Troy and gave the question more consideration than he normally would have. "Sure, son. Probably everyone has had that dream at one time or another, but it seems to be more than a dream that you're asking about, am I right?" Troy looked his father in the eye and calmly said, "I'm going to the stars someday, Dad. You'll see." Ben saw the man his son would someday become peeking through the little boy before him. To lighten the moment he grabbed Troy up in the classic "superman" hold and flew him into the house. "Alright, Spaceman, let's get on board the mother ship before the evil Spacemommy gets us both sighted in her laser beams." Troy howled with laughter as Mary swatted Ben on the behind and mumbled "I'll show you a spacemommy, acting all crazy in my kitchen and making me wait to go into town!" Ben put Troy down and yelled, "Every man for himself, the evil Spacemommy is on the loose!" Troy was lost in giggles as Mary shoved Ben towards the door and grabbed her purse. Troy, still laughing, raced past them and climbed into the back seat of the jeep. As Mary buckled her seat belt and Ben started the jeep, Troy whined from the back seat, "Mom, do we have to listen to that old music of Dad's?" Mary, laughing too hard to answer, could only look at Ben and helplessly shrug her shoulders. Ben, raising his eyebrows and pretending to be offended, looked at Troy and said, "Son, I know you're young and you don't know good music when you hear it, but your old Dad almost had a Motown contract." Ben began singing along to his music. Troy raised his voice over the singing and yelled, "Hey Mom, what's Motown?" Ben and Mary both turned and looked at him and then at each other and began laughing all over again. Troy seemingly embarrassed, shouted, "What did I say?" Mary smooched her son, "Nothing, baby, you just had to be there."

As they reached the end of the drive Ben noticed a cable van parked along the shoulder of the road. " Well, it looks as though progress has made its way into these old woods after all." Mary, looking skeptical, remarked, "All this beauty and serenity and all people want is their 57 channels and it's still nothing on." Ben laughed and patted Mary's knee. "Now honey, you know you love to watch those talk shows like everybody else. Have you ever missed an Oprah show?" Mary laughed and replied, "I guess you're right dear, but Oprah's show is about something!" Ben gave up this argument and continued to sing along to his Motown hits. Troy was in his own world in the back seat. He found his toy astronauts under the seat and was presently on a mission to conquer new worlds. Inside of the van, the so-called "cable guys" sat adjusting the signals on their high-tech listening devices. One of the agents grabbed a cell phone, "The company isn't going to like this, go ahead and catalog the tape. Yes, this is Agent Collins, the cat is out of the bag, awaiting further instructions." The voice at the other end was silent for a moment, "It's a go, proceed with elimination ops of the Bishops, keep this line open so we can advise you when they leave town." The agent turned to his partner who had already retrieved a case filled with devices. "Let's go, we should have about an hour to wire this place. Damn coon should've kept his trap closed." Down the road the Bishops were enjoying the music and their drive through the countryside.

As Ben approached the edge of town he could see the flashing of police lights. He slowed to allow a wave of people to cross the street. The road was lined with scores of camera crews and their news vans. Mary looked around not believing all the activity she was seeing. "I hope no one is hurt. Honey, pull over at the gas station." The scene looked like the circus had come to town. People stood along the street as though they were waiting for a parade. Horace, not one to be left out when things got exciting, greeted the Bishops in his loud booming voice. "Ya'll sure picked the right time to come into town, we don't usually have this much commotion goin' on!" Horace laughed and slapped Ben on the back as he walked around the Jeep. Horace continued, "Although, I'd wager what happened in them woods near your place last night would surely draw a bigger crowd than any little fender bender." Ben, his face covered with a look of confusion, asked Horace, "What are you talking about? We were up pretty late last night and those woods were as quiet and still as could be." Horace chuckled softly, "Wow, I know you're a city boy and all but them woods was anythang but quiet. It seems all them animals are actin' a might strangely when them blue lights land inside the woods." Ben laughed as he realized Horace was still carrying on about spaceships landing in the woods. "Horace, you know it isn't nice to scare your new neighbors with wild tales of spacecraft and eerie lights in the night." Horace replied with a serious look in his eyes. "I wish I was kiddin' with you Ben, but I've heard tales from people who was stone cold sober, bout visitors from another world who can cast spells on them woodland creatures with them blue lights of theirs. Most of the men round here won't hunt in them woods no more on account of how strange the animals are behavin'. My friend Jesse is the only one who still hunts there and he says pickin' them deer off is as easy as pie and he hopes whoever or whatever them visitors are, they just keep on puttin' meat on his table and trophy deer on his wall." As Ben started to answer Horace, Mary and Troy got out of the Jeep. Mary said, "Honey, Troy and I are going to walk around town and finish the shopping, so we'll meet you in about an hour over there at Molly's cafe." As they left the gas station Ben turned his attention back to Horace. "Horace, if what you're saying is true, about all these strange occurrences and aliens, how come no one is here investigating?" Suddenly Horace began an uncontrollable series of wracking coughs that ended in a long wheezing choke. He cleared his throat and pointed to the courthouse steps. "Who do you think them boys is? They sposed to have a secret base out near your place, but nobody's seen it," he tried to finish, but the coughing started back again worse than before. Ben, concerned at the sound of Horace's cough asked the old man gently, "Have you seen a doctor for that cough, Horace?" As Horace shrugged off Ben's kindly question he wiped his mouth with a handkerchief and Ben noticed the dark blotches on Horace's arm as his shirtsleeve fell down his wrist. Ben asked Horace to finish up with the jeep and he'd be back later to pick it up. As he began to walk through town, Ben's mind was crowded with thoughts of aliens and "men-in-black". Horace's apparent early symptoms of the disease and all the sudden increase in the activity of this small, normally quiet town didn't seem to be a coincidence. Could it have something to do with his return and the secret research he was conducting? Ben shook his head. "Now I'm being paranoid," he sighed to himself. As he passed the courthouse he looked across the street. The striking white-haired agent in the group that Horace pointed out earlier drew his attention. An overwhelming sense of recognition came over Ben. "Where have I seen him before?" he questioned himself. As the agent turned his intimidating gaze on Ben, it hit him like a bolt out of the blue! It was the same man who was at his hospital conference with the government. What puzzled him was why would he be interested in a UFO hoax like this. Ben's concentration was broken by the sound of Troy's voice. Across the way, Mary was loading his little arms with a few light shopping bags. Ben smiled and waved at his family and headed into Foster's drugstore. The tinkling bell above the door momentarily took him back to his childhood and Mr. Foster making the world's best sundaes. As he gazed around the store he could see that it hadn't changed much over the years. How strange that it comforted him to know this. Ben was feeling a little off center when he heard a voice behind him that was all too familiar. "Lil' Benny Bishop, son how long has it been?" Mr. Foster slowly made his way around the counter and grabbed Ben around the shoulders "Well look at you now, what brings you way back up here?" Ben composed himself after the good shaking he had just received. "Well, Mary retired from teaching a few years ago and we thought what better time to get away from the city so I could devote more time to my research." Mr. Foster secured his sliding glasses with one push of his finger, "Well we're mighty glad to have you back. So you gonna stay and work the land?" Mr. Foster nodded and smiled at Ben. "Try to at least," Ben laughed in reply. "So how is Mrs. Foster?" he asked the druggist. The expression on Mr. Foster's face somehow changed in that instant and Ben felt his sadness. He looked into water-filled eyes just as Mr. Foster tried to turn away, pretending to dust a perfectly clean display shelf. "Just don't understand it, the woman hadn't been sick a day in her life." Mr. Foster's voice began to choke up with grief. "Spent her whole life doing the Lord's work and worrying that I would catch a chill." Ben couldn't hide his emotions as his eyes too began to fill up. Mrs. Foster had been like a mother to him, always pinching him when he goofed off or fell asleep in Sunday school. Later the Fosters helped pay for him to go to med school. Mr. Foster took a deep breath and managed to go on. "Doc said it was the cancer, but she never said a word. Even made Doc Evans promise not to tell me, said I'd make too much of a fuss over her. And you know she was right. I did. You see, Doc told me anyhow. It all happened so fast; Doc said he'd never seen anything like it. Neither had I. What with the outbreak of sores and the burning fever, in a few months time my Becky was gone.

May the Lord bless her sweet soul." Both men stood silently staring out the front window of the store fighting back tears and clearing the knots from their throats. Ben was hurt by the fact that he had prior knowledge of the killer that had stalked those he loved. All he could think of was that he must step up his efforts to find the cure for this merciless killer. This had nothing to do with race, people were dying and fast. If only he had been able to save Mrs. Foster! And now there was Horace to worry about! Ben was determined to help those who still had a fighting chance, his own son included in that group. Mr. Foster brought him out of his reverie with words that meant the world to Ben. "Oh she was so proud of you and Mary! It did her heart good to see the two of you go out in the world and succeed the way you have. You know we never had any children of our own, so you were just like a son to us. Why I'll never forget how happy she was when you and Mary made us little Troy's godparents. She's gone now, but if you ever need help with the boy I'm not too old to take him fishin' or teach him to track in the woods." Ben smiled warmly at his friend. Just then they both caught sight of Troy out front surrounded by pigeons and loving every minute of it. "Well there's Dr. Doolittle now, we're about to have lunch at Molly's and I'd love for you and Mary to get reacquainted. You can get a taste of what you're in for as that boy's godfather." Ben patted Mr. Foster on the back as he extended the invitation. "Why I'd be delighted," laughed Mr. Foster, the twinkle coming back in his eyes. "Just let me lock up here and I'll be right over," he said as he took off his white smock and hung it on the same hook he'd used for years. When Ben turned to leave the store, the bell tinkled above the door. Agent Hunt walked casually in. Mr. Foster called out from the back, "Sorry, we're closed for lunch." Agent Hunt continued striding into the store as though Mr. Foster had never spoken. Ben was uneasy with the predatory air about this man. He walked around looking over everything as though it was beneath him to have entered here. Taking his finger along the counter and examining the dust he found, he finally spoke to Ben. "Seems as though you've forgotten about our agreement Dr. Bishop, the Five are waiting impatiently for your report." Ben's stare would have sent chills through a wiser man. He just didn't like this man. Hatred was something Ben hadn't known for another person, but with Agent Hunt it came easy, he was just plain evil, down to the core. Throughout his medical career he had dealt with all types of law enforcement officers, from prison guards, FBI, CIA and even soldiers of fortune. He could tell the good guys from the bad and this bad apple was walking death, a killer. A low growl emerged from Ben, "If memory serves me correctly the agreement I had was with the Federal Medical Association and not with the likes of you!" Agent Hunt arrogantly attempted to dust off his hands, "All matters of the state concern me, especially breaches of national security. I need not remind you of the functions of ICON Industries, only that your time is almost up!" He turned and deliberately knocked over a glass container as he left. Mr. Foster rushed from the back stockroom at the sound of broken glass, "What the sam dickens is going on out here?" Ben reached for the broom and dustpan and began to clean the mess, "I don't know but I think I'm about to find out." Mr. Foster assured Ben that he would finish cleaning the mess, but for now he couldn't wait to see Mary and his godson as he rushed Ben out the door. Mr. Foster led the way to Molly's, mumbling something about her apple pie. Entering the crowded café, Ben spotted Mary waving from a table in the corner. Mary greeted Mr. Foster with a big hug. He got a warm hello from the little fellow tugging at his waist. The group settled down to enjoy their meal and some of Molly's famous apple pie. Troy, smiling with ice cream around his mouth asked, "Mr. Foster have you ever been to Motown?" The threesome looked at Troy and began to roll with laughter. Still confused Troy demanded, "What did I say, Mom? Dad what's so funny?" Out of the corner of his weeping eye, Ben could see Agent Hunt across the street as he talked on his cellular phone watching them.

Chapter Three

Meanwhile, in deep space, another meeting of sorts was taking place. The wrap-around console of instruments surpassed anything known to man. Digital and geometric patterns appeared in mid-air as holographic images surrounded the programmers of this fantastic craft. The only sound audible inside this technological marvel was similar to that which an unborn child experiences inside its mother's womb. An air of calm serenity emanated from each being as they went about their appointed tasks. Each individual was surrounded by a thin blue vapor that seemed more an extension of his or her life force than an external phenomenon. There were two of these vapors near the forward command center. They appeared to mingle together and cast a softly brilliant azure pool around a throne. It was the being known as Kasha and her daughter Zenani just back from their latest visit to the planet Earth. To them it was their ancestral home, yet it remained largely a mystery that still offered much to investigate. Kasha reflected that her duty as chief medical officer and top-level research scientist was beginning to interfere with her obligation as Queen among her people. She knew that Balimar would be displeased with her last foray on Earth. Her brooding thoughts were dispelled at the sight of her precious daughter transfixed before the image of their mother planet, the Earth, on the huge telescreen. Kasha was pleased to see that her child was as taken with the beautiful cerulean globe as she had been in her youth. Truth be told, she still felt chills when she surveyed those billowing diaphanous clouds encircling the vivid richness so like the blue fluid in her veins. As the telescreen before her displayed the vision of her beloved homeland, Kasha gently stroked her daughter's silken hair. Suddenly the image faded and the majestic countenance of her King appeared on the screen surrounded by a vibrant sapphire glow that could only be her husband's aura. No other being, ancient or otherwise, possessed the magnetism or sheer beauty of his lifeforce. Balimar was directly descended from the Father of the Unspoken Ones. He was the first of their kind to fully display the strengths and talents of their blessed race. All heads in the room rose at once as if at silent command and all bowed in honor of their King. As one they rose and levitated from the chamber to give their King private audience with his Queen. Young Zenani also left, although reluctantly, and only after sending her father the mental equivalent of a hug and kiss. After dismissing his daughter with a fatherly smile and comment on her beauty and apparent growth in his absence, Balimar shifted his attention to his beloved Queen, Kasha. Unknown to either of her parents, Zenani had hidden herself near the rear of the room in a corner to eavesdrop on their conversation. There was a long silence between the two as Kasha lowered her head in reverence for her companion and king. She raised her palm, as did he, revealing their pulsating bloodstars. Both were bathed in the light of life. The soft-spoken words he telegraphed seemed to boom, "My Queen, your wisdom and kindness amaze me as ever. The lifeforce between us foretold that you have made another exploratory mission to the mother planet and at such a perilous time. The journey you embarked upon was so written by the Ancient Ones and you were entrusted to deliver them from the plague. My Queen, the disturbance that exists within their kind is very strong. You must proceed with utmost caution." Kasha nodded slowly in acknowledgment, "Yes, my King. As you have envisioned they are here, the children of the gift have survived. But there is more, the devastation of this planet over time has left them with a pathological deficiency that causes them to expire while still very young. I now have the antidote for the plague and wish to deliver it with your permission." Balimar listened intently to his Queen, then spoke, "Your discovery pleases me and though your travel has been far, your time in that galaxy has diminished. You must return through the portal before it is too late." Kasha, determined in her plea, "My lord, in the time that exists between our worlds humankind will perish and what of children of the gift?" Balimar stood and Kasha stopped. Knowing the compassion in her heart, Balimar held his hands in truce. "Queen Mother, your mission there has been one of peace. There are many things you still don't understand. I have dispatched my elite guards to meet you at the portal's edge. You were too young to remember the brutality and atrocities these duplicitous traitors committed against the Ancient Ones. As Queen you must now know the truth that was passed to me through the "Eyes of the Soul" of our Ancestors." Kasha's head snapped back from the brilliant light that shone from Balimar's eyes as hers also began to glow. The visions of the Ancient Ones were unveiled as her body stood limp. Her minds journey was but a blur as it transcended through centuries of light travel and galaxies afar known only unto Balimar. His voice was clear in her mind as she swirled in the vastness of time with flashing faces of the Ancient Ones guiding the path back to Earth's beginning, hurtling through time and space entering the atmosphere of the world that once was. Kasha's view was of super continents of lush green forests and captivating volcanoes flowing golden lava. The clear blue seas swept the shores with towering waves. Upon her descent Kasha thought, "This place of beauty could not be the same." Then hearing the voice of Balimar, "It is so, Queen Mother, the land of the Ancient Ones, Eden. It will later be known to the new order as Earth. Kasha could only gaze at the array of prehistoric life that surrounded her. Walking among creatures of such deadly power, she felt no danger. The wind blew the voices of the Ancient Ones. "The lifeforce here is one with nature. We once stood as guardians of this world. With this gift we helped man and beast live in harmony. Our efforts have spanned time and known only of peace." The images of the elders led her to a cliff's edge; waiting was a Pterodactyl, which she instinctively knew was their means of travel and companion. After Kasha mounted the winged lizard she knew its thoughts as they flew high among the mountains toward the land of the Ancient Ones. The place they reached was known as Machu, high in the mountains, adorned on top by the pyramid of the Ancient Ones. Kasha's mind was reeling from the waking dream journey her husband had planned for her. She knew the day would come when he would impart the sacred past. It would take all of her mind's will to fasten onto this wondrous legacy and retain all that was revealed. As the Pterodactyl glided silently to a sacred patch of ground lit only by a faintly glowing bluish star, the beauty of the majestic mountain peaks surrounding them overcame Kasha. None could compare to the magnitude of the pyramid that rose defiantly in their midst. She descended from the giant winged beast and placed her feet firmly on sacred ground. She could feel the lifeforce of all who had come before singing in her veins. There was the sound of weeping mingled with voices foretelling doom for all who would remain here past the time of the Unbelievers. Kasha tried to cover her ears to escape the tortured cries. She knew the Ancient Ones had suffered for their gifts and had become the outcast of society, but this was unbearable! Great streaks of blue tears marred her lovely panic-stricken face. "How could this be?" she screamed aloud and was shocked to realize she had broken the silence of this realm. As she lifted her hand to wipe the tears away, a figure approached from just above where she was standing. The mysterious being slowly took each step of the stone stairs with deliberate ease. As the shadow of the being fell upon Kasha, she was enveloped in a caress as soft as a cool morning breeze. She was transfixed when she looked into eyes so like her own. The familiarity was stunning! Standing before her was Kasha-La, her own grandmother's grandmother and her namesake. She was bathed in the golden blue-tinged light that was common to the Ancient Ones. She took Kasha's hand and led her to the stone stairs and bade her follow. She said only two words that seemed to ring over and over in Kasha's ears, "My Daughter". As they gained the top of the stairs, Kasha was amazed at what lay before her. There was a multitude of people below them standing in an unending concentric circle around the pyramid. Even more surprising, there were all the races of the Earth represented there. Before her on a dais in the shape of the sun stood Balimar in the attire of an Incan warrior. Thus she was escorted into the pyramid with her past and her present representing her. This was the way of the Ancient Ones. As they walked the last steps to the entrance, Kasha noticed that Incas were lining the path down both sides. It was clear they beheld Balimar with great respect. They had built this city in honor of the Ancient Ones and had given them shelter from persecution during the Great Tribulation times. As reward for their loyalty they had been taken with the Ancient Ones when the Unbelievers found the city. Kasha adjusted her eyes to the dim light of the altar room just inside the antechamber. Before her on a golden pillar encrusted with the lifestones of her people, lay an enormous black pearl that shone brilliantly in the void of the darkened room. Balimar stood with his hands outstretched above the beautiful jewel. As he called upon the Ancient Ones and his Father, Omed, Balimar began to gently caress the pearl as if to draw forth some long held secret. No sooner had this thought formed in Kasha's mind than it became a reality. A holographic history of her people began to unfold before her. As the mists of time swirled in the darkness, Kasha felt a strange yet comforting presence within her minds subconscious. It was the Ancient Ones communing with her in the time-honored tradition. Kasha had been told all her life that this sometimes happened to a lucky few. She never dreamed she would be chosen, although it was her fondest wish. A great joy was bubbling in her chest, determined to escape. Kasha suddenly heard laughter, deep and pure. The sound conveyed a feeling unknown to her before. She was delighted to find the laughter coming from inside her, flowing over her lips and nestling in her ears, bringing total abandon as well as fulfillment. Slowly she began to regain her composure as the Ancient Ones appeared before her. They were standing hand in hand in an open garden. It was night and Kasha could sense everything around her as if she were truly there among them. She heard the musical babble of a nearby fountain, smelled the exotic scent of jasmine in the warm night air. Jagged flashes of lightning ripped the sky in the distance. The Ancient Ones all raised their flashing ebony eyes and searched Kasha's soul. "She is our daughter," they confirmed through a mindlink unique among their people. Omed, her father-in-law and Father of the Unspoken Ones, took her hand in his and joined their bloodstars. In an instant Kasha was surrounded by people who no longer walked the Earth. The ground she stood upon was rich with lush vegetation and the smell of smoke and lava filled her nostrils. It was the dawn of time! The blood-curdling roar of a tyrannosaurus vibrated the ground. At the foot of a steep mountainside several cavemen began to panic and scramble back up the cliffside to the safety of their cave. Suddenly the t-rex crashed through the trees and roared again so loud that the climbers doubled their efforts at escape. It was futile, of course. The huge monster was in all his glory and obviously hungry. He began to pick them off the mountainside with the same ease as you would pick berries off a vine. The gory sight sickened Kasha, yet she was in awe of the mighty dinosaur. At the entrance of the cliffside cave the fortunate ones were struck dumb with terror. The t-rex was still raging below them, unsatisfied with the meager meal and wanting more. One of the older cavemen brought out a huge conch shell and blew repeatedly towards the russet colored sky. Suddenly, high above them, a Pterodactyl appeared with a rider on his back. As they slowly descended toward the cave, Kasha could see that it was Tal-or, Omed's brother. He was dressed in flowing robes of animal skins. The beast set down on an outcropping near the mouth of the cave. Tal-or dismounted and levitated to the gathered tribe. The t-rex was increasingly enraged at the sight of Tal-or and the traitor dactyl that bore him wherever he wished. Tal-or calmed the terrified tribe and raised an ornate scepter towards the heavens and whispered an ancient chant. The sky darkened into a blood red horizon. Tal-or raised the scepter higher still and sent a bolt of blue lightning from his eyes into the scepters crystalline orb. The t-rex continued his snarling and the snapping of his huge teeth. Tal-or trained his sight on the beast and released the lightning from his scepter. The humming of the bolt whistled through the air and pierced the t-rex in his thick forehead. The mind link was established. Tal-or communicated a message of warning: "Disobedient one, you have been on Ancient Grounds before. This is sacred terrain you so carelessly destroy and these are my people you terrify. Do you think I do not see your trespass or do you not care?" As the mighty beast trembled and tried to resist, Tal-or levitated him to eye level and commanded "You will not leave here as easily as you came, burn now for the violence you committed against these poor souls." Thrusting his scepter forward, Tal-or whispered, "Be gone" and hurled the giant lizard into the smoking lava of the volcano. His tortured roars echoed through the valley as warning to any other predators who would seek to violate the ancient pact. Tal-or floated down to the torn bodies that lay scattered below. He scanned the area and heard the faint moans of a small child. As he neared, he could see a deep slash across her small body, she was the only one to survive and was now dying before him. Kneeling over her crumpled body he could hear her pleas, placing his palm over the wounded area, the bloodstar pulsed with life bathing the girl in a blue light completely healing her. The young girl sat up and gave thanks to the guardian as the people slowly began to come back out into the open, shouting in cheers. Tal-or turned and nodded at the elder of the tribe as he mounted his beast of flight and waved good-bye.

The voice of Omed pierced the thoughts of Kasha, "This was the way of the unspoken ones, the creator's own divine intervenors of this world called Eden. The lifeforce was strong between the guardians, though separated by land and sea the winds carried their songs of peace. As man left the tribes and formed cities farther from areas that beasts roamed, they fell prey to forces more monstrous than nature, civilization. They became the property of the pharaohs and kings that ruled. Behold." In one magical moment Kasha was whisked through time and space in a blur. Standing now on the shoulders of a mountain, she bore witness to the splendors of man. As far as the eye could see in this vast land stood great Pyramids. Millions of slaves toiled in the sun appearing as ants in their daily grind. A beast of flight appeared and Kasha soon mounted to journey far. While in flight, she could feel the lifeforce of the guardians whenever she entered a different region or kingdom. The voice of Omed again seized her thoughts, "Our covenant was with the creator, not man. The web of deceit the pharaohs spun clouded the minds of men with the lures of false gods and wealth. They built great cities beneath the pyramids to protect them from the world's beasts. As great minds blossomed in these places, so did their imagination and technology. The greed for power grew within man at an alarming rate, as did their disregard for life. The advances of science and mathematics opened their minds to possibilities never before realized. Along with all the good that came with such knowledge came weapons of mass destruction, which began the murderous ways of man. Soon the scientists of their time harnessed the elements of the volcano's lava creating their own version of nuclear energy. From this process evolved mechanical birds of flight and a means to destroy their enemies. The pharaohs, convinced of immortality, joined together in the most diabolical plot of all time, the annihilation of the Ancient Ones. They poisoned the minds of man against us as being inhuman to ensure their grip over the people." Before her eyes, Kasha saw this evolution take place in moments. The sky was filled with spacecrafts blazing lasers in this ancient land and time. Then images of Ancient Ones being murdered around the world appeared before her. The deceptions and ambushes came in all forms as their pain and death brought blue tears streaming down Kasha's face. Unable to confront these atrocities, she stood mute as time marched on changing events and places in nanoseconds. The rich enchanted green land that once surrounded the pyramids had turned to deserts of sand from the atomic waste. The elders of the Ancient Ones assembled those still remaining to a land far away from the Pharaohs. For centuries their existence was a mystery as they lived in bliss in the mountains of a continent unknown to civilized man. The poison of the world now reached toward the heavens destroying all in its path, even the ozone. The deadly rays began to burn the very soul of man as death and pestilence besieged the world bearing the plague. The spirits of the unspoken ones could not bear the suffering of the people of the creator, thus they came forward. The pleas of the pharaohs for their people were answered, but as soon as the healing of the world began so did the betrayal. They blamed the plague on the Ancient Ones because of their jealousy. The spies of the pharaohs searched the world and finally located the land of the Ancient Ones. It was here in the land of the Incas that the armies of the pharaohs amassed and began killing all in their path. The elders had prepared for centuries for this day and they loaded the children of the gift and the faithful aboard a magnificent craft launching it moments before the onslaught began. Suddenly Kasha realized she was aboard the vessel as a small child, holding the hand of a boy she recognized as Balimar. The flying crafts of the pharaohs approached by the thousands as their lasers burned and scorched the holy land. In the courtyard of the Incas, she saw the Ancient Ones form a circle around the people. The boy now released her hand and with one motion of his, a force shield appeared around their craft as it continued to rise. As she looked below the elders had all raised their hands with bloodstars shining bright. Wind and twinkling lights engulfed them. The explosions of the lasers blasted the walls of the temple as the high winds swirled in the courtyard. The blasts occurred only feet from the holy circle, and then a brilliant light erupted and in a flash they all vanished. The pharaoh's warriors, unaware of these events, continued their attack, convinced of victory. Kasha's heart was saddened because she no longer felt the lifeforce of her people. She could only stare at the world below as the craft sailed to the edges of space. Her thoughts were interrupted by chants of the other children giving homage. As she stepped closer, a light surrounded the small boy that had held her hand earlier. While he spoke they all listened, "I am Balimar, the Unspoken One." At that instant, the same force that had brought her through the ages now reclaimed her. The light diminished and she stood as an adult facing Balimar on the screen. Her face was still stained with tears as he spoke, "Now you know all, my Queen, I will await your return." The image of Balimar disappeared and the stars of the galaxy returned in focus. Out of the corner of the room she heard Zenani call, " Mother are you okay? Is father upset? Are we going home?" Kasha took her daughter's hand and stared at the stars.

"No, my daughter, first we must save the little boy in the woods and all who are like him. The only way to do this is to deliver a cure to mankind, for the plague has returned and I fear that the unspoken ones will suffer greatly at the hands of the greedy." As the others returned to their stations, Kasha gave the order to return to Earth, but first she contacted the group to which she would reveal the cure.

Back at Molly's diner, the Bishops and Mr. Foster were on the sidewalk talking and taking turns embracing each other with promises to spend more time together. Across the street, Agent Hunt dialed his henchmen back at the Bishops in the "cable van". With an evil grin on his face he spoke into the phone, "Hunt here, has the package been delivered for the Bishops?" The reply he received brought a sinister laugh and praise for his sidekicks. "Excellent, all is ready and the prey is on the move. They are at the gas station now and I am certain they are headed your way. Report to me when they arrive. Out."

As the Bishops left Mr. Foster at the drugstore, Ben was in much better spirits. He put his arm around Mary as Troy skipped ahead in front of them. Mary, smiled at her husband, "Darling, everything is coming together for us here. It is wonderful to see Troy so happy and to get reacquainted with our past. This is the support we've always missed by living in the city. Now Troy can grow up with quite an extended family and we can draw on the strength of others who love us." Ben was filled with peace and optimism at Mary's words. If only these government goons would lose interest and leave this peaceful little town. Horace ambled off the porch of his small store/gas station and handed Ben the keys to the jeep. "I checked her out from top to bottom and everythang is a-ok." He rubbed Troy's head and told him, "Hey tadpole, go on in the store there and tell Bertha I said you can have anythang you want." "All right!" Troy shouted and scrambled for the storefront. "Now Horace, you'll have that boy spoiled

43

rotten in no time," Mary playfully scolded. "Now, miss lady, ain't nothing wrong with givin to the little ones ever now and again. 'Sides, he can help me catch some fish for supper tomorrow if it'll make you feel better." Mary smiled and thanked Horace for his kindness. "Oh, by the way, don't you think it's great we're finally getting cable up here?" Horace scratched his head, confused. "Well that's news to my ears, guess I'm goin to have to stop dozin at them town hall meetins." Ben glanced at Mary. Troy bounced out of the front door with a pirate hat and a patch on one eye, " Argh! Mateys!" "Dad! Mr. Horace got all kinds of neat stuff in there! Thanks, Mr. Horace." Ben opened the door for his swashbuckling son, and then shook Horace's hand as they went on their way.

On the way home everyone seemed kind of quiet. Ben glanced to see Troy switching his patch from eye to eye, but Mary was in deep thought, writing something on paper. Ben reached over, rubbing her knee to break the silence, "Hey baby, what are you writing? Let me see." Mary knocked his hand away huffing; "You need to keep you eyes on the road, with your nosey self!" Troy stuck his head between the two, "Dad, how bout some of that Motown stuff." Ben agreed, shaking his head in anticipation, "Son, you ain't said nothing but a word. Anyhow, I need to loosen your mother up a little bit. Fore I'm through she'll be screamin' "Eddie Kane! Eddie Kane!" Mary slapped Ben on the shoulder in play. Ben took one hand and started rummaging in his tapes. Troy looked confused, "How come we don't have a CD player and who is Eddie Kane?" Mary and Ben both looked back at Troy, but this time he beat them to the punch. "I know, I had to be there!" Ben smiled searching in the tapes, "Here I found it, The Temptations! Ball of Confusion!" He slapped it in and the fun began as he and Troy began their duet. "People movin in, people movin out, why because of the color of your skin. Why! Why! Why!" Mary shook her head feeling sorry for her fallen stars. A few songs and a mile or two later, Mary suddenly called for Ben to stop the jeep. Ben pulled over and Mary jumped out mumbling something about flowers. Ben and Troy exhaled together, "Girls!" Ben watched Mary carefully collecting the beautiful wildflowers and thought how lucky he was to have such a woman. Looking at the door Mary had left open in her haste to get out, he saw the pad she had written on earlier ruffle in the breeze. As he pulled it closer to the middle of the seat he saw the title of her poem, "Meant To Be." How he loved to read her poetry! "Surely she wouldn't mind," he thought as he began to read:

> Time is flying
> Like the birds outside my window
> Flitting through my hands
> Yet lately it has become
> Fringed along the edge
> With gold
> We are together
> A family
> We stand heart to heart
> Fighting demons, the luck of the draw
> Hand in hand
> We've always been
> And will remain
> My love, my friend
> The child you gave to me
> A perfect blend
> The best of both worlds
> Suffering with the worst in both of us
> Shows me every day
> With his smile
> That I was MEANT
> To dance with you
> That first night
> And let you steal my heart away.

As Ben finished the poem, he wiped the corner of his eye. Troy broke in, "Dad, are you crying?" Ben composed himself, "Naw, I just have something in my eye. Must be all the pollen in the air." Troy crossed his little arms in disbelief, "Yeah, right!" Mary opened the back window of the jeep and placed her bouquet inside. "Okay fellas, I'm finished, let's go home." Ben cranked the engine and pulled back onto the highway. When they reached the house, Ben saw no sign of the cable van as he pulled into the driveway.

At the Cape, far from the Bishops humble abode, the scurry of personnel was unbelievable. Space Command Center was on the highest alert. The news of alien contact had set all this activity into motion. There were live feeds directly to the White House and secretly to ICON Industries exclusive boardroom. Scientists scrambled to decode the message. ICON already knew the full details. They were so far ahead of the government on everything. The sun reflected on the solar panels on the roof of ICON Headquarters. The billion-dollar complex was unmatched in the world. From humble beginnings in the 1970's as Digicom computers, the company was shrouded in mystery. The strange disappearance of it's founder, Wil Nathan, along with numerous takeovers of major computer companies and buyouts of a string of medical labs, ICON had become an industry giant. ICON now controlled every government contract pertaining to space technology, human genome mapping, and pharmaceuticals. Little wonder that they were far ahead of the government on this occasion. Getting into the ICON complex was like getting into Fort Knox. There were never any unexpected guests. The list of appointments ran well into the next year. The whole building was glass and marble elegance throughout. A huge waterfall provided the only sound in the center courtyard of the atrium. Hovering robots acted as messengers. In the name of efficiency, a select few security guards ran the surveillance monitors eliminating the cost of needless surplus employees.   The extreme plush trappings of the upper level offices were lacking on the lower level. Not to say that the lobby was shabby, quite the opposite.   The imported marble and polished nickel seating arrangements screamed opulence, but also conveyed an austere quality that left visitors feeling rather cold. The chill induced by these surroundings hung over the entire building. Pervasive gloom stalked the halls of this cavernous space. The few humans in the employ of ICON Industries were visibly remote and evasive when interrupted from their myriad duties throughout the day. This was odd considering the lower level functioned as a sort of reception area; the reception here was always cool.   A person could spend hours wandering the echoing halls and never make contact with anything remotely human. This carefully orchestrated distance created total surprise for those finally being granted an audience with Arthur Kehoe, the man in charge at ICON. The coldness of his building emanated directly from his eyes. The only relief was that here on the penthouse level, warmth and luxury was the order of the day.   Inside the luxurious boardroom adjacent to Kehoe's office, four board members sat engrossed by the image on the huge screen in front of them. As they arranged the meeting time and place with the alien Kasha, they began to stare at one another as if trying to decide which of them would be the one to contact Kehoe. Seated at the momentarily vacant head of the table was Delores Bates. Word around ICON had it that she was the power behind the throne.   Only she knew the truth. Arthur relied upon her because the men in this room were totally worthless.   They did not possess the talent or the drive let alone the ruthlessness it took to reach the stars. The pressures of global acquisition and domination left her hungry for more and she was actually as shrewd and cold as Kehoe himself. However, this little project was beginning to become riskier than either had imagined. Yet the gains far outweighed the risk, besides, she was never one to lose her nerve when the stakes were increased. She glanced across the table at Stanley Winters. "What a joke!" she thought as she eyed him from Kehoe's seat. She often thought they should relieve him of his board seat. Arthur would have none of that! Stanley knew every dirty deed and shady deal. He had been Arthur's right hand man from the start. The funny thing was, he had been close with Wil Nathan as well. He had put the price on Nathan's head at Kehoe's urging. Now Kehoe held all the cards, but Stanley was a constant weight around his neck. He had been privy to every hostile takeover as well as the supposed "friendly" ones. Only he knew the lengths Kehoe had gone to in order to make ICON what is was today. If he were forced out and stripped of his status, he'd certainly make sure the ship went down with him. An unfortunate accident was also out of the question. Stanley made no secret of the fact that he had "insurance" in the way of documents and tapes hidden in a safe known only to him. Smiling at Delores like the Cheshire cat, he didn't seem the least bit ruffled by the matter at hand. Bill Ryeburg, on the other hand, was the most upset about potential difficulties presented by this meeting. Of course they had to proceed, the benefits were too great to stop now. Still, he would really rather not attend the actual meeting. If everything turned sour at the last minute and they were exposed he could save face and start his career over elsewhere. He wasn't about to go down for that bastard Kehoe! "Oh no, not me!" he thought to himself as Josh Gordon broke the silence in his usual cocky manner. Josh was so full of himself for no apparent reason. As "payback" to a former "business partner", Kehoe had been forced to put the young hothead on his board. This irked him no end, but there was really nothing he could do, his hands were tied. Any harm that came to the junior Gordon would bring swift recrimination from the esteemed Senator Gordon. Surprisingly, his influence was much stronger than Kehoe had bargained for and now this thorn in his side was festering. Josh knew all of this and played it for all it was worth. The numerous benefits gained and the opportunity to drive the rest of the stuffy board members to distraction gave him some twisted satisfaction. This was obviously an appropriate situation for him to start ruffling feathers. "Well, who is going to be the one to contact the mighty hunter?" he sneered as he looked around the room, sizing up the competition. He laughed and began pushing their buttons. "Let's see, why not you, Delores? You are his favorite, aren't you? Surely it should be our fearless "wannabe" leader. You know he'd love to hear from you especially if you tell him which panties you have on today and how moist they are with sitting on the "throne"!" Delores was fuming as the others barely restrained the gasps and chuckles this little scene had produced. "Listen, daddy's boy, I'm where I am for one reason and one reason only, my mind! We all know that you are sorely lacking in that department!" As Delores regained her composure, Stanley began to laugh sending Josh into his next tirade. "What was I thinking? The one he really wants to hear from is his snitch. As long as Kehoe carries your sorry ass he can continue to do his dirty deeds without fear of being found out. My, what that must do for your reputation in the corporate world! But you better watch your back, Stanley. A dark rainy night, bad brakes on that sweet Mercedes, and Kehoe could breathe a lot easier." At this latest outburst, Bill rose and tried to calm Josh's temper. "Don't bother, Ryeburg, I had no intention of suggesting that you be the one to call the old geezer. He already knows you'd be the first to jump ship at the slightest provocation. Afraid of your own shadow, "Mr. I don't want to get my hands dirty! Sit your ass down!" Josh shoved Ryeburg back into his leather seat and buzzed Ginger, Kehoe's executive secretary, in the outer office. "Ginger, baby, get your fine ass on the phone and bring Mr. Kehoe in. We've got big game for him right here at home. And Ginger, I'd like for you to be in my office hunting for your panties in about 20 minutes." Ginger buzzed back, "But Mr. Gordon, my panties aren't here, I didn't wear any. How'd they get into your office?" Josh sighed as he looked at the disgusted faces around him. "Never mind, Ginger, just be in my office in 20 minutes ready to take dictation." "Yes, Mr. Gordon." The girl was quite the airhead. However, her lack of secretarial skills was not an issue for Arthur Kehoe. She was built like everyman's fantasy, huge chest with a nice round ass and just a tiny waist in the middle. Ginger ran her manicured finger down the list on her phone. She pushed the number for Kehoe's pager and retrieved her pad and pencil from the desk, wondering why Mr. Gordon needed to dictate at a time like this.

Somewhere in the winter wilds of Alaska, Arthur Kehoe felt the frozen ice in his mustache as he continued to control his breathing. After being airlifted into this region, he had backtracked to the range of mountains that called to his gut. He had hunted every type of game in the world and had bagged them all, except one, the most evasive legend known to man, Sasquatch. Two days ago he picked up some tracks he at first thought were that of a bear. Couldn't be though, bears walked on all fours and whatever this thing was it was walking upright. It took over 10 hours to position himself across the valley from the small series of caves that dotted the mountainside. Along the way, he had found scat that resembled human feces. He had hunted enough bear to know the difference. A light snow had been falling since he reached the site under the cover of darkness. Now after 14 hours of leaning against a rock and being camouflaged by the snow, Arthur peered through his binos, watching the caves for movement. He could make out a few rams on the slope above the caves. They were locked in battle and the sound of their horns echoed across the valley. Out of the shadows of the cave Arthur saw something moving toward the slope. The jagged, snow capped rocks blocked his view. Perhaps it was just another of the herd curious over this duel. Suddenly the clash stopped and the rams raised their heads to catch a scent. Kehoe slowly moved his rifle into position, not wanting to make the slightest noise that would carry across the narrow valley. He kept the shadowy figure in sight until rocks blocked his view again. Just when he was about to lower his gaze, a huge furry beast appeared. The animal walked on two legs and stood at least ten feet tall. He watched as the Sasquatch stared at the rams. Expertly, he raised his scope and took aim. His beeper rang crystal clear across the valley. As he cursed and turned the beeper off the scene before him dissolved. The animals ran for cover, destroying his plan to bag a legend. Arthur rolled over in the snow and screamed "NOOOOO!" Lying there, he felt hot enough to melt the polar ice cap. On the way back to his base camp he began to plot revenge on the poor soul who had dared to interrupt him at his once in a lifetime shot of bagging Bigfoot.

Several hours later, plenty of time for the boss to stew in his owns juices, the helicopter landed atop ICON headquarters and heads started to roll. First he fired the pilot, next was the security guard at his office door and finally Ginger. His storm of rage preceded him and the members of his board were cowering in silence upon his arrival. The crashing slam of the huge office doors immediately brought everyone to their feet. Even Delores was trembling as if she had been the one to spend 14 hours on the snow-covered mountainside, instead of Arthur. He stalked into the boardroom eyeing each of them as if they were his prey. The silence in the room was painful. Arthur felt a headache settling behind his right eye. Bill Ryeburg chose this unfortunate moment to ask Kehoe about his hunting trip. Kehoe walked slowly over to Ryeburg and told him the hunt was far from over. "I may not have bagged Bigfoot, but make no mistake before this night is through someone's ass is going to be mine!" Ryeburg turned three different shades of gray and sank down in his seat, hoping to disappear off the radar. Josh Gordon decided to make his get away while Kehoe was threatening Ryeburg, but he wasn't fast enough. Kehoe caught him in a bear hug that was anything but a hug. "Josh, son, where are you going? I was just about to ask you why you had me paged against my strict orders, especially today of all days." Josh squirmed and searched the room for help. Of course his attempt was futile, the others were warming up to the idea of Josh being the object of Kehoe's rage. Josh stammered for an answer as Kehoe tightened his grip. Delores stood and began to speak before young Gordon was able to make a complete fool of himself. "Now Arthur, you know Josh would never dream of interrupting you on such an important occasion. I must apologize and beg your forgiveness. It was I. I knew you'd be so upset if we delayed. Everything is under control with the alien and our pharmaceutical division is ready for production. Once the alien gives us the edge on this cure, we can corner the market and watch the money roll in. You can see why I had to have you here. You've sacrificed so much for this moment." Kehoe released Josh and shook his head in amazement at Delores. He knew damn well that Josh had been the one trying to run things in his absence. Now he could see that Delores was the pretender to the throne. How cunning of her to protect the little twerp! Now she had Josh in a rock and a hard place and herself in line for his gratitude. He would have to keep an eye on her from this point on. The last thing he needed was one more board member with leverage against him.

As Kehoe seated himself at the head of the polished mahogany table he began to feel his anger subside. He was very disappointed to have missed the transmission. The excitement on the faces surrounding him as the discussion turned to the historic meeting fueled his emotions. He would assert himself so there would be no more power struggle within his motley little group. He planned for everyone to be at the meeting, just not as close as they would like. If one of them dared to put this opportunity in jeopardy, he would literally make heads roll. Delores, sensing the moment, spoke. "Arthur, would you like to see the transmission that Kasha sent?" The room darkened as Kehoe nodded silently. The ebony vision that sparkled on the screen enchanted Kehoe. He was enthralled by the divine truth that pierced his evil heart. The darkness scattered momentarily and regrouped in the seat of his soul. In that instant he knew his path would lead him to utter destruction or ultimate triumph over these dark strangers. He felt the adrenaline coursing through his body and laughed at the thought of destiny. He motioned for his burly bodyguard as the screen faded to black. "Cease all operations in Alaska. Have all personnel evacuated immediately. I don't want that area disturbed for a thousand miles! Everyone out!" He waved the guard away along with his associates and contemplated his next meeting with Bigfoot. The proof of its existence was no surprise. Legends and myths had always fascinated him. The only difference between Kehoe and the kooks of the world was that he had the inside track on information that eluded the common man. Such was the way for the Kehoe clan. The mysteries of time had been witnessed by each generation and held as a precious commodity that ensured their fortunes. Now he was poised to fulfill the dream fostered by generations of manipulation. He chuckled when he thought of the small minds that would be so surprised to find that "we are not alone". If they only knew he was the real threat! He switched the screen back on and increased the volume. The rich tone of her voice underscored the ethereal lightness of her melodic speech. He could hear in his mind the words she spoke in the tongues of many nations. "I am Kasha of the world known as Zion. Children of the new order called Earth, we are of the unspoken ones and wish no harm unto you. I have been chosen to eradicate the plague that has besieged your kind. Though you may think we are different, you are all my people. There is much to explain and so little time, I will transmit the following coordinates. Blessed are the children of the gift." The screen faded again as the transmission ended. The wheels in Kehoe's mind turned even faster, he and all the others that controlled this twisted world weren't about to have some black exiles from outer space come down as the saviors of mankind. It had taken centuries of mind control through religion to keep the peoples of the world killing and hating each other. The news that we are the progeny of benevolent darkies would rattle the very foundations of the rich and powerful. It could destroy the illusion that "anyone can succeed". Sure a few lucky saps could amass small fortunes, but nothing to compare to the entitled of this world. That's why Wil Nathan had to disappear! Kehoe was sick as he thought of all the "do-good" ideas, helping the poor and educating the masses. The masses didn't want help or education, all they wanted was a handout. His birthright assured him his position. The same families had controlled the world's fortunes since the beginning of time, pharaohs, kings, barons, and chieftains. The land barons and oil magnates. Diamond mines in Africa. He laughed out loud as he thought of all the greed and treachery practiced in the name of the almighty dollar. All the masses ever did was whine about the environment, the cost of living and education. That's why they had nothing and he was on top. His family had never flinched at the degradation of human life, the destruction of the environment or loose morals required to reach the stratosphere of success he now enjoyed. His great-grandfather was the founder of a certain racist organization in the South. His father had controlled a playboy president that ended affirmative action and then set him up with a dizzy broad who made oval office calls that almost led to his impeachment. Then there was great-great grandfather Kehoe, the seed of evil. He was behind the diseased blankets given to Native Americans. What a stroke of genius! Kill them with kindness. It was always affirmed that each Kehoe child was born with a billion dollar bank account. Kehoe called his board members back inside. "Here's what we're going to do."

CHAPTER FOUR

The Bishops were unaware of the events unfolding around them and the sinister plans that would change their lives forever. As they emerged from the vehicle, Mary noticed a line of helicopters above heading towards the top of the rise. Shielding her eyes from the evening sun, she remarked to Ben, "Honey do you see that? Maybe there is some truth to those wild tales Horace is telling." Ben, staring intently at the choppers above, felt a cold chill crawl up his spine. The feeling of impending doom snaked around his heart and took hold as he struggled to sound lighthearted in his reply to his wife. "Sweetheart, it's probably just some weekend warriors on maneuvers, nothing for us to be concerned about. Still, we should stay out of their way. Son, you stay near the house and clear of the woods this evening." Troy, put out by this restriction, began to argue. "But Dad, I was going to look for Zoë tonight." "You heard your father. You can see Zoë just fine from the porch or even the back yard. He comes right out of the woods for you anyway. No more arguing young man, I'm going in to start dinner and when I call, you'd better come right away," Mary told her son in no uncertain terms. Ben continued his gaze at the horizon as the choppers landed atop the distant rise. It was a military operation. Only Ben had no way of knowing it was far more serious than a weekend warrior mission. As top military personnel and government scientists set up their command center and perimeters, ICON Industries had moved into position in their own secret bunker near the military site. The meeting tonight would be intercepted and relayed back to ICON headquarters. Ben sighed and began to follow his wife inside. "Mary, I think I'll put in some research time if you don't mind," Ben said as he rubbed the small of her back and gently kissed her earlobe. "Of course not dear, you go ahead. I'm preparing a special treat for dinner and I don't need any distractions." She laughed and pushed her husband away as he tried to land another kiss.

As the sun slowly slid toward the end of another day, the activity on the plateau increased. Preparations for the historic meeting had everyone on nerve's end as scientists and security scurried about. The most advanced communications and computer systems arrived in record time all bearing the ICON logo. In the command center, representatives from around the world had met and decided on the members that would form the greeting party. Heading the party, Dr. Steinberg, noble prize recipient for his DNA research, Civil Rights Activist Dr. Robinson, Retired General Vanderbilt, and Father O'Malley of the Catholic Church. The briefing of these leaders covered all possible areas of concern, questioning whether motives were peaceful or hostile, and what would constitute an act of war. Never in the history of man had contact of this kind ever been made. As the members now had a chance to talk alone, conclusions varied from one extreme to the next. As the subjects covered scientific discoveries to devil worship, Dr. Robinson seemed delighted at the explanations he heard. Thinking to himself, "After all these years of green men and star wars, it turns out that brothers are running the universe. Miss Daisy won't be sleeping well in the big house tonight." A loudspeaker echoed in the background "T minus 5 hours". Looking around, Dr. Robinson noticed the man with white hair standing in the corner. The noise level of the room was so loud that Dr. Steinberg finally shouted, "Ladies and gentlemen, if I could have your attention please, from all known indicators the visitors are here to help us defeat the plague that is upon us. Their advances in science and medicine could be limitless, not to mention the technology they possess. This is a great opportunity for mankind and we must do everything in our power to make them feel welcome. I have met with the president and he and other world leaders are hopeful for the success of our encounter. Tonight, history will be made. Let's double check the coordinates at the landing site and tighten security on all levels. This is now a Top Secret operation and no further personnel will be granted access to the area." Dr. Steinberg concluded his speech and final preparations began in anticipation of the alien arrival. Agent Hunt strode purposefully out of the command center and positioned himself near a small stand of trees just to the left of the main operations center. He tapped the top button of his overcoat and began to relay information to Kehoe in the secret bunker beneath him. Kehoe instructed Hunt to stay close to Steinberg and the greeting party and be ready for any circumstance that could arise. Agent Hunt smiled as he lit up a cigarette and stared intently at the house in the valley just below where Bishop and his little family would spend their last night alive. He felt the thrill of the kill coursing through his body as he envisioned their impending destruction. "The doc has to go, never should have got involved in this in the first place. Uppity nigger trying to save the world," he said to himself.

Below in the Bishop household, Mary called Troy in for dinner as Ben lingered on the front porch lost in thoughts of this strange disease and the implications of his research. He couldn't help but notice the activity in the distance. "Sure hope they keep it down tonight, it's been a long day and I need some sleep," Ben thought to himself as he rubbed his tired eyes. Mary opened the screen door and watched her husband, "Baby, come on inside and let's get dinner over so you and I can snuggle up and drift into dreamland together," she whispered as she came up behind him and gently massaged his tired shoulders. Ben pulled Mary around him and held her close in the darkness lit only by an occasional firefly searching out a mate with its bright little glow. "Honey, isn't this place just wonderful? So peaceful and soothing." Mary sighed as she buried her head in Ben's chest listening to his heartbeat. "You're right, darling. This is just what we all needed right now. No hectic traffic jams and irate people everywhere you go. No crime or violence threatening our home and family. I don't know why it took us so long to come back. Just chasing our dreams, I guess, when all our dreams are right here in this house." Ben stroked Mary's hair and inhaled her scent that never failed to warm his heart as well as other parts of his anatomy. Mary reluctantly pulled away and took Ben by the hand, "Come on, lover. Dinner will be cold if we don't go in now." Ben reached past Mary and opened the screen door to let her in first. As he followed her inside and closed the front door, he took one last look at the bright lights on the distant hill. Ben shrugged as another cold chill passed through him. It felt almost as if someone was watching him.

The sound of Troy's giggles and Mary's surprised voice scolding their son greeted Ben as he walked into the kitchen. Standing at the back door with the salad bowl on the floor at his feet, Troy looked like he had just lost his best friend as the disappearing shadow of the young deer skipped across the dimly lit backyard. Mary was standing over him with her finger in his face and the other hand on her hip. "Boy, I can't believe you put my food on this floor and let that deer eat out of my bowl! Are you crazy? I'm gonna bust your little behind right here and now!" Mary, mad as a wet hen and about to grab Troy, was surprised when Ben came up behind her and held her in his arms. She was about to protest when he brushed her lip with his finger and turned his attention to Troy. In a stern voice he rarely used with his son Ben admonished Troy, "Son, you get that bowl off the floor now and put it in the sink. Your mother worked hard on this meal for us tonight and you will not disrespect her ever again in any way. That deer has plenty of food right out there in the forest. You may have meant well, but boy if you do that again I'll bust your behind myself." Troy obediently did as his father said and put the bowl in the sink. He went to Mary with tears staining his small cheeks. "Mom, I'm sorry," he sobbed in hiccups, "I only wanted to share with Zoë. I wasn't thinking about how it would make you feel." He broke into more sobs as Mary took his little hand in hers and wiped his tears with her other hand. "Baby, Mama knows you have a tender heart for that little deer, but she is a part of nature and you can't tame her like a pet. Now let's eat dinner and I'll tuck you in tonight with the story of a little boy and his forest friends."

The family settled down around the table as above them in the starry heavens out in deep space Kasha prepared her crew for their visit to Earth. Zenani approached her mother with a confused look in her eyes, "Mother, do we have enough time to help the people of Earth and get back through the portal before Father finds out?" "My dear, I have plenty of time to accomplish these tasks, but you do not. You will stay here and await my return. If your Father asks of my whereabouts you will not lie to him. Now I must leave. I will tell you all about it when I return." Zenani shook her head in frustration, "But Mother, I can go too, I won't get in the way or cause any trouble." Kasha looked at her daughter. "What a wonderful child." she thought. "Just like me, always choosing her own path and so headstrong!" "Daughter, you will remain here in your chambers, no more discussion. I have spoken." Kasha left her daughter in a silent pout and finished her preparation for the journey. Zenani had no intention of staying behind and headed for the star cruiser to find a good hiding place.

Back on Earth at the command center, Agent Hunt contacted the Five once more before the arrival of the alien spacecraft. "All is ready. You can patch into the government computer terminals at any moment. The main display cameras are set up and can be accessed now. You will be viewing the meeting from a front row seat. Sit back and enjoy folks, the party is about to begin!" Down in the valley below agent Hunt had placed his men near the Bishop home in the "cable van" and given them orders to keep an eye on the activity in the house. "This will soon be over and all the loose ends tied up in a pretty little bow." Hunt was very pleased with himself as he walked off to the edge of the forest to brief his men on the ambush. On his signal they would execute a single shot as the alien began to spill her secrets. Sure of himself and confident in his plan, Hunt strolled back into the main encampment and leaned against a military vehicle and took out a cigarette to pass the time left until the main event. He could still see a few lights shining from the house in the valley and wondered if Bishop understood the implications of their encounter at that rinky-dink drugstore this afternoon. "Probably not," he mused. "He still thinks he can save the world and his sick little son." An evil grin passed covered his face as clouds drifted in front of the full moon glowing brightly despite the momentary shadow over it's surface.

In the Bishop's living room, Mary and Ben were having a quiet moment alone when Troy squirmed between them and demanded his bedtime story. "Alright dear, up to bed with you and a short story to lead you into dreamland," Mary said as she led her tired son upstairs. Ben watched his wife and son and realized how lucky they were. Although Troy was ill, he really had been making amazing progress here and Mary was becoming the carefree girl he fell in love with once again. The look on her face as she saw her son filling up with energy and suffering less pain made Ben thankful to the powers that be. "Maybe we're really in for a bright future here," he hoped in his heart as he heard Mary's footsteps on the stairs. Mary tucked her son into bed and began her story. Ben relaxed on the sofa and drifted off to sleep. Troy started to yawn soon after Mary began her story and was sound asleep towards the middle of the forest adventure. Mary adjusted the blankets and picked up assorted clothing on Troy's floor. On her way out, she turned out the light and pulled the door till it was only slightly ajar. Satisfied that her son was down for the night, Mary went downstairs and saw her husband asleep on the sofa. Smiling, she crossed over to the sofa and gently sat down beside Ben and began to rub against him. Her warm curves slowly brought Ben out of his slumber. He grabbed her around the waist and pulled her on top of his reclining form. Mary, feeling the heat of her husband's firm body beneath her, became aroused and passionately kissed him. Seeing the desire in her eyes, Ben got up in a sitting position and struggled to remove his shirt as Mary, her skirt riding up around her hips, hurriedly unzipped his trousers. Mary, rising, quickly removed her lace panties as Ben saw her luscious hips and behind revealed in the firelight. Mary smiled as she saw her husband becoming aroused before her eyes. Ben caressed her behind. Unable to wait any longer, he gently positioned his wife beneath him as their bodies became one with each stroke. Mary returned his strokes with her own until they were both soaring on waves of passion. They climaxed together and gently drifted back to reality in each other's arms. "Umm...Baby that was wonderful as usual." Ben said and kissed her on the forehead. "Well sugar, it's wonderful because you make it that way." Mary sighed and held him closer as she thought to herself how much she loved this man. As the fire popped and hissed, Ben rose and collected their clothing. "Baby, let me get our robes." Ben said as he went upstairs. "Okay, honey. I'll make us some tea and we can sit by the fire."

While the Bishops finished their romantic evening and went to bed, Kasha and her crew were about to land at the appointed site. Just a few hours and this mission would be complete. Kasha steadied herself with the knowledge that she was operating on the premise of helping her progeny, even though Balimar would probably be furious when he found out. She had never once gone against her husband's directives, yet she was determined to fulfill this duty of the

Ancient Ones. Kasha turned and instructed her crew, "Prepare the star cruiser and activate the ship's cloaking shield before we enter Earth's atmosphere. Time is of the essence. We must complete our mission and return before the portal closes or we won't be able to leave this solar system for twenty Earth years." Kasha's crew obeyed their Queen's commands and readied the strange craft for the mission at hand. In a small chamber seldom used by any of the crew, Zenani had hidden herself and smiled as she felt the engines roar to life beneath her. "Mother will be so angry, but I've got to go! Maybe I can help her save the Earth!" With this thought she curled up and dozed with visions of her deer and the young human in her head. As the craft took flight, Kasha's thoughts were with the millions of people her gift would save. In her mind she could see the faces of the people from the past dying from the plague. She sighed, "Balimar, I must try."

The Command Center's alarms were deafening as everyone raced to their stations. Over the blaring PA, "We have contact and are receiving an incoming signal!" The members of the greeting party surrounded the command console. Their eyes widened in amazement as they saw Egyptian hieroglyphs appear upon the screen before them. Dr. Steinberg slowly placed his hand out as if to touch the symbols, "My God, they've returned, it can't be true!" The silence in room was broken as Dr. Robinson shook Steinberg's arm. "Stay with us doctor. Who has returned and what do the symbols represent?" As if in a trance Steinberg turned staring into space, "The Ancient Ones." The group converged on the good doctor for more information as the tension mounted. Wiping the sweat from his brow he began to explain, "It was only legend. As a young med student I traveled to Egypt on the opportunity of a lifetime, when no one realized the secrets that DNA could reveal. We were granted a chance to test the DNA of the pharaohs by the Egyptian government and were allowed a rare glimpse of the burial chambers in one of the pyramids. This one kid in our group named Mendez was convinced that some of the symbols on the walls were of his tribe in South America. We all laughed him off; he didn't even know how to read Egyptian. He wasn't amused and began looking around the chamber. We laughed when he started to chant some tribal song. Then, as he touched the symbols, they began to glow. The laughter stopped and we knew something larger than what we could imagine was happening. The walls began to tremble and a few of the floor stones parted revealing another chamber. There we stood in shock. Most of the students ran out. Mendez took one of the torches from the wall and went down into the chamber. After gathering our senses we followed. From the light of the torches we could see the walls and the floor were covered in Egyptian blue with golden hieroglyphics adorning the walls. As we walked further into the chamber, Mendez read the symbols, "These writings are of my people, and they speak of the battle of the beasts and the unspoken one, his flight on birds of prey and defending the meek, and how the greed of the pharaohs brought death and the plague. Banished to a distant land the Ancient Ones fought the giant beasts of the river and found favor with the Indian race. The Indians honored them and welcomed them into their villages, giving them sanctuary. As the pharaohs conquered and destroyed all in their path, they continued to spread the plague. The ground began to growl and spit fire and nothing could breath. The pharaohs sent a plea throughout the world for the help of the Ancient Ones. The elders responded by healing the world of the plague. They were once again cut down and murdered. The temple of the Ancient Ones was located in the land of my people; there they would mount their last stand. Here, these symbols show the children of Ancient Ones before the battle at the temple, then in the stars. This explains the disappearance of my people. The faithful were taken to the stars with them."

Above, we heard the others returning and the sound of soldiers shouting commands. "In the corner of the room, on a golden pillar, stood the largest black pearl I've ever seen in my life. The soldiers began to fill the chamber, shoving and shouting for us to leave. Mendez stood staring at the pearl. Unconcerned with the commotion, he reached out and touched the pearl and the whole room filled with this warm blue light. The soldiers became afraid and one of them shot Mendez in the back. The ground beneath us began to shake as the walls started to crumble. We raced out. Nothing remained of the chamber and the Egyptian government wrote it off as an accident. Never again have I seen the sign of the Unspoken One until now." A loud booming voice came over the PA system, "ALERT, ALERT, ALERT!" General Vanderbilt shouted over the noise, "Okay people, we have incoming, take your places and may God bless us all." Everyone raced into position, including the security personnel. Perimeters were secured and everyone was placed on standby.

Down below in the valley, young Troy sat up in bed. He could see the lights of the command center from his bedroom window. He began to think of Mr. Horace and his stories of the aliens. Maybe all these people were out there to welcome the aliens! Troy's mind began to race as he got out of bed and quietly dressed. "I've got to see if they're coming!" he thought to himself and rushed around his room trying to find his shoes. At last he was ready to go! Troy opened his door and peeked out into the hallway. He could see his parent's bedroom door was closed which meant they were surely in bed already. He crept downstairs and out into the cool night air. He could see that the lights were coming from a small hill not far from his house. Troy set off in the direction of the lights. Soon he could see all the soldiers and the other people rushing around like something important was about to happen. Troy hid in some bushes and watched as a soft blue light appeared in the night sky high above them. For a moment Troy felt as though he had seen this light before, but the feeling passed and the excitement mounted as he saw the alien craft coming closer to the encampment before him. "Wow, Mr. Horace was right!" he whispered and tried harder to stay hidden in the bushes. It wouldn't matter if he jumped up and out of the bushes. No one would have noticed. Everyone was glued to the sight above. Even the security guards and soldiers were lax in their duties because of the unbelievable sight before them.

As the craft landed, operations began in earnest. All personnel came to their senses. They were still in awe, yet they knew the importance of this meeting. The accurate performance of their duties was paramount in this instance. Troy sank deeper into the bushes and began to tremble at the sight before him. He was overtaken by a sense of deja'vu. How could it be that he had seen this before and didn't remember? His mind tried to shake off the familiarity of the scene, yet Troy wasn't convinced. The sight of doors sliding silently open and the rush of swirling blue light from within the craft brought the sound of a chorus of inhaled breath from those assembled outside. Time seemed to stop for everyone as the anticipation overtook them. What would they see? How could it be that other life actually existed? All those wild stories of abductions and little green men, were they true? How would mankind deal with the presence of an alien group capable of coming to Earth whenever they pleased? Surely the government had known all along. Our airspace was covered with radar. How could they get through without us knowing? All these thoughts were spinning through the minds of the people assembled at the command center. Kasha could feel the doubts and fears of the humans waiting outside and realized how their weakness could drive them to kill what they couldn't understand. This was why the Ancient Ones had become victims. The old fears, distrust, and hatred had been passed down from their ancestors. When would they ever learn that differences weren't threatening? If celebrated and encouraged diversity would enrich their lives and their culture. The achievements to be gained from harmony and acceptance would always be hidden from them. Kasha's heart was heavy with the sadness of knowing her aid to these humans would be in vain. They would continue to destroy themselves regardless of any effort made to protect them. Time was foremost in her mind. After instructing her crew to be on their guard, Kasha led her small group outside.

As the alien Queen began to step from within her ship, all eyes were riveted at the sight of her. The shock was palpable in the air. Everyone had expected the worst and here before them was the most beautiful, vibrant, clearly black female they had ever seen. It was obvious that she was of African descent. Her face was magnificent to behold. Eyes as dark as the night sky drew attention to the serene quality this woman seemed to emanate from inside. The same blue light streaming from the ship behind her lit her skin. The blue-black sheen of her complexion suggested a warmth and comfort that immediately surrounded all those in her sight. A party of five other females slowly floated from the ship and surrounded their Queen. Their mystical black eyes shone with adoration and respect as they looked upon their Queen. The assembled humans were still overtaken with shock at the sight they beheld. Never had they imagined the aliens to be like this. So human-like in their appearance, yet it was abundantly clear that they were not of this Earth. Strangely, no one was fearful. The surprise presented by the alien's physical appearance had replaced the fear of the unknown. Dr. Robinson was probably the most shocked of anyone. Tears of joy shimmered in his eyes at the sight of these majestic beings. His people, the used and abused, subjected for hundreds of years to cruel enslavement and harsh circumstances had descended literally from the stars! For the rest of his life he would remember this moment, not because aliens had landed, but because they were just like him! His heart was singing as he stepped forward from the group. He bowed before Kasha and addressed her with the utmost reverence. "Queen Mother, you honor us with your presence and we are deeply grateful that you wish to bestow this wonderful gift upon us that we may heal our sick and stop this terrible plague." As Robinson spoke, Kasha's crew drew closer to their Queen as a force field began to hum to life around the entire alien party. It was the same blue glow as the light from inside their ship. Fearing that he had been misunderstood, Robinson raised his hands in a placating gesture and backed away from Kasha. Father O'Malley stepped forward and spoke gently to the aliens, "Please, we will cause no harm to you. We only wish to welcome you and learn your most valuable lesson. Many of our people are suffering and dying from this strange disease. We are unable to offer them treatment or even comfort them in their final hours. Your knowledge is our only hope." Kasha, still surrounded by the force field, slowly stepped toward Father O'Malley. "We have no fear that you will harm us. However, these people are my responsibility and I cannot risk their safety in the pursuit to save a dying planet. My people know this plague of which you speak. We have been keeping watch over our ancestral home from beyond the stars. We can only offer the knowledge to cure the plague, but nothing more. You see, even if the plague is stopped, mankind faces a more serious problem. Your fear and suspicion of what you do not understand will be the end of this planet and all who dwell here. We felt the shock and confusion our appearance caused in the minds of all assembled here. That is the reason we have remained hidden from you, our offspring. We were killed and driven out from your presence thousands of years ago because of fear and hatred, yet we have continued to care for you and keep our home always in sight. Now I know what the Ancient Ones came to learn. We can never return to you, but my heart will not allow me to leave you with no means to fight the plague. But heed my words; unless you learn to live together and tolerate those different from yourself, you are ultimately doomed. This plague is only an indicator of the sorrow that is to come if hardened hearts and polluted minds are not cleansed. The key to a world free of the plague lies within those known as the children of the gift. They suffer here for their gift and are weakened by it. Your callous treatment of their race has demeaned them and led them into sickness and frailty. Because you have not respected them for their natural abilities, they are unable to use their gift or even realize their importance to this planet." Kasha finished her speech and motioned for her second in command to step forward. In the aliens' slender, graceful hands was an ornate silver box. Kasha lifted the lid to reveal a small crystal vial of serum, the antidote for the plague. Everyone's attention was drawn to the box, even Troy was straining from his hiding place to try and see what gift the aliens had brought.

Just then he caught sight of a small figure emerging from the ship and fading into the woods just a few feet from where he was sitting. Apparently no one else had noticed, the box still held them mesmerized. Seeing this opportunity to leave his hiding place and follow the small alien, Troy quietly slipped away towards where the figure disappeared. On the other side of the clearing Agent Hunt was transmitting the scene to Kehoe in the secret bunker below. Kehoe instructed him to tighten the perimeter and alert his men to be on guard. In the woods Zenani found Zoë and her family amid the dark shadows. She stretched out her hand and Zoë obediently approached. Suddenly, Zoë's parents were startled into a run by the sound of approaching footsteps. Zenani froze as a gunshot rang through the silence. She jumped as a figure parted the bushes; it was the young human boy! More shots rang out as Hunt's men fired upon Kasha and her crew in the resulting confusion. Kasha had been explaining the antidote when the deer bolted and the first shot was fired. She was hit by the following shots. Her frightened crew levitated their fallen Queen and rushed to the safety of their ship. Zenani could see the ship closing and preparing to leave. "They don't know! They don't know I'm out here!" As the ship departed for the stars, her heart cried out to her mother. Kasha could feel her daughter's cries and tried to regain consciousness but drifted into darkness. Her crew placed her into a hyperchamber to save their Queen and set a course back before the black hole closed. Light-years away in a distant galaxy, the pain of his Queen was felt by the Unspoken One, Balimar, as he cried out in horror, "Kasha!!!"

The members of the welcoming party shouted in anger, unheard by the soldiers and agents as they secured the perimeter. Dr. Steinberg grabbed Agent Hunt, "You fools, the only chance of defeating this plague and all you can think of is destruction. We had the antidote in our hands! Have you all gone mad?" Agent Hunt's punch was so quick it knocked Steinberg to the ground. "Don't ever touch me again! You and others like you make me sick. This world isn't ready for saviors. We control this planet and everything on it, and besides we have something better than the antidote, we have the darkies! Get them out of here!" One of the agents yelled to Hunt, "Sir, team 1 reports sighting a small alien child and are in pursuit!" Agent Hunt snatched his radio, "All teams this is Hunt. We have a code red in sector G and I want it dead or alive! Close off this mountain, and get rid of that damn welcoming party and the Bishops. Then leak it to the press they were killed by the aliens."

The flashlights flooded the woods as Troy watched from his bush. The small alien figure stood lost and confused. Shots rang out landing at her feet. Something came over Troy as he leapt from his hiding place and pulled the alien to the safety of the bushes. They could hear the men running past. Troy could feel his heart racing then realized the warm hand he held was softer than any he had ever felt. It reminded him of his Mom's hand. "Troy, we have to make it to the river!" When they dashed toward the next closest bush, Troy searched his memory trying to remember how she knew his name. The barking hounds were closing in as they crouched in the bushes. Holding her hand, Troy turned to her knowing he had never been this close to a girl. Still something inside of him was strong to protect her. Though he felt no fear, she was so different and he had never seen eyes like hers. He could only ask, "Who are you? I mean what are you and how did you know my name?" "Troy Bishop, I am Zenani, daughter of Balimar. I know much about you and your people, but there is little time. You and other children of the gift are in much danger. We meant you no harm. You are my companion." A look of embarrassment came across Troy's face as he thought, "Companion? Was that like a boyfriend or something?" Now his hand really started to feel clammy. Whatever it meant, he felt it too as he squeezed her hand affirming their bond. He heard the dogs coming down the path. "Zenani we have to make a run for the river, are you ready?" She replied, "Yes my prince." The sound of her soft voice eased his fears as they sprung into action and began racing down the hill. Troy ran as fast as he could. He finally noticed Zenani wasn't running but floating as he pulled her along. A voice behind them shouted, "Over here! It's heading for the river!" Almost unable to stop, they came upon a 50-foot drop at the edge of the trees. Down below Troy could hear the roar of the river. He looked around for another way down but they were running out of time. As the lights danced around them he saw Zenani floating in the open like a deer caught in headlights. He heard the gunmen open fire. Diving, he pushed Zenani behind a tree. The pain! His small chest felt as though it was on fire. When he rolled off Zenani, he could see she was hit too. Blue blood oozed from her arm. They looked into each other's eyes both knowing the end was near. Zenani took his hand as her palm began to glow, "My prince, you cannot die, your gift is most needed to lead your people to freedom. You must take my strength, my Father will protect my spirit." Troy couldn't move, he could only hear her soft words. The bloodstar now pulsed bright as it's light went from his hand and engulfed his whole body, levitating him off the ground. He could feel the pain leave as new strength surged into his veins. It was happening again. Troy felt sad knowing he would not remember, would he lose his friend once more? The lifeforce transfer was complete. It's power repelled his levitated body out over the river like he had been shot out of a cannon. Though it happened in a blink of an eye, to Troy it was slow motion, seeing Zenani's outstretched hand and then, splash! The cold rushing water swept Troy downstream as the soldiers now surrounded Zenani where she lay wounded. The agents stood above her reporting her capture. In a whisper she spoke to the stars, "Father my prince is safe. Now I shall sleep until your return."

Across the galaxy a star fighter the size of a small planet raced at light speed unimaginable to man. Balimar stood as his daughter's lifeforce found him. "Rest now my child the spirits of the Ancient Ones shall watch over you. Your pain is now mine. They know not what they have done but in you they hold the fate of their world. The plague is the least of their worries now. For their betrayal and attack on my wife and daughter they will feel the wrath of the Unspoken One!"

Down below, the agents carried Zenani carefully back to their van and tied her small hands and feet to prevent any further escape. Farther down the river, Troy regained consciousness and gingerly sat up. Shivering in his wet clothes and disoriented, he tried to clear his head. "What just happened?" He was frustrated as tears traced their way down his dirty, scratched face. "I've got to find my way home." Shakily Troy got to his feet but vertigo overtook him and he sat back down. Scared and alone, blood on his clothes with several bruises and lacerations on his arms and legs, Troy sat still and tried to remember how he got here and why his clothes had traces of blood all over them. All he could remember was the warm glow of a blue light and then, nothing! Troy got up, determined to get home to the safety of his family. As he made his way slowly through the woods, he was unaware that his parents had awakened and found him missing.

The sound of gunfire awoke Ben and Mary. They immediately went to check on their son only to find an empty bed. Frantic and filled with fear, Mary raced outside in her nightgown with Ben close behind, trying to catch up with her and calm her down. At the edge of the forest Ben caught his wife and tried to hold her and reassure her that they would find Troy and that their son was okay. As they began to enter the forest calling for Troy, headlights cut across the lawn illuminating the couple briefly before the vehicle braked to a stop a few yards from their front porch. Ben and Mary started toward the vehicle as agents piled out and searched the area. Throwing open the back doors of the van, Agent Hunt stepped down and stretched out his arms to prevent the Bishops from coming any closer to the van. Mary rushed at him, babbling about Troy. Agent Hunt grabbed Mary's hands and tried to assure her that her son must be inside their home. He and his men had combed the woods and there had been no sign of a small boy anywhere. Ben got in Hunt's face and demanded that he take his hands off Mary. As Hunt released her, Mary ran to the house calling for her son. Just then Ben saw the small alien girl in the back of the van. "What in the world?" His mind raced to figure out what was going on. He started to demand answers from Hunt when the little girl held out her bound hands and a blue light began to glimmer in her palm. Ben was amazed as he began to receive a mental picture from the girl of Troy nearing the house. His son was hurt, but he was alive. Then Zenani showed him the C4 and a digital clock with the red seconds counting down. The explosives were inside his house! Mary! Hunt had grabbed Ben when he realized the girl had been seen. Now Ben broke free of Hunt and leveled him with an uppercut to his chin. Troy watched from the woods as his dad fought with the white-haired man. "What was going on?" Troy was scared as he saw his father running to the house screaming for his mother. "Mary, Mary, get out of the house! There's a bomb! Mary!" As Ben opened the screen door a huge explosion filled the night. Zenani began to weep for the Bishops. She felt Troy's presence nearby. As she searched the wood line she saw the boy standing in the darkness with a look of stunned disbelief on his face. The pain in his eyes went straight to her heart. "I cannot leave him with this memory." Zenani whispered in her small broken voice. With the sheer will of her love for Troy, she connected her mind with his and promised him he would never be alone. She once more erased his memory of this night and sent him into a deep trance. She saw him fall to the ground unconscious. Through the back windows of the van she watched as tears streamed down her face. The agents were laughing and patting one another on the back. As they piled back into the van making fun of the crime they had just committed, Zenani was sickened by their presence. "Father knew exactly what these people were capable of. Oh Father, how could they do this? How could they?" her heart cried out as the van and it's secret disappeared into the night.

Moments later the local volunteer fire and rescue teams appeared on the scene and began to hose down the smoldering remains of the Bishop home. Mr. Foster was there as soon as he heard about the explosion over his scanner. He stood off to the side shaking his head and praying that the Bishops weren't home when the house went up. Suddenly a young volunteer fireman confirmed the worst as Mr. Foster overheard the report to the fire chief. Two remains had been found, adult male and female. The woman was inside the house and the man had just reached the door before the explosion. Well that just didn't make sense! Ben would never have left Mary in a burning house! Mr. Foster scratched his head and walked over to the chief and began to ask questions. "Chief, how did this happen, what could have caused this destruction. This is much more than a simple house fire. I know Ben would never have left the house ahead of Mary. Something isn't right here." The chief placed his hand on the old man's shoulder, he knew how close Mr. Foster and the Bishop's had always been. "Now, Seth, I'm not supposed to give out information to just anybody, but this is the exception. The FBI agents claim that this was the result of some gas leak. Me personally, I smell a rat. There's no way this was gas related. Nothing was reported to Chester down at the gas company and in all my years I've never seen a gas related fire blast the foundation clear out of the ground. And you're right about Mr. Bishop. He wasn't leaving the house; he was trying to go in. Now didn't they have a little boy?" Mr. Foster grabbed the chief and affirmed that the boy, Troy, was with the Bishops when they first came to town. "My God, they haven't found his body, have they?" Mr. Foster began to sob and break down. The fire chief assured him that the boy hadn't been found, though his men were still searching. "Please chief, search outside the house. Maybe he got out or was blown free of the house." Just then two firemen approached with a stretcher. A confused and shaken Troy was moaning quietly on the stretcher. Mr. Foster rushed forward to hold his hand as the emergency med techs loaded Troy into the waiting ambulance. The EMT's tried to shut the doors but Mr. Foster insisted on getting in back with Troy. "I'm all the boy has now. His parents died in the fire and I'm his godfather. Get this thing moving! This boy needs to be at the hospital!" Mr. Foster felt all his energy drain away as he slumped beside the semi-conscious boy. "Don't worry son, it'll be alright. Me and you, we gonna be fine." he whispered as he rubbed Troy's head with a trembling hand.

As the ambulance rushed down the driveway, another searched for their injured loved one in the depths of space. Balimar was racing towards the portal to save his wife and daughter when he saw her ship approach. He commanded his crew to make contact with Kasha's ship and instructed them to dock inside his ship immediately. As his commands were carried out and obeyed, the portal closed for another twenty years and Zenani was lost to the mighty King and his wounded Queen. Knowing there was nothing he could do for his daughter, he turned her over to the protection of the Ancient Ones. Balimar attended to his fallen wife.

CHAPTER FIVE

The celebration at the ICON headquarters was a different story with the press corps interviewing each executive in the main ballroom. The champagne flowed freely while movie stars danced the night away. ICON was billed as Earth's victor against an alien invasion. When Bill Ryeburg gave his version of ICON's role in the encounter, the world was not prepared for what would happen next. It started as any press conference of an executive ready to blow his company's horn. Ryeburg went straight to the point. He proudly told how ICON's research department developed the communication technology responsible for the reliable audio/visual link with the aliens. He then showed the cleverly altered video that was later released to the press. It showed Kasha receiving a box then producing a weapon that started the battle. The press absorbed his story like a sponge until a young Asian reporter named Susan Woo began her questioning. "Mr. Ryeburg the footage that ICON provided wasn't very clear. For example, when the alien drew the weapon her motions seemed a bit exaggerated. From the video images it's clear the aliens fired no shots. It's almost as if the tape was interrupted or possibly even doctored. The events leading up until that point prove them to be rather peaceful." Ryeburg cleared his throat, "As a corporate head of ICON, I can personally vouch for the validity of the tape. I resent the insinuation that ICON has misrepresented the events of last night. We were all taken in by their deception. We were fortunate that none of our people were killed." The feisty reporter poked her mike even closer, "Well sir, how do you explain the fact that your men were the only ones actually firing rounds on the tape?" Responding like a politician, he calmly adjusted his tie, "Young lady, shots were fired and my men returned fire!" Unconvinced she fired back, "So we are to believe that a superior race with advanced technology that could produce a weapon that would potentially do more damage than any weapon known to man came out blazing with guns instead of lasers?" Sticking to his script, Ryeburg responded, "As I stated, shots were fired and we returned fire!" The flashes from the cameras were blinding as other reporters yelled for their chance. Ms Woo stood steadfast, "Mr. Ryeburg! Mr. Ryeburg! Please, one last question! If there isn't an antidote, what did they mean when they said the children of the gift were the key to the plague? Mr. Ryeburg! Who are the children of the gift?" Frustrated by the tenacious reporter, Ryeburg lost his cool and angrily responded, "The alien intruder was making reference to African-American children afflicted with the dreaded sickle-cell anemia gene. Of course our own data has borne this supposition out. We have been funding private research that would seem to link the sickle-cell trait directly to the cure for this plague." The room fell eerily silent. Ms. Woo, clearly shaken by this obvious breach of company secrecy by a top official and the repercussions to the children afflicted with sickle-cell, gathered herself and pressed on with her questioning. "Mr. Ryeburg, am I correct in assuming that you are implying that the blood of African-American children who have sickle-cell anemia carries the cure for this plague?" Ryeburg stared intently at the young reporter. "I am not making any declarations to that effect. I simply said that we are researching many avenues and the sickle-cell trait is only a possibility. No further questions!" he stated and stormed from the podium. As reporters rushed out in search of phones and fax machines, Agent Hunt grabbed Ryeburg in the shadows and shook him hard. "You fool! You better thank your lucky stars that Kehoe is busy elsewhere, now you have time to dig a hole and crawl in it. As soon as he hears this, he'll have your head on a platter! Maybe I should save him the trouble and do it myself!" he threatened. Ryeburg felt a cold thin point against his neck and then the sting as a blade drew blood. Shaking violently, Ryeburg pulled free of Hunt and rushed to the nearest exit rubbing at his wounded neck. Looking back, he saw Hunt cocking his hand towards him as if it was a gun, laughing with an evil gleam in his eye.

While everyone else focused on parties and swollen heads and botched press conferences, Arthur Kehoe was personally supervising the containment of Zenani. Under the guise of governmental affiliation with the world not knowing of her existence, Kehoe placed Zenani in a missile silo at the Cape. Kehoe spared no expense or expertise in her confinement. Walls were lined with titanium in the hope of deflecting her telepathic abilities. The greatest medical minds were assembled to construct a life support environment. After the Bishop incident, Zenani lapsed into what seemed to be a self-induced coma. The challenge to the scientists was to accommodate the levitation state she remained in. Attempts were made to take blood and tissue samples for DNA studies, but upon being taken the samples would immediately dissolve, leaving no trace. It was as if she were content to sleep and wait, but for what?

Seth Foster was given custody of Troy as they made the long drive in the limousine to the cemetery. The death of his parents had taken a toll on young Troy. He was unable to eat or sleep. In moments of exhaustion he would drift to sleep and have the same nightmare, flashing bits and pieces of that night but always ending with the laughter of a white-haired man. The townsfolk and friends of the Bishops all gathered around the gravesite to give their last goodbyes. Mr. Foster comforted Troy after he broke down crying, clinging onto the coffins that held his parents. At the Cape a technician recorded blue tears from the alien child.

In the days and weeks that followed the press was relentless in covering the encounter with the aliens, with headlines jumping off the front page. "Alien vampires seek blood of humans!" "Children of the Gift hold the Key!" "Blacks may have cure for plague!" Kehoe slammed one of the papers down on his desk "I leave for a few hours and you idiots allow Ryeburg's fat mouth to leak out information that could destroy us all, then he vanishes without a trace!" The ringing of Kehoe's cell phone shattered the silence in the conference room. "Yeah! Where are you? Argentina! Hunt I don't have to remind you whats at stake, just do it!" The look on the faces of the three seated before Kehoe slowly registered what was said and they knew the fate of their former board member was sealed.

Agent Hunt flipped his cell phone closed with satisfaction, "Oh Ryeburg, Mr. Kehoe has just ordered your head on a platter, and I am to be his waiter tonight!" Hunt laughed at his own wit as he adjusted his headphones to speak to his men. "All teams this is Hunt, what's your status?" he whispered into his microphone. As he gazed through his binos, he did a sweep of the magnificent estate ranch spying the guards on top of the roof and walking the garden grounds. The Spanish-style villa was beautiful. Nestled at the base of a small majestic mountain range, isolated with a breathtaking view of the crashing ocean waves. When the sun was setting as it was now, there probably wasn't another place on Earth as close to heaven as this. Ryeburg, unaware of the surveillance in the night shadows, felt himself finally relaxing after his hasty departure from the cutthroat world he had become a victim of. He paced the elegant marble halls wishing he could undo all that had transpired in the last forty-eight hours. It was useless though. He'd wanted out, but not like this. Still, it felt good to have his future secured. His private Swiss accounts would afford him a life of luxury. All that was left was to grab his hidden stash of jewels and ready cash and be on his way. As he stepped out onto one of the many terraces surrounding the villa, the warm night air caressed him. The heady fragrance of the exotic flowers blooming all around wrapped him in fantasies of this tropical night. He heard soft footsteps approaching and turned to see a lovely young woman dressed in a bandeau top and sarong, her bare legs appearing briefly with every step. Ryeburg surrendered to the exotic thoughts whirling in his mind as he watched the thin fabric of her sarong pull across her shapely hips as she passed him and bent to set his drink on a low table. As she straightened and turned to leave, he was lost in his fantasy as he saw the sway of her long silken hair brush her hips and surround her in a fragrant curtain about her shoulders. He wanted nothing more than to drop everything and feel the heat from her luscious body consume him and as she passed him again he reached out to touch her. She moved sensually against him and whispered in his ear and laughed sweetly in the night air. The shrill ringing of his cell phone brought Ryeburg back to reality as he sent the girl reluctantly on her way.

As Ryeburg spoke with his pilot, Hunt received confirmation from his teams and slowly lowered his gaze from his view to a kill. The first team finally reported in, "This is red team leader, we're in place and I count four on the roof, two on the terrace and a total of ten on the grounds, over." Hunt looked over the grounds to confirm the count, "Roger, red team leader, ensure that your snipers take the ones on the roof at my signal." Moving his binos to look down the road, he watched as one of his crew dressed in black climbed up a telephone pole carrying a pouch. "Blue team leader, is the charge set to blow all power?" An answer came back, "We are ready!" Hunt then refocused on the villa, "At this time recheck all night vision devices. I want a clean sweep of this place with no witnesses. Leave Ryeburg for me!" As darkness quickly approached, Hunt checked his watch. He noticed an elegantly dressed man walk onto a balcony overlooking the pool talking on a phone. Speaking into his mic Hunt asked,

"Red team leader can you confirm target?" Trying to adjust his binos the reply came back, "Roger sir, have eyes on objective, it's our man." As the man turned and walked back inside still talking, Hunt had one of his men aim a listening device toward the room. In the library Ryeburg spoke to his pilot, "This is Ryeburg, is the plane fueled? Good! Be ready to take off as soon as I arrive." He paced the room and began to talk to himself as he checked his briefcase, "I've got to keep moving, think Ryeburg think, can't use my bank accounts till this thing blows over. This ten million in diamonds and cash should hold me until I can figure my next move." Outside, Hunt grinned as he gave the order. "Red team this is Hunt, take out the roof now!" The head shots from the snipers were followed by the thud of bodies dropping to the ground below as Blue team's explosion knocked out all power. Fear gripped the guards. They ran for cover unable to see, and were hit as they scattered. The luxurious sparkling pool turned red with blood and the manicured lawn became a killing ground as the ICON teams swept across firing their silencers. Upon reaching the house, Red team, equipped with night vision devices, dropped the remaining bodyguards like flies. The explosions and gunfire rocked the house as Ryeburg locked himself in the huge room with a few guards. Within moments Blue team had reached the room and blew the door off the hinges with charges, in seconds the remaining guards were dead. Only Ryeburg was left alive, pleading on the floor as the team had their weapons trained on him. Suddenly the group spread apart and Ryeburg found himself crying on the dress shoes of his captor. Looking up he recognized the white hair of Hunt. Smiling as if being reacquainted with an old friend Hunt began to chide him, waving a mocking finger in his face, "Well, well, well, what do we have here? Looks like you can run but you can't hide!" Hunt and his men laughed as they watched Ryeburg squirm. With the briefcase still in his grip, Ryeburg opened it, begging, "There's over ten million here in diamonds and cash, take it, it's yours. Please don't kill me!" Hunt reached down and examined the case, "OK, I won't kill you." Hunt took the case and began to leave the room as his team backed out. Seemingly relieved, Ryeburg rose to his knees still sobbing, "Oh! thank you, thank you!" As Hunt stepped away from the window, Ryeburg noticed a small red dot climbing from his chest to his forehead. Ryeburg cried out, "You promised you wouldn't!" as his head splattered against the wall behind him. Agent Hunt calmly closed the case, "Well I said "I" wouldn't kill you," laughing as he looked at the waving sniper on the roof. When the phone rang in the ICON conference room, Kehoe stood silently at the window watching the tiny dancing lights below. He wondered what consequences would come from such stupidity. He answered the phone without a word and hung up. Staring emotionless out the window he sighed, "And then there were four."

Across the country and around the world shock waves could already be felt as people crowded hospitals coming forward with symptoms of the plague. Soon the children with sickle cell trait became their focal point as hospitals now offered free medical treatment for reasons unknown. Fear and panic became the new epidemic as the public learned of the supposed "cure" for this strange disease. What would this mean for the children with sickle cell who were already weakened by their affliction? Would they be put through more agony to save the world? Would black people around the world be used as "guinea pigs" in the search for a cure? How would all the radical groups in the country be controlled? The safety of the public at large was now in question and black people all over the world began to fear for their families as well as themselves. History had shown that they would be used and treated as animals if there were any gain to be made by the ruthless people of the world. Who would protect them this time around? A call went out among the black community for solidarity when only days after the press release the unthinkable happened.

Two young black girls were abducted from their neighborhood in broad daylight. It was a humid day in Los Angeles and in the area of South Central, children were running and playing in the streets. Fire hydrants gushed cool streams of water as music blared from cars slowly circling the block. Angela Green and CeCe Hightower were playing jump rope together as they did every day since they had first met in Kindergarten. Now that they were in the second grade they tried to hang around with their older sisters, but that never worked out so they just stuck closer to each other. Tired and hot from all the jump rope, Angela squinted up at the sky trying to see through the thick smog that trapped the heat. CeCe wiped the sweat from her small forehead and jerked on the rope to get Angela's attention, "Ange, let's go down to Vaughn's and get some slushee's!" she demanded in her little girl way. "Shoot C, you don't gotta whine like that, anyhow we ain't got no money for slushee's!" CeCe rolled her eyes and blew air through her little lips with her hands on her hips, "I didn't ask you if you had money, girl. I asked did you want to get some slushee's!" Angela looked at CeCe like she had lost her mind, "I know you ain't got enough money to get us both a slushee." CeCe laughed and said, "I got enough for one and we can share!" Angela perked up at this and said, "O.K., but I'm gonna pick the flavor!" The girls skipped hand in hand down the street and around the corner to Vaughn's. They were not supposed to go there, but they did anyway. They hadn't noticed the dirty gray van creeping slowly along behind them. Nobody did. There was no such thing as a suspicious character in this part of the neighborhood. The only suspicious thing around here was when the 5-0 rolled through and didn't stop to harass anyone. The girls continued down the street ignoring the abandoned buildings and the gangs of teenage boys and girls marking their turf.

Vaughn's was at the end of a dead-end street with a vacant lot on one side and a rail yard on the other. The girls knew not to go into the rail yard, but they didn't hesitate to cut through the vacant lot on their way to the store. The gray van slid into the lot and followed the girls halfway across till both the van and the girls were hidden behind the old partially burned glass factory. Noiselessly, two white guys jumped from the back of the van and caught up to Angela and CeCe before they could reach the end of the building. "Hey little girl, where ya goin?" one of the guys asked Angela as he grabbed her around her waist. His buddy already had CeCe and was putting one hand up her blouse while he covered her mouth with his other hand. CeCe was struggling and bit his hand. He cursed her as he let go. She started to scream. "You little black bitch, your ass is mine now!" he shouted as he grabbed her again and punched her, knocking her unconscious. Angela began to scream at the top of her lungs, "Mama! Mama! Please no, Mama!" The men slung the girls in the van like rag dolls as two other thugs muffled and gagged them. The van made its get away. The store clerk at Vaughn's ran out of the store as the van bounced out of the lot. He was able to get the license plate. The men in the van were in jubilant spirits, shouting, "Yahoo! Got that black ass now, baby!" In back of the van the four men passed bottles of booze and weed smoke billowed from the open windows. Their laughter stopped when they heard the moans of the small children. Seeing the tears streaming down the girls face brought a chorus of twisted laughter. One of the men slipped his hand under Angela's dress. Her reaction came natural as she kicked, hitting the man in the face. He landed on the rear doors causing them to swing open. A car behind the van slammed on the brakes seeing the man hanging out the rear. A woman in the car composed her husband then pointed at the van, "Did you see that? Those men had a little girl tied up in the back of that van! Pull over, we have to call the police!" The driver of the van shouted, "You stupid assholes! What you trying to do, get us busted? Leave em alone til we get to the docks!" After closing the doors, they all began to beat the girls. When the van finally pulled up to an abandoned warehouse on the dock, the drunken men piled out laughing and pulling up their pants. The driver looked nervously around to see if the coast was clear. They lifted the small naked girls and carried them inside the warehouse.

While the girls were strapped to some old mattresses on the floor, two of the men closed the warehouse doors and slid a large wooden bar into place to keep anyone else out. They worked hurriedly on the girls. Their laughter echoed in the empty building. "Hey man, I know how to do this!" one of the hoodlums slurred as he grabbed Angela's small arm, looking for a vein. "Hurry up, dude! The cops are probably lookin' for us right now!" his buddy nudged him and staggered, almost falling. Soon the men had Angela and CeCe hooked up to a crude blood transfusion system and were draining the girls, each taking their turn infusing their blood with the girls'. Beaten, raped, and now drained of life sustaining blood the girls lay near death. The men danced around drunkenly, talking nonsense and taking turns mutilating the girl's bodies. Angela passed into death with these words ringing in her ears, "Hey man, if I'd known these niggers was able to cure this shit, I might not have killed so many of them!" Laughter echoed around the building and CeCe finally succumbed. As their tiny spirits left their bodies, they joined hands in death as they always had in life and floated free, away from the horrible sight beneath them. The men, high on drugs and alcohol and still excited by the violence they committed, continued their gruesome mutilation of the girls, spreading blood and body parts around the room. They soon became tired and slumped one by one down to the floor into the carnage they had created.

Meanwhile, at a nearby gas station, the couple who saw the van and its occupants waited for the police to respond to the call they placed nearly an hour ago. Finally a cruiser appeared, slowly pulling into the station. The couple rushed over trying to report what they'd seen. The policeman stepped from his car with his hands up, gesturing for silence and trying to calm the couple. "Now folks, calm down please, and tell me what happened," the officer said as he pulled out his notepad and prepared to take their statements. Near hysteria and angry over the time that had passed since a report was made, the woman began to urgently tell the cop what happened, "Officer, we saw a girl bound up in the back of a van with a group of white men fondling her and trying to hurt her! They were driving in front of us when the back doors of the van flew open, startling my husband and causing us to nearly wreck our car. I saw a young black girl in the back! She was tied up and her mouth was taped, but she was struggling against the men. One of the men shouted at us and managed to get the doors shut. The van sped off towards the docks! Lord knows what they've done to that poor child by now! You've got to hurry! It was a dirty gray van, maybe 85-86 model Ford with license plates from Arizona. Please officer, you've got to do something, it's probably too late by now!" The policeman tried to calm the woman and get her husband to take her back to their vehicle while he called for back up. "Ma'am, we'll do the best we can to find this girl. With your description, it shouldn't take us very long." She reluctantly got into the car with her husband. "Officer, I don't want to seem ungrateful, but if the police had responded sooner, it might have been possible that you could have caught these crazy men and saved this girl. Now, I don't think there's any hope." She shook her head and turned away as tears began to roll down her cheeks. Her husband hugged her and tried to comfort her as the policeman hurried to his car and called for backup, repeating the information given by the woman.

Soon the neighborhood was crawling with police. Word had leaked out over scanners and soon the press as well as the public was aware of the abduction. The Greens and Hightowers soon discovered that Angela and CeCe were last seen headed towards Vaughn's and no one had seen them since. They were frantically searching for the girls when police officers found the van outside the warehouse. After a quick reconnaissance of the building, the police forced their way in and began searching and shouting as the suspects were seen. The four men had recovered from their stupor and were fleeing the scene in every direction. Confronted by the police, two of the men pulled guns and were shot point blank. The other two were caught just outside the warehouse. They resisted arrest and fought violently until police subdued them and placed them in cruisers. News teams were everywhere trying to get footage of the arrest and the inside of the warehouse. Police quickly set up blockades and police tape as the violent crimes unit was brought in. Head detectives photographed the grisly crime scene. Many of them went back outside weeping and sick, trying to compose themselves in order to continue collecting evidence and get the bodies out. This scene was being broadcast nationwide as two officers knocked on the doors of the Green and Hightower homes. Wailing and cries of anguish were the only sounds coming from their homes as the police left, shaking from the horror they'd seen and the grief of the families fresh on their hearts.

The neighborhood streets were packed with people outraged by the murders and the slow police response. Susan Woo stood with mike in hand preparing to broadcast live from the warehouse. She began her report with the facts. "Today two young African American girls were playing and having fun when their world and this neighborhood turned into a dark killing ground in broad daylight. Angela Green and CeCe Hightower were classmates and best friends. They were in the second grade at a public school here in South Central. Allegedly on their way to a local store, the girls were abducted and taken here to this abandoned warehouse. What went on inside is too violent and inhuman to imagine. The girls were raped and beaten by a group of young white men apparently bent on murder and mayhem. Sketchy reports from several sources indicate that the suspects drained the girls of their blood in an amateur blood transfusion attempt. Direct links to the ICON press conference of a few days ago is evident. Citizens, angered by reports that police were notified by an eyewitness and still failed to respond in a timely fashion, have taken to the streets and are protesting the handling of this crime. The city is under curfew for fear of riots over these murders. This is Susan Woo for Channel 6." Shaking and saddened by the news she had just reported, Susan Woo walked to her news van, ignoring questions and pleas from the crowd gathered on the docks.

As broadcasts went out around the nation and the world in millions of homes, people watched horrified and disgusted by the brutality committed against the two young girls. In some homes, there were other black people who had disappeared mysteriously or who wouldn't be missed because they were all alone without family or anyone to care that they were suddenly gone. Their captors were white people from every walk of life, young or old, rich or poor, it didn't matter. Fear of the disease and lack of human kindness had turned them into hunters. They stalked and kidnapped unsuspecting blacks and kept them in basements, cellars and attics. Their hands and feet were bound and they were gagged with duct tape, ripped up pieces of sheets, and any other thing a person could find around the house. There was even a farm way out in Illinois that held blacks captive and shipped them around the globe in private planes to rich and famous buyers worldwide.

Back in Los Angeles vigils were held for the murdered girls and around the world parents bluntly told their children what had happened to Angie and CeCe. They hated to put this fear into their children, yet there was no other way to ensure that they understood why they must stay together in large groups and never leave the sight of a parent or teacher. The Nation of Islam provided escorts to and from school as a resurgence of the Black Panther Party consumed the adults who were tired of sitting locked in their houses fearing every white face they saw. They knew this was how their ancestors must have felt. Hunted and used for the gain of a race that hates you because of the color of your skin, all their emotions boiled to the surface as black people worldwide struggled to live their daily lives, fearing for themselves and those they loved. A siege mentality overtook many and they turned to their communities and built trust and hope together. Their ancestors had overcome persecution to lift their children up and give them hope for a better tomorrow, they could now do no less! The government made many announcements about the freedom and rights of every citizen. They assured that the abductors would be prosecuted to the full extent of the law as the Aryan Nation and the KuKluxKlan marched and rallied in the nation's capitol, spreading hate and making light of the murders. Any racial harmony that had been gained over the years went down the tubes as the world fell back into strictly divided sections and fear and paranoia gripped everyone by the throat.

This was the world in which Troy Bishop grew up. In his small hometown, people had pretty much always kept to themselves and had a "live and let live mentality". This was because everyone had roots there and knew everyone else. There were pockets of trust and respect throughout the country as black and white came together and upheld peace and the safety of everyone in their community, yet they were in the minority. Luckily, Troy grew up with kind and wise counsel of how the world could have been; yet he was also made aware of the dangers that the outside world held for him. Since he was a child of the gift, Mr. Foster kept a vigilant eye on Troy while trying to give him as normal a childhood as possible. He grew up like any child would, he had chores and helped out at the drugstore. He was a Boy Scout and Eagle Scout. He went to church every Sunday and mowed lawns on the weekend as he got older. He played basketball, baseball and football all through school and excelled in academics. His first love would always be the stars above and his dreams of exploring space as an astronaut. He had several close friends and yearned for his mother and father, especially at the holidays when it was only he and Mr. Foster. To everyone who knew him, he was the all-American kid. Mr. Foster was always amazed by his keen sense of nature and his true love of animals. He knew so much about the animals, it was as if he was part Indian and loved to track and fish though he would never hunt. What scared Mr. Foster most of all was the boy taking off in woods alone with all the madness that was going on. He would always find Troy sitting in the back yard in a lotus position meditating, surrounded by animals. It amused Mr. Foster seeing the squirrels climbing on his head and deer licking his face, sitting there like a young Bruce Lee. So it was no surprise when he enrolled Troy in Kung Fu classes and he quickly absorbed the teaching and earned his black belt. By all appearances Troy seemed to be a happy, active teen, even though at times he became silent and somewhat introverted. Some nights dreams would come that would bring him abruptly awake filled with a fear that he couldn't understand. There always seemed to be a piece missing that was the most important part. If he could remember that part, he would be free of the occasional dreams that left him grasping at straws. Always in every dream there was a mind link with someone else that he felt physically even though he was asleep. It was as if another person was whispering in his ear, or actually even there in the room with him. Always he woke up with the same name ringing in his head, Zenani. This puzzled him to no end because he'd never recalled knowing anyone by that name. Yet there it was, as clear as crystal, always Zenani. He never told anyone about these dreams, not even Mr. Foster. Partly because his parents were always in the dream and that was still too painful to talk about and partly because he was scared that if he told someone the dreams might get worse or come more frequently. He knew that didn't make any sense but he still kept them to himself. Exhausted by the emotions the dreams aroused in him, Troy decided not to fight them any longer. He sought to define his unconscious state while dreaming. He practiced his martial art and deeply studied yoga. He researched everything he could find on hypnosis and psychology in hopes of unlocking the secrets in his psyche and revealing the portions of the dream that always eluded him. Little did he know that someone was there with him in mind and spirit. Someone else had the same dreams at the same time.

Miles away at the Cape, the girl Zenani was growing and changing into a young woman just as Troy was becoming a young man. She was monitored day and night around the clock and studied by the most brilliant scientific minds from every nation in the world. They were mystified and actually had discovered very little about the young alien who was growing up right before their eyes. Amazingly, she was growing as a human female of relative age would have done; yet she remained in a comatose type of suspended animation. Her clothing also "grew" with her. From all analysis it seemed to be an organic molecular structure that changed to accommodate her bodies changing shape. On one of Kehoe's visits, the scientist briefed him of frequent activity of her brain waves then mysteriously nothing. As he stood over her in the room, the pearl black eyes flew open sending his mind whirling through ancient Egypt until he came face to face with Balimar, then they closed. The guards rushed in to see the shaken executive sweating, trying to loosen his tie. "Mr. Kehoe, Mr. Kehoe! Are you O.K.? What happened?" Kehoe stared at the child, "Just meeting the family, I suppose," he murmured absently as his mind raced to sort through these images. The guards looked at one another confused and left the room behind Arthur Kehoe, shaking their heads.

CHAPTER SIX

The streets of New York City were almost deserted. The few people walking around were cloaked and wore heavy sunscreen with dark glasses and hats. Most businesses were now underground and the windows of corporate offices were blackened. The strangest occurrence was the absence of the bums and homeless, all was silent not even the streetwalkers were out. The police remained a constant presence in full force with black officers demanding they be teamed together. People filled the local hospitals. The majority was very light skinned to white instead of the usual large representation of darker skinned patients. Fear was the master of their emotions as many neglected the usual healthcare system and opted for home remedies or trusted family physicians. Most feared their blood would be taken against their will or worse fates, such as death would await them inside those antiseptic halls. The entrepreneurs began collecting their own blood in small amounts, bagged it and sold it, much like "nickel bags" of dope, in the streets backed with heavily armed enforcers who took their fair share of the profit. Many blacks found it easy to "trade" quantities of their blood for any number of goods and services. Most actually were living quite well materially, but the constant danger to their lives made it difficult to enjoy any of the "trade-offs". They knew it was only a matter of time before their numbers came up. Nobody likes to pay for something they can just as easily take by force. Now the plague had taken a new turn as it started to attack the heart of America, the young. The ozone surrounding the Earth was now dangerously depleted and allowed UV rays through that were not only affecting the elderly but the young as well. The symptoms of dark blotching and sores followed by high fevers and bleeding ulcers that soon surrendered to death's grip defied all treatment. As much as people of the world wanted to unite, the sought-after anemic blood became more precious than gold. ICON's boldest move was to bring the flock back into the fold, knowing they needed the support of the black community to continue their research. The offers were unimaginable. They provided security and wealth to those that agreed. Soon underground facilities sprung up around the country and the world as others followed suit. Now united as one, the world was trying to come together to combat this awful plague...or were they? The governments of the world combined their efforts to help find a cure, from primitive potions to space medicine.

This is where the platform was set for ICON Industries. With space programs in effect for the last few decades, they had recently completed a space station that could support over 5000 people. ICON had secretly been constructing a moon colony for future mining operations. The world's leader still hadn't accepted the fact that another race of beings had visited their world. The problem in question, when would they return? Billions of dollars were spent developing high tech weapons and more advanced space shuttles to combat future encounters. The space program was being swallowed up into ICON Industries and the ultimate control of all operations fell to Arthur Kehoe. Throughout the country and around the globe, many blacks were still being abducted. None were ever found, not even remains, as the fear and mistrust mounted despite all the "wonderful" programs designed to find a cure and promote harmony among the races.

It was in this surreal world that Troy Bishop would soon begin to realize his dreams of space travel. At his high school graduation, he was of course the valedictorian. Mr. Foster stood proud with tears glinting in the corners of his eyes as Troy walked across the stage to accept his diploma. He whispered his thanks to Ben and Mary for this precious gift that had filled his lonely days with so much wonder and now the pride he felt as he watched Troy, strong and filled with promise. The boy had been accepted at Tuskegee and would be pursuing his dream of becoming an astronaut. Mr. Foster felt the presence of the Bishops' as he embraced Troy in a big bear hug. "Boy, you done good! Your mama and daddy would be so proud! Lord knows they're up in heaven with the missus right now, just smiling and tellin' all the angels what a boy they have down here!" Troy blushed as he hugged the old man tight and tears began to form at the mention of his parents. To this day he still couldn't deal with the pain locked deep in his heart. Mr. Foster sensed Troy's unease and remained quiet as they walked to the truck in the school parking lot. On the way home, Troy began to talk about his future and all his plans. He was anxious to get home and pack for his visit to the campus at Tuskegee. He worried about leaving his grandpa all alone, but he knew he had to leave his small hometown to get his chance at reaching the stars. Troy became quiet again and his mind wandered to the dream he had just last night. It was the same as always except this time he had seen his parents as never before. They were standing together surrounded by a soft blue light that seemed so familiar. Although he couldn't see their faces, he felt their love enveloping him and his heart surged with all the emotion he'd held inside for so long. When he awoke his pillow was stained with tears he never knew he'd cried. Now in the fading light of the afternoon, he pulled the memory of his dream around him and promised himself as well as his parents that someday he would break the mystery surrounding their deaths and let go of all the pain in his heart. He came back to the present as Mr. Foster pulled into the driveway and they got out and went inside to celebrate this momentous occasion. Inside his friends waited to surprise their favorite classmate and celebrate their day together. Troy jumped as the door opened and everyone yelled, "Surprise!" The party got into full swing as he and his friends danced to the latest hits and shared their good news of future plans and all their hopes and dreams. Everyone was excited about going away to school. The world had definitely changed, but they still held all the promise of youth can. The celebration lasted well into the night when finally everyone began to head for home to get in a good nights sleep before they "conquered" the world. Out on the front porch, Troy joked and laughed with his friends and they all promised to stay in touch.

When the last car pulled from the drive Mr. Foster came onto the porch and took out his pipe. They stood in silence together as the night wind began to pick up and lift the tree branches gracefully in the moonlight. Troy shuffled his feet, trying to think of how to say all the things he held in his heart for this man who had loved him and raised him like he was his own son. Even though the path he would take to his dreams excited him, he knew he would be homesick immediately. If it weren't for his grandpa, he'd probably never have been able to get past that awful night when his life had turned upside down. As much as it hurt to talk about his parents, Mr. Foster had always understood and never pressed him to talk about it. He had kept his parents alive by sharing memories and talking of them as if they were always watching over him. Mr. Foster cleared his throat, also wondering how to say all the things he needed to tell this young man. For so many years, Troy had brought him companionship and a sense of family at a time in his life when he had lost the woman he loved most. Somehow, they both had helped one another through the hard times. Now came the moment Seth had both dreaded and looked forward to. He had brought Troy through the trials of boyhood and was very proud of the young man he had become. All that was left now was the send-off to college. This was harder than either of them had expected. Mr. Foster finished smoking his pipe and sat down on the porch swing. The silence was interrupted by the occasional squeak of the old swing. Seth cleared his throat again and broke the stillness of the moment by telling Troy about the first time he'd met Ben. "Your father couldn't have been no more than six or seven at the time. He'd come into the store with your granddad and started nosing' around in everything, same as you did when I first brought you in to help out. He was such a polite child, though. Wasn't a mischievous bone in his body. He always struck me as being so much older than he was, you know, like he had an old soul. He went straight for my medicines and books on pharmacology right off the bat. He asked so many questions, your granddad finally made him go sit at the soda fountain with a comic book. He didn't like that, no sirree, I tell you! Imagine that, havin' to make a child look at a comic book! My wife, Becky, she took him under her wing from that moment on. See, your grandmother had died young and it was just your dad and your granddad for the longest time and the missus, she naturally started in motherin' him since we'd never have any young'uns and here he was without his momma. Made perfect sense to Becky. Well that boy was at the store forever after. He grew up right behind that counter, askin' questions from sunup to sundown, and he was a quick learner just like you. I see so much of your father in you, son, and it makes me feel so proud. See, your father was a real good man. He was smart as a whip and always stood up for what was right. He couldn't stand to see any kind of sufferin', whether it was humans or them forest creatures. He devoted his life to helpin' others in his own special way and I know you'll do the same. I'm sad to see you goin', Troy, but I know you won't forget what I've taught you. And you know you can come home anytime, the more the better for an old lonely man like me! There's some things I've been savin' for this moment, cause I know you wasn't ready for them till tonight. I've always tried to protect you from everything that happened the night Ben and Mary died, but I have to tell you that they had no idea what happened to them. Something happened that night that had to do with the work your dad was doin'. I don't know how or who was involved, but believe me when I say the explosion was intentional. I thank God every day that you was out in the forest messin' with them animals when it happened. I don' know what I'd have done if I'd lost everyone I love." Seth wiped the tears from his eyes and continued, "Your dad brought me some of his research papers the day before the explosion. I kept askin' him why, but he couldn't say. He wanted me to put them up in case he needed them later was all he said." Mr. Foster got up and went into the house. Troy sat on the porch trying to compose himself after hearing all these things about his dad. It hurt so bad to remember all the good times. It only made him wish for times that he would never have. Now there were papers that his dad had left behind. Did he know his life was in danger? Why had he stayed here risking everything and leaving his son an orphan? Troy began to get angry as he thought how selfish his dad had been. In the same moment, he knew his dad wouldn't have put his family in jeopardy. He was just so mad that he'd lost everything, left only with dreams that tortured him instead of giving him an escape. When Mr. Foster came back out, he saw Troy shaking on the top step and went over to him. He set a box beside Troy and spoke to him softly, "Son, I never meant for you to get upset tonight. I guess I wanted you to know how much of your father is in you and how much I still miss him, too. He loved you more than anything and I know he never wanted things to end up like this. He came here to continue his research to end this awful plague that's still upon us, but it was mainly because of you and the sickle cell. Why with the grant money he got to do his research out here, he knew he was bound to find a way to cure you. That was his main priority, you and Mary. His family was everything to him and he was trying to continue his search for a cure to sickle cell while developing a cure for the plague. Maybe these papers can help you see what I mean. You'll understand some of it, I'm sure, but still it's a mystery. Whatever the case, he didn't want them gettin' into the wrong hands. You be sure that you keep these safe no matter what. I'm convinced that if the people responsible knew of these papers or of your existence, all hell would break loose around us."

Troy's head snapped up at this news and he began to go through the box in the pale glow of the porch light. "Now Troy, there's one more thing I want to give you before you get caught up in these here papers," Seth said and gently held out a small velvet box in his rough palm. Troy took the box and opened it, puzzled by the contents. Mr. Foster began to explain in a teary, broken voice of how he'd come to find the golden band cushioned inside the box. "It was the day after the explosion. I'd gone back up to look for anything that may have remained after the fire. I was siftin' through the ashes as the sun caught this ring and the glint drew my eye. If you read the inside, you'll see it was your mothers'. It was all I ever found, the only piece of your momma that you've got to hold on to. I've wanted to give it to you many times before, but like I said, I know you wasn't ready until now. I've put it on one of Becky's golden chains, cause she loved your momma and daddy so much and she would have loved you too. Wherever you go, the love of those two women will always be with you and mine too. Son, just don't let the pain and the bitterness win out. Think of the good, of the love and legacy they each left with you. And know that they are watching over you." Mr. Foster finished his speech and left Troy on the porch to sort out his feelings. Troy lifted the chain and ring from the little box and held them in front of him, dangling and glinting in the night. He read the inscription in the ring to his mother from his father, "always and forever", and tears once more ran silently down his face. He took the chain and fastened it around his neck. As he turned the ring around and around in his fingers, he felt a peace surround him and for a moment he flashed back to the image of his parents in his dream. Mr. Foster was right. He was going to be all right because these people who he missed so much were watching over him and it was their strength and love that would sustain him through the hard times. Even though he couldn't see them, he could feel them. He dried his eyes and picked up the box containing his father's papers and went inside to look them over and try to understand what had happened all those years ago.

Most of the papers were scientific thesis and research his father had obviously been working on for quite some time. He had been getting closer to a breakthrough when he had brought this box to Mr. Foster. Troy began to wonder about the events that could have prompted his father to feel as if his work needed to be kept secret. Mr. Foster had come into the room and sat by the fireplace with a mug of cocoa for himself and Troy. "Are you finding any answers in that box, son?" he said to Troy as he handed him his cocoa. "Actually, I'm finding myself more questions about why my dad felt he needed to leave his most important research here instead of at home. There must have been something going on that I never knew about. Do you remember any strange events or unusual encounters my father may have had with anyone?" Mr. Foster sat quietly going over the days when Ben had first come back and recalled how the government had them FBI men everywhere because of that alien attack. Suddenly he recalled how Ben had reacted when that white-haired fellow had come into the drugstore. "Come to think of it your dad did have an unfriendly conversation with one of them agents that was swarmin' all over town cause of that alien scare that was goin' on. I didn't catch all the conversation, but I do remember hearing something about ICON Industries and national security. Your dad did not like this man at all and I could tell their talk had upset him. He tried to hide it from me, but I knew him better than anyone and I could always tell when someone had got on his bad side." Mr. Foster finished and looked at Troy. Troy tried to remember all the dreams and pieces of that night and he recalled the white-haired man laughing, always laughing. It wasn't just dreams but actual events that really took place that dreadful night! Tears began to form in Troy's eyes as he asked, "Grandpa, I can't remember anything except bits and pieces, but I know ICON had my parents killed. Why?" Grabbing his hands, Mr. Foster tried to explain, "My son, I tried to prepare you the best I could, this is a cruel world and now even more, they won't hesitate to kill you, do you understand?" Troy looked into his grandfather's face knowing the words he spoke were the truth. "Yes, grandpa, I'll be careful." Troy looked back into the box of tapes and papers hoping he would find some answers. He stayed up most of that night trying to piece together a picture of his father in his last hours before the explosion.

Most of that short summer passed for Troy in that box. Try as he might, he just couldn't make sense of all the information in front of him. Sometimes it seemed as if his dad was finding that his sickle cell somehow repelled the plague. But how could that be? Was his father finding that blood from a black person could save the world? If that were the case, the repercussions for anyone of color would be numerous, and not necessarily good. He had heard stories all his life about mysterious disappearances and the much sought after commodity that his blood would become if he were in the larger urban areas. But growing up here had in no way prepared him for the reality of life out in the world. After seeing all the papers his father left and the warning his grandpa had given him, Troy began to feel as if he had better start to watch his back, even at Tuskegee. The last piece of paper he had found was at the bottom of the box and seemed to be part of a journal. It was clearly his father's handwriting and it was about Troy and his illness. His father had written of his amazing recovery shortly after the move. There were chartings of his blood analysis and notes on his improved physical condition. His father had determined that he had somehow gone into a type of remission from sickle cell but could find no medical explanation. There was a strange notation about a small star shaped imprint on his left palm that had never been there before. He wrote of how Troy had loved the woods and always wanting to see the aliens that everyone was talking about. He wrote of how good life was here and the love for his family driving him to finish his research. The last line chilled Troy to the bone; his father had written that he feared for his life and that he might soon have to leave so his family would be safe. There were notations about ICON doing experimental research on blacks and a possible moon base operation where subjects would be taken for more extensive medical research. It was clear that his father feared that his findings could lead to genocide for his race. That entry was dated the day before the explosion. Troy pondered these monumental discoveries and realized his father was right to fear the ultimate path his own research would blaze. Already blacks and whites were more polarized than ever and the plague had changed the world so much. There seemed to be little hope that mankind could close the gap, ever widening, threatening to swallow this planet whole.

Troy finished out his summer helping at the drugstore as he always had and taking some extra fishing trips on weekends with Mr. Foster. On their last night together before Troy left to begin his studies, both men sat outside late into the night reminiscing and joking. Troy finally felt a sense of peace for the first time in a long time and he hugged Mr. Foster tight and told him he loved him for helping to unravel the mystery of his youth before he went away and undertook the pressures of college. Tears came to

Seth's eyes as he watched his boy head inside and prepare to become the man he was destined to be. He sighed heavily as he sat on the porch swing and lit his pipe. Upstairs Troy double-checked everything to make sure he hadn't forgotten anything. Tomorrow his future would begin! The knowledge of his past strengthened his resolve to achieve his goals. Someday he would have the chance to reveal the truth about his parents and why they had died in vain. He felt his father's presence in the room and the urge to turn and search the shadows overtook him. As he turned toward the window he saw his curtains stir as if a light breeze had disturbed them, but there was no wind outside. Troy broke into a cold sweat and whispered his promise to the stilling curtains, "Someday, dad, I'll expose the cowards who took you from me." He turned and got into his bed, tears lightly tracing his face and fell into a deep sleep.

As the mists of sleep shrouded him, Troy began to dream. This time the dream was different. He felt no sadness or anxiety, only peace and wonder. He was in the forest and there was a glowing blue light just ahead. A figure stepped from the shadows and with the light surrounding her she motioned for Troy to come to her. She was the most beautiful person he'd ever seen, but she most definitely was not human. Troy was lost in the warm ebony sheen of her skin and the love that shined from her mysterious pearl black eyes. She drew him into her arms and gently kissed his lips. A melody that turned into a voice inside his head came from her full shapely lips. "My Prince, you have grown as have I during our time apart, I wait for your arrival. There is much we must do together. When the time is right, I will lead you to my side and you shall free me from my bonds. My love and light will guide you in your quest to the stars." As the dream faded, Troy stirred in his sleep and rubbed his left palm. When the morning sun came streaming through his window, he sat up and tried to remember the dream girl and the words she had spoken. He felt a mild sensation in his left palm and suddenly remembered the notation on his father's journal page. Troy looked at his palm and tried to make out some sort of shape there, but it was no use. Anyway, he had to get up and get ready. Today he would leave for Tuskegee and he couldn't keep his future waiting!

CHAPTER SEVEN

Arriving on the campus of Tuskegee was a dream come true and Troy soon absorbed the vast knowledge that was available. His professors were amazed at his IQ and he soon found himself on the dean's list. Troy loved being on campus and continued to work hard toward his engineering degree, but he couldn't shake his need to fly beyond the stars. After his second year he transferred to the Air Force Institute of Technology and it was everything he had hoped. The time seemed to fly by and Troy earned a master's degree with distinction and a Ph D in aerospace engineering. Mr. Foster was so proud of his son, Dr. Troy Bishop the astronaut, that he and the whole town threw Troy a welcome home parade. Troy couldn't believe his eyes when he arrived that day, but it did his heart good knowing somewhere in this crazy world there was still a place to call home. He had made a point to call every weekend and always returned on his breaks. On every break he would always visit his parents gravesite.

When Troy pulled his car up to the curb, the high school band started playing as town folk rushed up to greet him. Many of his old friends patted him on the back as they led him to the center of the town's square. There he could see the smiles of Mr. Foster, Molly and even the mayor. As he climbed the stairs of the gazebo, Molly gave him a big hug, "Baby we're all so proud of you, welcome home!" The mayor shook his hand and gave him the key to the city, "Son, we knew you had it in you!" Troy thanked everyone as he looked over at the man that risked so much and had raised him as his own. The roar of the crowd brought tears to his eyes as he hugged his grandfather. Chants of "speech, speech, speech" echoed from the crowd. Looking around, Troy wiped the tears from his face, "I don't what to say, but when I look among you I see my own family, and many friends. I know I couldn't have done it without your help." Suddenly a shout from the crowd, "Troy, bring us back some moon rocks!" The laughter erupted and everyone looked at Troy on the small stage. Blushing from the excitement, Troy was soon surrounded by his family of friends as the celebration began. The band started to play and the scores of well-wishers shook the hand of their hometown hero. Today was a good day and the fun lasted well into the evening.

When Troy and Seth returned home they were both exhausted and didn't make it past the front porch before flopping down for a rest. The country view flooded Troy's memory with his childhood, the stars in the sky seemed brighter than he remembered. The fresh country air was a far cry from what he had just left in the city. It filled him and invigorated his mind. In this moment, each man seized the opportunity to let his thoughts wander as if enchanted by the night. Seth finally asked, "Son, so what you gonna do now?" Troy slowly rubbed his hands together thinking, "Grandpa, everything has been happening so fast. That's why I just wanted to come home for a while and leave all my troubles behind." Scratching his head Seth asked, "Boy are you having girl problems? I mean you've never talked about having someone special in your life." Troy laughed, "I guess I've been so busy with training and school that I just haven't had time for that kind of stuff. Besides the dreams of her that I have, they're so real. I can't see her face, but I know she's there with me, always." Confused by the rambling Seth continued, "Who son? Are you still having the dreams from that night?" Troy struggled to find the words, "Grandpa I could never love another, she's in my every thought, my dreams, and I feel her energy all around me. Something happened that night for sure, something that has lived with me my whole life but I can't remember a thing. I must be going crazy! From the first time she came to me in a dream, her eyes so dark and piercing and when I woke my hand was burning as if someone had placed a hot iron in it. I feel like one of those alien abduction nuts in an old B-movie. I'm about to begin my astronaut training and I'm on the brink of insanity! There's no way I'll get through those battery of tests. Grandpa what am I to do?" Seth patted him gently on the shoulder, "There, there my boy. First of all, you did right coming back home to think things through. After all that has happened over the years, I' m now a true believer that nothing is impossible. I'm sure there is a connection between your story and the visitors from space. When you were a child I wouldn't sleep at night so that I could stand guard over you. The times were crazy as well as the people after that night. I never told you before that I sat in your room in the dark with my shotgun. It was exactly one year after your parents were killed. As I sat watching over you, I saw the blue light that seemed to come from your small clenched hand. I thought maybe it was a trick of light from the hall, but then I got up and walked over to you and opened your hand and there in your palm was the source of the light, a small raised star shape that seemed imprinted into your palm. This phenomenon would happen every year on that night. Besides promising your father that I would watch over you if anything happened, I never from that time on told of your gift. As I would often wipe the sweat from your brow, I would hold your hand and as the Lord is my witness I have never been sick a day in my life since. Although many nights I pray just to join my Becky, something inside guided me over the years to see to your safety. No son, you aren't going crazy, but rather evolving into someone very important to all of us. I think somewhere in your father's papers there was some kind of shorthand that may hold some answers. As for now, you must get some rest." Troy agreed as the two went inside for the night.

The bright morning light broke through like spotlights shining in Troy's face. Cheerful sounds of songbirds heightened his senses to the welcomed smell of breakfast. Seth had always been an early riser and was through cooking and getting ready to head to work when Troy strolled into the kitchen in his robe. "Good morning son, I was just about to head out, the foods on the table and the coffee is ready, if you need anything just call me at the store." Seth said. Still rubbing the sleep out his eyes Troy replied, "Thanks Pops, I should be okay. I'll stop by about noon to take you to lunch at Molly's." Seth reached and grabbed his arm, "Son it's great to have you home. Get some rest, alright?" Troy agreed and watched him till he drove out of sight. His eyes began to search across the countryside. This was a special place. It was a haven, even the town folk weren't as affected by the unknown disease like the outside world and the few cases reported were of newcomers or folks that had left town for a while. "Why would beings from another world choose a place like this anyway?" he thought. "The world was going to hell in a hand basket!" he chuckled. After getting his fill of country cooking, Troy turned on the television while getting dressed. A reporter was standing near the Grand Canyon and from what Troy could see, a new volcano had emerged and violently erupted. The camera zoomed in on an ash cloud towering up into the sky, blocking the sun and turning the day into premature night. Troy shook his head, "Mother Earth just ridding herself of all the poisons we've placed inside of her." Troy couldn't shake the feeling he had, only that the time was near. It felt as if an apocalypse was coming, but wasn't that what every generation felt as they became aware of the frailty of man? The news stories changed from one report to another, from wars in distant countries to more murders of black people, kidnapping and mutilations. The sad looks on faces covered with creams and wearing hoods trying to hide themselves from the sun. Troy flicked off the set and walked outside on the porch and felt the warm morning sun on his face, its warmth somehow relieved him of the sorrow he couldn't escape. Maybe a walk in the country would help clear his thoughts. As he stepped off the porch, he looked back at the still open door. "Couldn't do that in New York, be lucky if they didn't steal the screen door," he smiled. Walking in the woods was nicer than he expected, smelling scents he had long forgotten, hearing the innocent sounds that only nature could bring and seeing life in harmony with the colors all around. Nothing could have been more breathtaking as Troy walked deeper into the coolness of the woods. Even though most of the paths had disappeared with overgrowth, he still knew them like the back of his hand. Troy hadn't noticed how far he had gone until he reached the clearing. For a second he felt a little dizzy, then a tingling sensation all over his body. He stood there in a daze as a jolt went through him, falling as if in slow motion to the carpet of fragrant pine needles covering the ground. The morning dew felt wet upon his face as he rolled to his back seeing the pale blue sky, then darkness. In his dream, her beauty unfolded coming so closer. A satin darkness unmatched in his world bending closer with a kiss. Troy knew it was here they had first met and now a kiss, even better. As their lips met his heart felt as if it would melt, then small drops of water hit his face and his eyes began to open. A ray of sunshine made him blink as the kiss came again and again but more like a lick. Struggling to focus his eyes as the licks became more playful, Troy rose and looked into the face of a baby bear. Thinking it was all just a dream, he gently pushed the baby back and braced on his elbows, noting that they were not alone. The loud roar sounded that mother wasn't far away. In an instant the clearing was filled with the sounds of a zoo. Looking past the baby, his eyes soon saw the mother, then a wolf, an owl and other flocking birds. Out walked a mountain lion with cubs. They had him surrounded! Then it stopped, not a sound could be heard. The crackling of twigs broke the silence and Troy thought, "What now?" Odd as it seemed, he didn't feel afraid of the animals as they moved next to him and the sound got closer. It seemed to come from all directions, but no farther than behind him. Still sitting on the ground, he turned. There stood the grandest buck he had ever seen in his life with twelve points or more, a hunter's dream for the Whitetail Hall of Fame. Although he wasn't a hunting man, Troy knew one for the record books and this one would score a 205 easily. The buck slowly continued to step closer as Troy rose to his feet to ensure that he wasn't still dreaming. This buck had to be the size of a small moose and how he could have escaped the hunters this long was amazing. The animals stood motionless at the sight. Moving slowly forward as if in a dream, Troy finally recognized the buck as his childhood friend, Zoë! Troy stepped forward with tears streaming, "How could this be possible? It's been almost twenty years, this can't be!" As he looked into the eyes of his dearest friend, he knew it was true and embraced the buck as he cried. The other animals quietly left the clearing as if in respect for this private reunion. Troy felt himself spin back through time, feeling like a child again, trying to believe in this miracle. As he dried his eyes, he inhaled the spicy air, marveling at the beauty of nature and the return of his dear friend. He looked into the bucks' eyes and spoke softly as he stroked the strong neck of the animal. "Do you remember her or am I crazy? Was she here with you, too?" The buck looked at Troy and cocked his head as if he understood. Suddenly a blue light flashed in the large brown eyes of the deer. Troy froze in disbelief. Then he laughed out loud and startled the buck. "I'm sorry, Zoë. It's just that I came here to find some sanity and this is anything but sane! Standing here, talking to the most magnificent deer ever about an alien who loved us both a long time ago, enough to risk her life to save ours! I just can't shake her from my memory, if only the bits and pieces would come together. If only I could find her, if only we were together. There is something she wants from me. What is it? And my parents, how are they connected to her blue light?" Again the tears flowed as Troy watched the buck turn and finally leave the clearing. He noticed that the sun had risen higher in the sky as he dried his eyes. "Time to head back and pick up Pop's for lunch, but I think I'll keep this meeting to myself!" he thought.

As Troy drove into town on the sunlit, curving country road, his mind wandered. He had his career and all the accomplishments he still had to achieve. The visions of the girl haunted him. How could he take his dreams and turn them to reality if he didn't solve this puzzle? He needed to find a way to unlock the secrets buried in his subconscious. He felt like he was coming closer to the answers, especially after seeing Zoë today. He shook his head as a smile crossed his face. "Imagine that, after all this time!" Maybe it was destiny. Maybe if he just followed his heart and pursued his dreams, the girl would guide him to her side. Those were the words she had spoken in his dream. He remembered those words as if he'd just heard them, "My love and light will guide you on your quest to the stars." Troy decided to trust in those words because his heart told him it was the only way. Feeling as if the weight of the world had been lifted, he pulled into a parking space right in front of the drugstore. He was still smiling as he walked into the store. "Well son, you seem awfully happy this afternoon. It wouldn't be because of that big breakfast, would it?" Seth chuckled and slapped Troy on the back as he came behind the counter. "Oh, I don't know, could be." Troy replied as he jabbed a phantom punch at the old man. "Come on, son. Let's go on over to Molly's." Seth laughed as he dodged Troy's jab. As they left the store and locked up, Seth remarked again on Troy's new attitude. "I don't know what happened at home this morning after I left, but I sure am glad to see you in such good spirits, son." Troy's smile widened as he walked down the street, obviously enjoying the sunny afternoon. "I took a little walk in the forest and cleared my mind. It's amazing what a little fresh air can do for a guy's head." "I'll say! Well, I don't know about you, but I'm past due for some of Molly's chicken and dumplings," Seth remarked as they neared the diner. As they approached the front of the diner, they could see some young men Troy's age standing around. Their laughter grew louder and Troy heard their remarks, "Well, well, well if it ain't the hometown hero, another chimpanzee in outer space, that's all we need!" Three of the five men deliberately stepped in front of Troy to block the door. Troy recognized the one making comments from his high schools days, Tommy Hodges still up to his bullying ways. The guys all roared with laughter at their play, "Boy, Molly don't serve no monkey food in there, so why don't you run back to the zoo?" Troy just smiled and patted Seth on his shoulder assuring him everything was all right, "Grandpa it's okay, these are some old friends of mine from high school, go ahead, I'll meet you inside." Seth hesitated as Troy urged him on, "Don't worry, I'll be right in." Seeing his grandfather safely inside, Troy turned to face his old high school bully, "Well Tommy, looks as if you're still up to your old tricks. I see you've started your own chapter of the KKK." The smiles disappeared and the group slowly surrounded him as Tommy spat tobacco juice on Troy's shoe, "Boy, I never did like you and you won't be so funny talking with no teeth." Troy felt the presence of one of the men sneaking up behind with a two by four. He ducked the instant the man swung causing the board to hit Tommy square in the mouth. All the years of martial arts training came forth in Troy as he went into swift and deadly action, breaking the board as the man now swung back at him. In one motion he gracefully sidestepped and backhanded the guy while side kicking one of his buddies. His hands moved expertly as he worked over the next two. In a matter of seconds it was over. Troy stepped over Tommy, who was spitting blood and teeth out of his mouth, giving him some friendly advice, "You may want to try eating something a little softer, like bananas." Molly and Seth rushed to Troy as he entered the cafe, "Son are you okay?" asked Molly. Troy looked back outside as the men helped each other to their feet, "I'm fine, but I can't say the same for them" he laughed. Molly grabbed Troy and Seth leading them to a table, "Well now, after all that commotion I think you both deserve a good hot meal, so sit down before I use some Karate of my own." They obeyed Molly without question. After they ordered Troy was puzzled by the look on Seth's face, "Pop is everything okay?" Taking a sip of his coffee, Seth replied, "This used to be a quiet community. These last few years have been taking their toll. Recently they found some bodies out on the old county road, drained of blood. Wouldn't surprise me a bit if that crew wasn't behind the killings. Of course they were people of color. You know, as long as I can remember no one in these parts wanted to recognize their Indian heritage but I believe that's why these folks haven't been affected as badly. My grandfather was an old medicine man. I guess that's why I chose to bring modern medicine to these mountains. When your father chose the medical field, I was overjoyed. I would never have thought his work would one day prove so important it would cause his death." Troy replied enthusiastically, "That's it!" "What's it?" Seth asked. Troy clapped, rejoicing. "My dad's notes, you know the shorthand we couldn't make out, that's because it's written in an Indian language. I remember some of the symbols from my studies of tribes and customs." Shaking his head Seth said, "If it would have been of any tribe here, I surely would have recognized it." Troy jumped from the table, "You're right, but that's the only lead I've got. At least we know we're not looking for an American tribe. I've got to get started, tell Molly I'll take a rain check. See you back home!" he yelled as he dashed out of the cafe. The ride home had Troy filled with excitement, hearing Seth talk about the past jogged his memory. He thought of his mother. He remembered all the wonderful times she used to talk about, growing up in Panama and her family roots. There had to be a connection between his dad's notes and Indian tribes of Central or South America.

Troy was so lost in his thoughts that he didn't see the dust cloud rising up behind him and the truck that caused it. Before he knew it, the bullies from the cafe were tailgating him. Shouts of "yahoo" and the loud blaring of the truck horn indicated that these good old boys wanted their revenge. Troy grew more frightened as they sped up and rammed the jeep. His mind raced through terrifying thoughts of what could happen out here in the middle of nowhere if these rednecks ran him off the road. He sped up and tried to outmaneuver the big four wheel truck, but there was no way he could outrun his pursuers. As the chase wore on, the men in the truck grew more excited and one of them pulled a deer rifle from the rack on the back window of the truck. "Let's see if we can bag us a coon, boys!" he shouted through his tobacco stained teeth. Spitting a stream of nasty brown juice onto the truck bed, he sighted Troy's back window and shot several times. The blast broke out the window and a few of the shots embedded themselves in the rear of the vehicle. Troy almost lost control of the jeep. He couldn't believe this was happening! Just a few hours ago everything was perfect and now this nightmare was being played out in the hot midday sun. Troy could see the men had their faces covered in bandannas like bandits in an old western. They were so close he knew the next shots fired would not miss their target. As he gunned the engine and pulled away in a desperate attempt at escape, he saw the flash of huge antlers in the brush alongside the road. "How on Earth?" he thought. He looked in his rearview mirror just in time to see the horrible collision and hear the sickening thud and squeal of twisting metal as his own screams began to spiral out of control. Zoë had leapt in front of the truck full of hateful men and lay broken in the dusty road, a pool of deep red blood seeping into the parched ground. The truck had skidded sideways and thrown the men in the back several hundred feet into the air as it flipped and slid in what seemed like slow motion, crashing into a huge oak tree. The men inside were killed instantly as the cab collapsed against the tree. Troy pulled over and got out of the jeep. He ran to Zoë and knelt in the road cradling the big deer's head. He sat there crying like a small child and feeling like he had lost his last true friend. His vision blurred as he looked around the scene of the accident. He sensed that no one had survived the crash. He gazed down at Zoë as he felt a warm moist roughness against his hand. The big deer was licking his hand and Troy felt his friend becoming limper in his embrace. "No, Zoë! Don't leave me! Why did you do this? Why did they have to hurt someone? This whole world is crazy!" Troy began to come unraveled as he ranted there in the dirt, soaked in the deer's blood. Zoë raised his head with great effort and looked straight into Troy's eyes as if trying to calm him. The same blue light that had flickered in Zoë's eyes earlier in the day, flashed once more as the star shape in Troy's palm began to pulse and grow bigger. In an instant Troy saw the scene of Zoë, Zenani and himself in the forest on that night so long ago when they were all just children, of the forest, of the stars and he, a child of the gift. Slowly his focus shifted to his brave friend on the ground, breathing his last breath. Zenani's light curled like smoke from Zoë's wet, velvet nostrils and like a magnet flowed to Troy's hand. He felt a surge of love and peace surround them as Zoë's soul took flight, free of pain and transformed into an iridescent light that streaked towards the sky, prancing joyfully within the clouds above. He began to cry softly once more as he laid Zoë's head down and searched the skies again for his beauty. Troy's tears flowed freely and openly as his cry echoed throughout the forest. The minutes seemed like hours before he could muster enough strength to move Zoë from the roadway. He felt the twisted bodies of the wreckage had met a deserved fate, he couldn't bring himself to care for them after what they had tried to do to him and it sickened him to realize that was just exactly the level of ignorance they had operated on. Hate begets hate, and love conquers all. Troy started to laugh out loud as the cruelty of man sank in, he scared himself so much that he didn't remember how he made it back to the jeep. He could only rest his head on the steering wheel. He heard a vehicle approaching but was too exhausted to care. Seth careened to a stop just a few feet from the jeep and jumped out, yelling for Troy and shaking all over. "My Lord, if something has happened to that boy, I don't know what I'll do!" he said over and over as he saw the truck smashed against the tree and the smear of blood in the road where the deer had lain just moments before. He ran to the jeep and looked inside. "Thank you Jesus!" he yelled as Troy lifted his weary head and looked at his grandpa. Seth's voice broke as he spoke, "Son, are you hurt? A cold chill went over me when I saw them fellows burnin' tires out of town right after you left. But when I reached the house and you wasn't there, I backtracked hoping you took the outer road. My Lord, what happened?" Troy sat back and took a deep breath, "I don't know Grandpa, they came out of nowhere ramming the back of my vehicle, trying to run me off the road. I had no choice on this outer road but to try to out run them and they started shooting at me. They would have killed me if Zoë hadn't jumped in front of their truck." Seth, still unsure of Troy's condition repeated, "Are you sure you're okay? We've got to get out of here, can you drive?" Looking where Zoë' laid in peace, Troy nodded, "Yeah Grandpa, I can follow you back to the house." When they arrived home, Seth began to check Troy over and treat the few abrasions he had. "Son, why don't you go upstairs and get cleaned up, you're covered in blood." Seth gently nudged Troy toward the stairs as he spoke. "Come on, now. I'll have some of Molly's dumplings warmed up and we can sit down and talk calmly about what happened." Troy obeyed his grandpa and went upstairs to take a shower. He looked down at the bloody clothing he had on and hurried his steps up the stairs. As the steam from the hot shower filled the tiny bathroom, Troy felt the tension leave his body. He stood under the hot stream of spray for a long time when finally he decided it would be best if he went back to the Cape tomorrow instead of staying on for a few more weeks. Seth didn't need to be worried about him and he definitely didn't want anyone to start harassing him at the store. No, it was time to get on with his life and let the past go. Staying here would only bring more trouble and that was the last thing either of them needed. When he had dried off and finished dressing, Troy opened his laptop and sent an e-mail to his friend and fellow trainee, Lou Stryker. He wanted to send Lou some examples of the hieroglyphics and the code he thought some of his dad's papers might be written in.

Going through the papers again, he could see that he was onto something and he knew with Lou's help he could surely crack the code. He closed his computer and packed his clothing and shaving kit and went downstairs. He could see Seth in the kitchen shaking his head and mumbling to himself. He took Seth by the arm and guided him to a chair. Sitting down at the table with his grandpa, he could see the worry etched in his forehead. "Grandpa, I know what happened today has really upset you and I'm sorry. I should have ignored them at the diner, but I get so sick and tired of being at the mercy of ignorant people. It seems as if every black person in the world is on an endangered species list and I guess I just wanted to fight back. The color of my skin is all some people will ever see, they won't acknowledge that I'm human and that I have value and worth just because I'm different than them. I've decided to go back to the Cape tonight and get on with my training. I don't have to prove anything to anyone except myself. The only family I have left is you, and I won't stay here and put you in harms' way." Seth shook his head and dried the corners of his eyes. "Son, I don't want to see you go, but I know it is best for you to go on and start your training. I don't know what got into them boys. You know we've never had any problems like that here, before. I wish things were different, but the truth is the world is filled with good and bad people. You can't run and you can't hide, but you can use your head and I'm glad to see that you know the difference." He hugged Troy tight and they sat in the pale glow of the lamplight and finished their dinner, laughing over old times and talking excitedly about the future. As they finished cleaning up the kitchen, Seth told Troy he was personally taking him to the airport in Centerville. "You'll never get a flight out of our small airport tonight and I'll feel much better seeing you off myself." "You'll get no argument from me grandpa, besides with the long ride we can talk some more. I want you to stay overnight in Centerville and come back home in the morning though." " All right, son. Sounds like a plan!" As Seth went outside to have his after dinner pipe, Troy dashed back upstairs and went over his dad's papers one more time. He couldn't wait to show them to Stryker, it was only a matter of time until the secrets would be revealed. He made a last check of the room and gathered up his things. He felt as if he finally could deal with his past and build his future without fear. When he got downstairs, Seth was waiting for him with the truck running. "Let's get this show on the road, son! You know, I haven't been to Centerville in ages. A little traveling sounds good this evening." Troy laughed as he threw his suitcases in the back of the pickup and climbed into the seat next to Seth. Time seemed to fly and before he knew it they were at the airport. Waiting for his flight to depart, Troy and Seth had coffee in on of the small cafes and talked about Troy's future and the store back home. As his flight was called to board, Troy hugged Seth and promised to keep in touch. The night sky flashed brightly on the horizon from a distant storm as Troy looked out his window of the plane. He could see Seth standing, silhouetted against the huge glass windows, waving his hand, hoping Troy saw him. Troy felt a glow from within that he had never felt before. Watching his grandfather brought a rush of emotion and he finally realized how much love he had in this life instead of feeling loss. "Time to go forth," he thought. "Sir, we're about to depart. Could you buckle up, please?" Her smile was more pleasing than her voice. "Sure," he said and made the necessary adjustments. The plane started its taxi toward the runway and Troy continued to watch Seth's figure in the distance. It seemed strange being on a plane in virtual darkness but most flights were now booked at night anyway. Dark glasses and heavy sunscreen were the norm when people traveled during hours of light.

The flight to the Cape was nice, considering they were flying faster than light and were landing fifteen minutes later. As passengers disembarked, Troy could smell the ocean, even in the airport. Everyone moved along the mobile sidewalks. Tinted windows exposed the breath-taking views of the sea. The Cape's airport was typical of most coastal cities that were underground as well as undersea. Looking out of the windows of the lower level was wonderful, seeing the ocean-life swim by and domed cities in the distance. Waiting for his luggage took longer than the actual flight, and he got caught up in people watching. Troy thought how odd it was... all the lighter-skinned people in dark glasses just chillin and the people of color doing the jobs that would expose them to the sunlight. The government had ruled that white people didn't hold jobs that exposed them to the suns rays, but rather supervised. How convenient, how the cycle continued. All his life Troy dreamed of traveling in space and now the opportunity seemed tainted because white pilots and astronauts came down with the plague so quickly and were removed from flight status, leaving only minorities as viable aviators. Glancing about the airport, he noticed all the black pilots and service workers. Still only a hand full of blacks were astronauts, but that was changing with the need for more personnel in space medicine and moon mining. Space exploration had been top priority for the last twenty years along with star defense weaponry. How that dreadful night changed not only his life but also the way of the world!

CHAPTER EIGHT

"YO! Troy, over here!" Nothing could change the big mouth of Lou Stryker as Troy turned to face the booming voice. "What's up big guy, had to cut your visit short?" Lou laughed, embracing Troy with a huge grin on his face. Troy replied, throwing up his hands, "What can I say, it was time to pop smoke, what are you doing here anyway?" Lou watched as luggage started to fall onto the revolving platform, "Oh! Its like that! First you e-mail me all this sci-fi crap out of a Spielberg movie. Hey man, your pops was into some weird shit, but come on we can't talk here." The two went down the walkway talking over old times. Troy was taken in by the sea's view as robots flew lifelessly by, "It's always amazing to see nature as it truly is, for centuries man has longed to conquer the stars when space is here around us." Lou pulled out his cell phone ignoring Troy, "Your old man was dealing with some heavy players, its still going to take awhile to break his code and from what I can tell, for good reason. What do you know about ICON Industries?" The words struck a nerve with Troy, "Not much other than my father did some research for them years ago and them owning a few companies." Lou waved his hand before Troy, "Well my man, take a good look around you because all this is ICON, and I need not remind you who spearheads the astronaut program here at the Cape. We've got a lot to talk about. I've got your room reservations squared away. Let me just call and check on tonight's dinner reservations." Troy laughed, "Well you just do that."

Through the glass window he could see a large whale in the distance. Troy stepped closer to the glass and closed his eyes to hear its pitch. Slowly the giant came closer and locked eyes with him. Troy stood in a trance. He smelled the sounds the whale was making. Soon more whales came and hovered by Troy. Their echoes could be heard through the glass. The excited glee of several children caught Lou's attention. His back was turned to the whole event. Shocked by what was unfolding before him, he rushed over and grabbed Troy's shoulder, "Dude, snap out of it! Those things are looking at you like fish food!" Lou escorted Troy past the crowd that had gathered and into the elevator. After the doors closed, Lou sternly shouted at Troy, "Earth to Bishop! Man what do you think I've been trying to tell you? ICON runs this show and probably had something to do with your parents' death and you come in here acting like an alien from another planet, communing with nature and shit! Why do you think I'm here early? After I used the university's computers, the place was surrounded by government agents asking all kinds of questions." Troy whirled around to face Lou, concerned for his friend, "What happened, how did you get away?" Lou smiled, "Are you kidding, half of the nerds on campus are hackers, wasn't nobody talking. You never said anything about Dr. Bishop's work with the space program." Troy stammered, "All I knew about was his work for the hospital, later I found out ICON was funding some of his research, before the accident." Lou stared at his friend, thinking that Troy actually believed his parents' deaths were accidental. His voice lowered as he looked at his friend and shook his head, "The death of your parents was no accident, you're dad was onto some dangerous information. The pictures you sent of the house that was definitely C4. They don't use that stuff anymore, but I remember back in SF training how buildings would blow when we trained with C4. ICON snuffed your mom and dad out, how did they miss you? Oh man, Troy! If they ever connect you to that night, you're finished!" Troy was about to respond when the elevator came to a halt.

The natural light was blinding when the doors opened. "Welcome to the real world partner!" Early morning sun glared off every available surface. The sounds of traffic and loud voices could be heard as black workers and other people of color hurried about their jobs. Troy watched all of the cars with tinted windows. Lou flagged a cab, "The Cape Inn" he told the driver. "Troy we'll talk later. Let me show you the town." Troy sat back as the cab dashed into traffic. Compared to the country and small towns left unprotected, sections of the city were under huge glass domes with pollution clouds hanging close by. The people on the streets hurried along with coats, hats and the familiar dark shades. Even then you could tell what side of town you were on. The whites that couldn't afford the niceties bore the marks of the plague with their heads hung low, trying not to show their sores and blistering skin. When they entered a domed area checkpoint, the vehicle was scanned. Troy looked over at Lou, "So what's that all about?" Lou shook his head, "They haven't found a cure but they are damn good at detecting the virus." Troy couldn't help but think about how strong his feelings were here and the strange encounter with the whales, what did it all mean? No time to worry over it now, they were pulling up in front of the hotel and Lou was motioning him out of the cab, "Come on, man. I'm ready for breakfast!"

After finishing a huge morning meal in the hotel restaurant, Troy and Lou went their separate ways, with the promise of dinner later and a cram session on Dr. Bishop's papers. Troy entered his hotel room and fought the immediate urge to sink onto the sumptuous king-sized bed. He wanted to call and see how his grandpa was doing, but Seth wouldn't be home this early. He was probably on his way home from Centerville right now, another hour and he would check on Seth and then go to bed. He was drawn to the sparkling waters that shimmered as the sun climbed higher in the cloudless sky. The view from his room was spectacular. It seemed as if he could touch the sun from where he stood. His mind drifted to the ancient peoples who worshipped the golden disc as their most powerful deity. He could definitely see why they were attracted to the life-giving orb crossing the sky on a daily voyage. The sun never failed to come up each morning, and that was pretty impressive to mankind, even in today's modern, plague-ridden world. The sun still held its reign supreme. Troy shook his head at the irony of man always trying to conquer and control the world. Nature was a force all it's own. When will we ever harken the wisdom of our ancestors and honor the Earth and all the elements? What once gave us life is now taking it back, and we wonder why? The balance has long since been destroyed and now our life source is retaliating. How's that for justice? A sea bird flew across the sky and Troy began to daydream about someday taking flight himself. All the hard work was going to pay off. His lifelong dream was so close. He could feel the currents lifting him into a world where his skin wouldn't matter. His joy overflowing, Troy slowly came back to the real world as a freighter whistle blew on the waters below. He began to put away his clothing and arrange his things in the bathroom. He took out a few folders with some of his fathers' papers and sat on the edge of the bed and took off his shoes. As he looked through the paperwork, he realized the depth of his fathers' work. This had been a life-long project, one his father had been curious about even in his teenage years. Although he had never been able to devote enough time to his research, not until ICON had funded him anyway, he had never given up on it. Troy found some papers dated about a year after his birth. The research seemed to intensify right after his parents had discovered his sickle-cell anemia. His father had made notations about sickle cell in the margins of his research. This was why his dad had taken the grant from ICON. Just a hardworking man trying to save his only son. Who would have thought it would lead to all this? Now the nightmare continued. ICON was directly in charge of the entire space program. How could he possibly escape the notice of their far-reaching power? He dropped the papers onto the floor and rose to stretch himself. He rubbed his temples and walked to the phone. He placed a call to his grandpa and made sure that everything was fine. He hung up and immediately crossed back to the huge bed and fell into a deep sleep.

As dream mist swirled in his head, Troy began to toss and turn fitfully. He felt himself falling through space, but was strangely unafraid. He began to see the Earth coming closer and closer into view and realized he was high above, floating on a gentle breeze as if he were as light as a feather. Soon he could see the land and waters below and there were tribes of people everywhere. Only they were from a time long ago. The sheer numbers fascinated him. He'd always assumed tribes were just small groups of people, but this was different. They were much more civilized than modern men had believed. Temples and altars were magnificent and extremely well crafted. Clothing was minimal and totally functional. However, those who held high positions were adorned accordingly. There was a group of people who were different from the rest, yet somehow the same. These people were known as the Ancient Ones. The people held them in high regard. These holy men cared deeply for their fellow tribesmen. Everyone shared huge food stores and the work was equally distributed. They were supplied with food and clothing in return for their labor. Grand pyramids dotted the landscape. All of the people were content and carried on their lives in much the same fashion as we do today. The scene shifted and Troy felt as if he were watching a documentary. Peace and harmony began to be replaced by chaos and distrust. People began to fear those who were different. Illness and death began to corrupt their Eden. Soon they began to perform rituals and worship the elements of nature, thinking their miseries were related to the Ancient Ones. They offered sacrifice to the sun and worshipped all manner of gods to no avail. The Ancient Ones soon separated themselves and departed from their tribesmen. They traveled far and everywhere they established new tribes, teaching all they had known. Eventually, these tribes branched out and covered the Earth. The Ancient Ones settled on the Nile and began to teach their tribes how to live according to nature and how to use the intrinsic creative powers that lay in each human. From the Ancient Ones and the daughters of men came the line of rulers known as pharaohs. They were esteemed as gods and treated as such, although possessing no special powers. Their lineage established them as revered sovereigns. Over time they became proud and boastful, resenting the favor with which their Fathers were showered. When a terrible pestilence came upon the land they began to whisper about the Ancient Ones. They placed fear in the hearts of their subjects against the Ancient Ones and poisoned their minds to the benevolent Fathers. Soon the Ancient Ones were driven out again and once more they traveled and settled on an island. There they flourished and lived for years until the pharaohs found them and sank the island to rid the earth of the Ancient Ones. They escaped and roamed the earth until they found a remote tribe in the Andean Mountain Range. Here they were welcomed and cherished for many decades. Just as the scene was about to change, a persistent buzzing sound awakened Troy.

Waking up not knowing where he was, Troy lurched out of bed and looked around confused, trying to get his bearings. The loud, sudden banging on the hotel room door made him jump. Lou's voice boomed through the thin door, "Hey, man! Are you in there? We're gonna be late for dinner and these folks won't hold a table forever! Come on, open up!" Troy rushed to the door and opened it to find Lou standing there with his big hand ready to deliver another rain of knocks to the door. "Wow, you really been knocked out, huh bro?" Troy nodded and motioned Lou inside as he headed for the shower. "Hurry dude, we're barely gonna make it as it is!" The warm water washed over his stiff body and Troy began to relax. His mind was still grasping at the dream images but they were as elusive as the steam from his shower. All he could remember was pyramids. He felt as though some important clues had been revealed in that dream world. Or maybe he was just trippin' on his dads' papers. He got out of the shower and quickly dried off. He dressed in his best silk shirt and trousers and rushed out to the bedroom to find Lou looking through the folders he'd left out. "Your dad was meticulous with his research, that's for sure. We need to crack his code, though. I have a feeling it holds the key to a whole lot of things ICON would rather keep under wraps!" Troy put on his blazer and watch and slipped on his dress shoes. He looked at Lou as if he wanted to discuss the subject further and then changed his mind, "Come on, I'm starving! Since you're buying, I'll have surf and turf and the best wine in the house!" Lou laughed out loud and slapped his buddy on the back, "I know that's right, man! But seriously, I'm really worried about you and this ICON cover-up shit. From now on you're bunkin' with me." Troy looked at Lou as if he was about to protest and then thought better of it. "Hey, not a problem, bro. I mean that is if you've matured since we last roomed together in college. I hope you've changed your funky ways since then. Man you used to be the king of funk. You've cleaned up you're act since then though, right?" Troy laughed as he watched Lou pretending to get offended. "Man, what kind of friend are you, anyway? Of course I've "matured" since those days. As I recall, you weren't always smelling rosy back then either."

The two men left the room laughing and still trading insults as they moved down the hall toward the bank of elevators. The conversation turned serious as they exited the elevator and hailed a taxi outside the hotel. "For real, Troy, we've gotta break your dads' code soon and we have to keep everything on the down low till we know exactly what we're up against." Troy shook his head as they got into the taxi and Lou took the hint to keep it quiet until they were alone again. The streets were teeming with people and Troy was amazed at how everyone enjoyed the darker hours so much more than they used to. Life had turned upside down. The things people used to do during the day were now done at every hour of the night. Women were outside on the stoops talking and hanging out their laundry as children ran between the shadows of darkness and the occasional streetlight. Teenagers were cruising the streets and hanging out, riding skateboards or just talking and horsing around on their front porches. No one seemed leery of the night as they used to in the old days. I guess you have to live no matter what the circumstances, Troy thought as he watched all the people going about their daily, make that nightly, lives.

As they pulled up in front of the restaurant, Troy saw two black men dressed all in black handing out pamphlets on the sidewalk. They looked like preachers to Troy. He hoped they wouldn't harass him and Lou as they entered the restaurant. As soon as they exited the taxi, the two men walked over and stood in front of them, blocking the entrance. Both men were well over six foot and didn't look very much like preachers now, Troy thought as he tensed up ready for a confrontation. "My brothers," began the larger of the two men in a voice as soothing as his stature was intimidating, "We represent the Brotherhood. We are a group of young brothers such as yourselves who are trained to conduct surveillance and practice tactical maneuvers in our neighborhoods to protect our people." He handed Troy and Lou the pamphlets as he continued talking, "Are you aware of the growing numbers of blacks who mysteriously disappear daily in our streets? How about those who volunteer to serve ICON on their moon bases and never return or even contact their families? ICON releases footage of workers happily performing their duties, but we never see their faces. What is really going on? We are in the streets daily and nightly patrolling, trying to protect our people. Yet they are still disappearing. We need more operatives to cover more ground. Our number is on the back of the pamphlet if you would like to contact us about signing on. Thank you for your time." When he finished, his partner stepped to the side to allow Troy and Lou to pass. They shook hands with the men and then continued on to the entrance of the restaurant. Troy began to comment on the men out front. Lou opened the door and followed Troy inside commenting, "Those guys are serious about their organization. It's not some street gang, either. The top black college fraternities around the country are their main source of recruitment. They go for the best and brightest, and they train hard. The only catch is they keep their membership completely private and no one is guaranteed admission. You gotta earn your status in the Brotherhood. They have done a remarkable job protecting our neighborhoods, but they are up against a menace so pervasive, it goes all the way to the top of corporate and government offices. Everyone knows what's happening, but the Brotherhood is the only group doing anything about it." Troy shook his head. "These guys are the black panthers of the 21st century. I know you remember back about 15 years ago when some crazy white boys took those two young sisters in broad daylight. They were beaten and raped and then those sonofabitches drained their blood and mutilated them. Man, that was a wake up call for the black community about how serious the plague was and the lengths some white folks would be willing to go to save their asses. Anyway, one of the girls father, Rueben Hightower, started the Brotherhood."

When Troy and Lou finally walked into the restaurant, it seemed they were on the menu, all eyes held looks of approval. Although they were not the only blacks in the place, Troy insisted on a table near an exit. The two men ordered before they began their conservation. Lou leaned back in his chair with a look of confusion, "You know Troy, we've been friends for years and I guess when you're younger, shit like conspiracies by the government, men in black, is kind of hard to swallow. It was a long time before you even talked about anything. Your parents' involvement in all this and so far ICON seems to be smack dead in the middle of this madness. There's no doubt in my mind that ICON was behind the death of your parents, but my brother what gets me is, why were you left alive? Really, I've seen these guys on a bad day and something had to have been awfully important for them to overlook any loose ends. Since that night have you noticed that not one paper or news agency has mentioned one word about any aliens? All our lives we've dreamed of the stars and now the wondering is over. It's funny how fighting around the world has stopped and it's not because of this damn plague either. These white folks can't stand the thought of a higher intelligence being black. The world is more involved with star wars technology than ever. They've got shit you wouldn't believe. Well I don't have to tell you about the spacecraft that's out there. Which reminds me, I'm waiting on a program that will help us analyze your father's hieroglyphs. For an old dude, your pop was pretty damn brilliant. The bits and pieces I can make out, he speaks of these travelers and the meetings of the tribes and some strange rituals and sacrifices." Lou noticed the trance like stare in Troy eyes and snapped his fingers to bring him out. Troy blinked at the snapping fingers, "My mother was of Panamanian descent and she and my dad studied the different tribes and cultures during their college days which may explain why his notes went from Egyptian time to some strange Indian hieroglyphs. How does this all tie in with ICON and the government?" Lou was about to answer when their waiter arrived with their meal.

Rubbing his hands together at the arrival of their meal, Lou was ready to get down to business. Troy laughed aloud, "Man, you don't believe in missing no meals! With all the training we have coming up you may want to practice some push-aways." Lou looked at Troy with his mouth full, "What you mean push-aways?" "Push your fat-ass away from the table!" Troy said roaring in laughter. Still punishing his steak, Lou responded, "Oh, now you want to be a comedian! Well you won't be laughing when your little ass floats off in space somewhere!" The men both needed this lighter moment and each rejoiced at the wise cracks, trying hard to keep their mouths covered and hold their sides, hurting from the laughter. Troy struggled to catch his breath, but every time he saw Lou attempting to wipe the tears of laughter it seemed a lost cause. It was a while before the two realized again where they were and noticed the stares around them. But it was all good, you had to be there! Troy enjoyed the blow, it had been so long since he had a good laugh, "Same old Lou! I do want to thank you for your help on my dad's hieroglyphs, though. I hate getting you involved with this mess. You can see why I never talked to anyone about all this." Lou became serious waving off the thanks coming from Troy, "Hold up pal. Now we go a long way back and we both flew in the Corps to help pay for this higher education. You still haven't explained how you knew I was in deep shit after losing my wingman. Hell, I know I'm one of the best and I always thought the Top Gun award was bullshit. I had heard about your flight skills but I had written you off as another boy genius. Man I just knew we were dead meat with all those fighters closing in on us, till this day I don't know where you came from, but I was thanking my lucky stars. The flying you did that day was unbelievable! I never knew a V-fighter could do the stuff you were laying down. If it hadn't been for my video camera they would have never believed my story of the incident. The only thing that has changed is the battle. We are no different than those brothers standing out front. We have to fight this thing the best way we know how."

The one thing Troy had always followed was his instinct and the always recurring visions. His thoughts flashed quickly on his parents and his grandfather, together his life's foundation. Then there was Zenani reaching and touching his very soul. There was a voice, a being. He felt her presence unified him mind and soul. She had always filled his heart with the light. All his strengths and weaknesses were alive and guided by an unknown he trusted blindly. It gave him such a sense of his fellow man, and the truth. A quest that was bringing him to serve a nation knowing their motives. When Troy blinked, Lou came back into focus, "Man, you alright? I wasn't trying to choke you up, what we need is a nice hook. Come on, the bar's upstairs besides there's something I want you to see." The two friends rose and paid their bill. They headed toward the exit, weaving through the dinner tables. Lou found he was talking to himself and turned to see Troy rushing to another table across the room. He figured Troy had recognized someone. Then he realized what was happening when a man at the table stood up clutching his throat and staggering back. Troy quickly got behind the man and performed the Heimlich maneuver and a large piece of meat flew out of the man's mouth. The relieved, coughing man suddenly started shaking Troy's hand and thanking him profusely. The members of his party watched speechless, unaware that their friend had been choking in the first place. Troy rejoined Lou who looked totally unsurprised, "That's what I mean! First you have a conference with talking whales, and then you spot a choking man across a crowded room! You are one spooky dude!" Lou patted him on back for a job well done as they entered the tinted glass elevator.

The lights of the city jumped out like tiny glinting diamonds on a jewelers' black velvet showcase, as Lou pointed in distance. "There along the coastline, the blue and red lights on those towers as far as the eye can see, launch pads, baby boy, that's where we'll earn our bread and butter!" Troy watched in amazement at the endless chain of lights that dotted the coastline. He felt as though he had waited a lifetime for this moment, his dream come true. The pressured stop and ding of the elevator announced their arrival to the lounge. The sound of music flooded the elevator when the doors opened, followed by fragrances of perfume. Lou rubbed his hands together, seeing the ladies and partying going on in the place. Smiling like the cat that ate the canary, "I think I need to do a quick recon, I'll meet you at the bar." Troy looked knowingly at his partner following after a passing lady, when a twinge of pain surged through his hand. Gripping his wrist, he attempted to open his hand. The music changed to the sounds of the whales. His hand seemed to turn his body to again face the city lights as the pain began to cease and pulse with the soothing sounds. Touching the cool glass brought a calm he hadn't felt in a long time. He could feel her, she was here. He knew it! She was reaching out to him, searching his heart for the strength he would need to find her. Did he understand the importance of the moment? Zenani wept in her chamber as she found the seed of doubt and confusion buried deep in his soul. He had to let go of his logic and follow his heart or they were all lost! How to make him see? She searched the lounge and connected to Lou. She put the assurance Troy would need into Lou's subconscious. Now every time Troy doubted or tried to turn away, Lou would be there to believe in him and urge him on to accomplish the impossible. She could see that Lou would be a great influence on Troy, so she breathed her blue mist throughout his soul to protect him in the troubled times ahead. Lou turned to see Troy standing at the glass wall looking out into the night, rubbing his hand. He approached Troy and patted him on the back to get his attention. "Hey man, we came up here to relax and check out the honeys, right?" Troy turned and smiled, "Lou, you're always checking out the honeys no matter where we are!" The two men crossed to an open table and ordered cocktails as a jazz band began to play. They passed a couple of hours with Lou collecting phone numbers and Troy smiling politely and making conversation, but never taking any numbers. As they got up to leave, Lou ribbed him about his lack of prowess, "Bro, you had a couple of fine shorties all over you, and still you played hard to get, what's up?" Troy laughed and shrugged Lou's teasing off, "Man, those girls were fine, but my mind is on my money and I've got all this other shit happenin too! I don't have time to love' em and leave' em right now. I'll leave that to you!" Lou laughed and cocked his head in the direction of one of the prettier girls watching them leave with a look of loss on her face, "Mmmm.... I'm definitely calling her. Hey, it's all good with me if you take yourself out the game, more tenderoni for me!" Troy laughed and shook his head as they headed toward the elevator. "Man, you are some piece of work! You better get all these girls out of your system before we start training next week, that's for sure!" Lou grinned as he stepped into the elevator behind his friend. "Shoot, man, you know I ain't even worried about training! I've waited all my life for this and nothing, I mean nothing, not even the ladies, is gonna stop me from reaching my dream!" They bumped fists as Troy replied, "I hear you, dog. Our dreams are about to become reality!" The two friends exited the elevator and hurried across the room and out the door to hail a taxi.

When they arrived at the hotel, Lou recognized a lady in the lobby. He rushed to catch up with her and left Troy staring after him. He began to laugh and follow Lou. He watched as Lou came up behind the attractive young woman and placed his hands over her eyes in the familiar "guess-who" gesture. As Lou took the liberty of whispering in the woman's ear and leaning in closer, she whirled and slapped him full across the face. Troy rushed towards the pair, trying not to laugh too hard at his friend. He saw the woman's face as he approached and let his laughter break free. It was Katie Kimball, one of their college classmates! Troy remembered her feisty ways in school and laughed even harder to think of Lou trying to put the moves on Katie. Poor Lou was in over his head and didn't even realize it! Katie saw Troy and forgot all about her tirade that was in full swing against Lou. She left Lou standing, holding his slowly reddening cheek and nursing his huge ego. She caught Troy in a warm embrace and graced him with a soft kiss on the cheek, "Troy! It's been so long since I've seen such a handsome man! How you doing, sugar?" Troy grinned from ear to ear as he watched Lou staring in disbelief. "Katie, girl, you are looking even better than I remember! It has been a while, what are you doing here?" "I'm down here to accept a position at the Cape, how about you?" She smiled warmly as she began to walk with Troy back over to the desk to continue checking in to the hotel. She ignored Lou as they passed him. Troy told her about beginning his training and she was thrilled to know they would be in town together. She told him how much she had missed their friendship and hoped they could continue to be as close as they were in college. Lou, unable to keep quiet any longer, joined them as Katie got her room key. "Hey man, I didn't know you and Miss Kimball here were and item!" he said rolling his eyes at Katie as if she were a python. Troy laughed and tried to soothe his friend's bruised ego, "Lou, Katie and I go back all the way through college. We were just friends then and we're just friends now, like you and me, okay?" " Yeah right, a lady this fine and you are " just friends", hey that's cool. I won't tell a soul." Katie turned on him again and if looks could kill, Lou would have been a steaming pool of DNA. She put her well manicured finger in his face and began to go off, "First of all, it's not even any of your business what Troy is to me. I'm frankly disgusted that he even knows you! Secondly, Troy is a real gentleman. He and I were very close in college, but not in the way your filthy mind would imagine!" Troy began to laugh again, "Did you two have words before you fell out?" Lou started to say something but Katie had invited Troy up to her room to catch up with each other and the two were headed for the elevators. Lou yelled out, "What about me?" Troy and Katie turned to see Lou standing there like the kid that no one picks for the kickball game and took pity on him. "Oh alright! You can come too. Pick up my bags and come on!" Katie said with obvious irritation in her voice. As she turned her back, Lou started making faces and pretending to walk as prissy as she did. Katie turned, catching him in the act. She shot him another "death-ray" look and he quickly straightened up. Troy was laughing so hard by this time! He had forgotten how much fun he always had when Katie was around! Lou grudgingly stumbled into the elevator with Katie's suitcases and fumed, "Must be full of rocks!" Katie covered her smile and tried to muffle her chuckle so Lou wouldn't see that she really did like him after all, it was just that he could be so damn confident. She liked his air of self-assurance, but did he have to be so cocky? Troy watched his two friends and realized there was an attraction there. He decided he would have to help it along in the future, "Lord knows Lou could use all the help he could get with this one!" he thought as he made a mental note to himself. The elevator glided silently to a stop and the doors slid open. Katie and Troy stepped into the hallway and started toward her room as Lou struggled with the bags. "Hey man, you could help a brother out!" he griped at Troy. "My man, I thought you had everything under control. I didn't want to interfere, I thought you wanted to impress Katie!" Lou shot him an eye roll and gestured toward the bags, "I could hurt myself with all this mess and she wouldn't even bat one of her sexy long eyelashes about it! But if I dare scuff up her swanky luggage, she'll have my head!" Troy and Katie tried hard not to laugh at Lou, but it was so amusing to see Mr. Macho fighting with suitcases and the elevator doors! Troy excused himself and walked back to the elevator to help Lou. "Man it's about time!" "Hey don't get your shorts in a knot, dog. I came to help and you want to stand here snappin at folks!" Lou handed Troy the last of the luggage and mumbled something about what kind of friend he turned out to be. Noticing the rough handling of her bags, Katie sounded off, "If you two characters damage any of my things, this might be your last elevator ride!" A look of disbelief crossed both of their faces as Troy whispered to Lou, "Kinda rough around the edges, wouldn't you say?" Lou whispered back, "You ever seen the eye of a hurricane? Well she's the before and the after. But she was smooth and calm when those agents came through the lab."

Clearing her throat to halt the ill-advised conversation, "Gentlemen, this is neither the time or place for this." She cast her eyes at the camera mounted in the top corner of the elevator. Both men were exhausted when they reached her room. They dropped the bags as soon as they entered. Katie placed her finger up to her lips for silence as she casually looked over the suite and turned on some music. She then pulled a laptop out of one of the bags and made the necessary connections and waited for it to boot up. First order of business was to remove Lou's hand that had found its way so innocently to her exposed knee. She looked squarely at Troy, "I didn't think it was a big deal when Lou asked me to hack ICON's security system to unravel your dad's notes. But the more I structured the symbols, here take a look, I found that rather than a formula for a cure, it's more like a story, which I'm certain was probably the foundation of your father's work." The three watched intensely as the symbols of a forgotten language lit the screen. Katie leaned back in thought. "I spent countless hours and hacked so many systems trying to decode the hieroglyphs until it just smacked me in the face. Normally each symbol makes a statement and if you follow along instead of letting words lead you, you will see a legend of sorts emerging. I think possibly we're dealing with text older than time as we know it. The translators over time evolved, as did their language and interpretations, so words must be seen, not read." It all made sense to Troy, his whole life his gut had told and forewarned him to trust his heart. A lifetime of visions that until now didn't make sense. Katie pointed at the screen as she continued to explain, "If we examine the earlier writings they resemble cave drawings and like many, they show the tribe or family. We see the celebrations of the hunt, the plights they endured; cold winters, the birth of children, harvest of crops, war and death. See how the land and animals change in this next segment? The animal seems so large and they appear to be on the defensive." Lou smirked, "That don't look nothing like Bambi and if you ask me, those dudes look like they are hauling ass!" Pushing his hand off her leg again Katie huffed, "As I was saying, the drawings go on to show a gathering of the people in prayer or counsel with a priest or holy man, I can't be sure which, but ruler he is not because here they show a man of the crown on which they are bestowing their harvest. Here, the holy man is kneeling before the beast in prayer and the ruler is standing behind his army. Next, the beast has fallen and then the soldiers thrust spears in the back of the holy man and he is carried away by more of his kind with the ruler in chase. As the people shown again here are paying homage, you see the coming of locusts, destruction of crops and again death and slavery. What's funny though is the symbol for the holy man is unlike those around him. Look real close at this, people being sacrificed like lambs then the last entry is that of the ruler and the holy man. As we look at the changes of the symbols we are watching the evolution of man, from his first steps through days of Egypt and the Romans to Indian tribes of our era. Each always showed death, plague and people being sacrificed. As the symbols changed, so did the rulers but the symbol for the holy men remained the same. A coincidence? I think not." Katie paused and continued to view the symbols before her. Troy rubbed his temples and looked over to Katie. "I don't understand what all this could have to do with my dad or this ICON cover-up. Unless we can parallel these picture stories with the times we are living in what could they mean?" Katie took his hand in hers and tried to explain, "Troy, your dad was a scientist as well as a doctor. He had gained access to some pretty alarming data from ICON. Most of the information I've found so far comes from ICON's archives. There is a history that has been hidden from the world. It sounds crazy, but if the truth of these records is ever transcribed or revealed, world order would shift and life as we have known it will be a lie. The repercussions of the truth will negate the power that a segment of the population has held dear and guarded through the ages to pass on to their children. Don't you get it? Your dad found through his research that the race issue of the 20th century would become the war that it is now because of the plague in this century. Minorities, especially blacks, are the hunted. And for what?" Troy answered in a whisper, "Our blood!" Katie shook her head sadly, "That is the key, Troy. Our blood." Lou interrupted, "What do you mean, our blood? Girl, you saying you're black?" Katie started to leave, but Troy grabbed her arm. He shot Lou an angry look and said "Man you know you can be an asshole sometimes!" Troy sat down next to Katie and rubbed her back, "You know you can't pay any attention to him. What does he know?" Katie smiled at Troy and glared at Lou. "As I was saying before Casanova insulted me, your dad must have stumbled onto the secret controversial research about the effects of a black persons blood on the plague. He had to have been horrified to realize that his own research would be used against his race. That had to be why ICON decided to fund his private research. They pretended to care about a cure or vaccine for sickle cell. They knew your dad was the man for the job. His expertise in his field and the fact that he had a son with sickle cell, it all fit together perfectly." Troy looked at her astounded, "How could you know all this?" Katie squirmed in her seat, her face heating up at the prospect of having revealed too much of what she knew. Troy demanded that she tell him how she knew all these things about his dad. Katie relented and made both Troy and Lou promise never to breathe a word of what they were about to hear to anyone.

Katie pushed her hair back and began, "My father and your father were colleagues and friends Troy. I always heard my dad talk about Dr. Bishop, but when we met in college I never connected the names. Dr. Bishop and his wife and son were killed in an explosion on the same night that my dad was shot down during the alien invasion." Troy and Lou looked at her as if she had just landed from Mars. They both started to speak but she silenced them and continued, "My father is Dr. Eugene Robinson, he was part of the greeting party the night the aliens came. The story that was fed to the media was false. Someone who had a lot of power changed events around and blamed the aliens for the massacre that followed. The truth was that the aliens were fired on first and their leader was badly wounded. Everyone who witnessed the exchange was lined up after the aliens fled and shot dead. My father was gravely injured and believed to be dead like everyone else, but hours after the attack before any authorities came, my dad managed to crawl to a hunters blind and lay low until the area was abandoned. He has been in hiding ever since. He secretly works with the Brotherhood and he has only revealed the events of that night to his family. It was years before he even contacted my mother in fear for our lives. He and my mother were lovers and were to be married but even then society frowned on interracial couples, especially that of a Black civil rights leader to a white lady. My mother was crushed and frustrated by the government cover-up that followed in the name of national security. It was so hush-hush they didn't even release the bodies to the families, knowing an autopsy would reveal that bullets instead of ray guns killed them. She didn't even know she was pregnant with me until she had moved back to her hometown. She was left as a single parent to raise me. I was almost fifteen years old before I met my father and was told the truth. Lou shook his head, "I remember the first time I saw you on campus. I was like, damn, look at the ass on that white girl and come to find out you are a sista." If looks could kill Lou would have been a goner. Katie just pointed back at the computer, "This computer is the only link I've had with my Dad and all these years we have met in secret. My mother died of the plague when I was in high school and my aunt kept me until I started college. I guess Dad would sneak and view some our science expos on campus, because he later asked me about a young man he thought looked familiar. When I told him your name, he was shocked and said you looked like a chip off the old block. That's when I connected that the old friend he often spoke of was your father. Like you, my life has been shrouded in secrecy. The day Lou asked me to check the hieroglyphs, the government had denied access and after I hacked it I found that the program belonged to ICON. Most of what I saw of the file was similar to what the press released but there was something else. It wasn't clear what it was, only that something was recovered and that extreme measures were taken for its containment, it could have been a weapon or nuclear waste for all I know. While I was trying to break ICON's code, all hell broke loose and I realized I had been traced and agents were all over the place. Troy's eye's widened at the thought, "Could it been one of the aliens?"

Uncertain of what to say Katie remarked, "I'm not sure, I only remember something about a small package being extracted at the river by a decon team." Troy rubbed the back of his neck as he racked his brain trying to remember, "The river, the river? Why the river? That's almost a mile away from where the aliens landed. This makes no sense. Look Katie, is there any way I can talk to your father?" Katie hesitated, "I don't know, it's been awhile since even I have seen him, but I'll try." Troy reached and gave her hand a gentle squeeze, "Thank you, I couldn't ask for more than that. I'm sure you're tired so I'll be getting along." As he walked toward the door Lou called out, "Hey my brother, we'll see you in the morning." Katie jokingly laughed, "If you want to see another morning I think you better leave now." Lou raised his hands in defense, "OK, I can take a hint but I'll be right down the hall if you change your mind." She playfully pushed him out the door and waved goodnight. Troy stood by the elevator looking at Lou smiling from ear to ear. "She knows she wants me," he replied. Troy waved as he stepped on to the elevator, "Yeah right! See you tomorrow." Troy thought how sly Lou was to ensure that his room was on the same floor as Katie's. When he entered his room it finally hit him just how tired he was. He went straight to his bed and barely had strength to kick off his shoes. Drifting like a dance of peace he welcomed the sleep. The events of his lifetime were never far away, always painting a canvas of a lost memory.

A night at the Cape would be no different. The familiar black backdrop of his sleep melted into a sea of blue. The soft sounds of the whales, serene in song, transformed into the voice of mother earth. Troy found himself adrift amongst them in the depths of the ocean, moving fluidly in and breathing the liquid life. He felt so alive and blessed with each brush of the mammals. The gam of whales parted with one blue whale emerging toward him, the low-pitch sounds he could now hear as words. "We welcome the child of Zion, all that lives returns to the sea. We, the watchers of the mother, have awaited the arrival. Millions of years have passed since the first washed ashore, but they knew not of their own. Among them were the guardians of life to witness their evolution and bear their burdens. In any order there is one who knows, sees and is. Aware are the few of the gift of many. Heavy are the mother's tears unable to change the ways of her children. All that they do comes back to the sea, nature's journey of life. Your path is shared with another who waits to reunite. Together there is light, hope for the future. When you hear our song or the cry of a baby, which is it you don't understand? The mother's gestation period was over 16 million years and welcome you are, child of Zion." Then the sound of their pitches Troy could hear from all directions, inside he felt honored and humbled. Their numbers were too many to count as in the jubilation, streams of air bubbles came from their spouts and surrounded him. Troy felt joy as he tumbled around in the bubbles that caused him to start floating to the surface. He tried to laugh from the tickling when water entered his mouth and nose. The quick burn in his head forced him to race to the surface. He looked above and could see the light, but he was already out of breath. Struggling, still too far under, he tried to breathe, water, then blackness. It's often said there's no pain in death, just dying. The water jolted him like a bolt of lightning. With his eyes lit in fear, suddenly there was air. Troy coughed and choked as water came from his mouth. Fresh air finally reached his lungs, he tried to clear his vision. Troy looked around him, shocked to find he was sitting in the tub. He reached for a towel thinking to himself how stupid he was to fall asleep in the tub. After drying his back he wiped his face, seaweed, what was going on here? Troy scrambled out of the tub throwing the seaweed every which way. He sat down on the closed toilet seat and calmed himself. Dreams were one thing, but waking up in the tub when the last thing you remembered was falling asleep in bed, well that was something else altogether! Troy stood up and looked into the mirror. He rubbed his face and began to shave. The monotony of this morning ritual settled his nerves and by the time he had taken a quick shower, he convinced himself that Lou had probably tried to pull a prank. Nothing else made any sense. He quickly dressed and went downstairs for a big breakfast.

As soon as he stepped into the bright, welcoming dining room, he felt his spirits lift. Lou and Katie were already seated and devouring a fruit platter between them. Troy stopped at the coffeemaker for a fresh cup and picked up one of the courtesy newspapers from the counter. Lou saw him and motioned him over. Troy sat down and opened his paper. He glanced at Lou over the top and said, "Nice job with the seaweed man, you so need to grow up pal!" Lou looked at him as if he was going crazy, "What are you talking about, Troy?" "Come on, you know what I'm talking about. You came in my room this morning and while I was asleep in the tub, you put seaweed all over me! Where did you get that stuff, man?" Lou and Katie stared at one another and Lou started to laugh, although he looked a little disturbed. "Troy, bro, I don't have any idea what you're talking about. I haven't been to your room since yesterday. Believe me I've had much better things to do than sneak in your room and play jokes!" Katie kicked him under the table and Lou grimaced at her. Troy, tired of Lou's innocent act, became angry. "Look Lou, I don't care what you say, I know you did it! Who else would pull such a stupid stunt? I'm not mad at you for doing it. Lord knows someone has to pay attention to you, and if it makes you feel good to pull my chain well then go ahead. But please, no more seaweed!" Lou turned to Troy, "Buddy I'm really worried about you. I haven't been near your room. We slept in this morning, too. We just got here right before you did." Katie threw her napkin down, "Big mouth! I knew

145

you wouldn't be able to keep your mouth shut!" Troy completely forgot about the seaweed as he looked from one friend to the other. He laughed in spite of himself and gave Lou a fist bump. "I guess I won't be bunkin with you after all, dog!" Troy remarked. Katie blushed deeply and whispered between clenched teeth, "Can you two wait to celebrate Lou's conquest till I'm at least out of the room!" She rose to go to the ladies room and Troy tried to apologize. She waved him away and with as much dignity as she could salvage, walked gracefully to the restroom. Troy patted Lou on the back, "Man I knew you were into her, but I didn't think she was going to give in to you! She's just what you need. Maybe now you will settle down and start to act right." Lou held up both hands as if to fend off the words, "Wait up, now dog. Nobody's talking marriage, here. We just got better acquainted last night." Troy took a sip of coffee and looked Lou squarely in the eye, "Look Lou you are my best friend, but I'm telling you now...don't hurt Katie. I mean it. If you cause her one minute of sorrow, I'll be on your ass, you got it?" Lou shrugged, "Hey man, calm down. I don't intend on hurting her, ever. I've been watching her for a long time. It's just that we are beginning our relationship and after shooting off my big mouth this morning, well maybe now she would rather forget about it." Troy smiled and tried to reassure his friend, "That girl has a very good head on her shoulders. She knows how you are and believe me if she went that far with you last night, she's serious about getting to know you better. It was bound to come out sooner or later. Hey you two are my closest friends, right? Don't worry. She'll be mad for a little while, but if you try to smooth her ruffled feathers and let her know you didn't mean any harm, it will be fine." Lou sighed in relief and attacked his breakfast platter. Between mouthfuls he reminded Troy, "Katie got in touch with her old man last night. I think maybe we'll get to meet with him soon." Just then Katie returned to the table. She didn't look as mad as she had a few minutes earlier, but both men decided to tread lightly for the time being. "He's right, Troy. I did speak with my father last night and it seems that he has been thinking of contacting you. So we talked and as we were about to say goodnight he told me to have you waiting outside the hotel and he will send a car for us this evening around ten." Troy took Katie's hand and began to thank her when Lou broke in with plans for the day, "Since you haven't seen the town, let's make the rounds today and have some fun. I have a feeling that we are in for some strange times ahead. Why not try to enjoy ourselves before the shit hits the fan?" Katie smiled warmly at Lou and remarked, "I think we should take Troy to our favorite spot." Lou shook his head and said, "Now wait a minute girlfriend, twos company so three would definitely be a crowd, besides he's my best friend. I didn't know you were so kinky!" Troy laughed as Katie gave Lou the cold shoulder, "Never mind him, I meant the botanical gardens and the marine exhibit and he knows it. I think he was trying to compliment my skills in some off-handed, twisted way." Troy and Katie both enjoyed Lou's surprised expression at Katie's sudden feisty sparring. Troy folded his paper and whispered to Lou, "I told you she was a handful. You better watch your step, dog. Maybe I should be worried about her hurting you instead of the other way around." Lou laughed and continued eating, secretly delighted to see that Katie's sense of humor matched his. Although he would have to remember that she was a lady first and foremost. The three friends finished their breakfast and headed back upstairs for cameras, brochures and sunglasses for their day out and met back in the lobby. As Katie placed a colorful wide-brimmed straw hat on her head she laughed and nudged Troy in his ribs, "Think anyone can tell we're tourists?" Troy smiled as he pulled on his sunglasses and replied, "I think so. With all this stuff, it sure would be hard to miss

us." Lou turned his hat to the back and slid his glasses
down on his nose, giving Katie a caressing look from head
to toe, "Girl with that pretty yellow sundress huggin' your
curves, you're the only attraction I see!" Katie blushed and
tiptoed to kiss Lou on the cheek. Lou grabbed her and
caught her lips with his instead. "Come on you two, let's
get going " Troy laughed as he walked out into the bright
sunshine. He hailed a taxi as his friends walked out behind
him. Troy and Katie sat back discussing how pretty the
weather was while Lou gave the cabbie directions. As they
passed through different neighborhoods and shopping
districts, Troy again noticed how the races were obviously
separated. He saw the wary eyes of the blacks and
minorities as they went about their daily lives. It suddenly
hit him how real all this cloak and dagger stuff really was.
When you're young and trying to live life, the real world
sometimes slips away and you only see what you want to
see. These people lived day to day in fear for their lives and
for those they loved. Amidst the throng of people stood the
vigilant members of the Brotherhood. Troy shook his head
proud, "These brothers ain't no joke." "These are no joking
times. These brothers are on the front line, without their
help our people would have lost hope long ago," said Katie.
The cab came to a sudden halt and the driver didn't unlock
the doors until his fare was slid through the protective glass.
They stared at the large pillars of the magnificent building
that stood like a silent giant in the noise of the city. Lou
smiled, "Katie thought you would enjoy a little culture."
Already half way up the stairs, Katie yelled back, "You
guys coming or what?" Troy and Lou, each gesturing to the
other, "After you, my dear fellow," Troy insisting, "By no
means kind sir, I insist." Interlocking elbows the two
comedians skipped up the stairs. After entering the
museum, they raced to catch up with Katie. Troy looked
around in amazement, "Impressive, these can't be originals,
I mean here in the hood and all." Shaking her head in pity,

"You're starting to sound like Lou, both of you act like you've been locked in a cave somewhere," Katie replied. "I'm sure you remember the Mandela Act of 2005 unifying the nations of Africa. The United Nations awarded them rights to treasures hidden in museums around the world to include the mummies of Egypt. It shouldn't be a surprise to find our art back home." They continued their tour with Katie as their guide, each step echoed in the marble palace. It was so overpowering to be in the midst of so much history. Troy stopped in his tracks expressionless as Katie placed her hand on his shoulder. Her soft voice spoke what his heart felt, "The Butchulla people of K'gari, an island we now know as Fraser Island. One of many Aboriginal groups, their peaceful existence was shattered upon the arrival of European settlers. Sounds all too familiar, huh?" Lou stepped closer to his two friends and angrily reflected, "It always comes back to world domination and brute force. I'm so sick of this bullshit! When will it stop?" Troy and Katie turned to see Lou storming away towards an exhibit on basket weaving. "I'm afraid no time soon." A voice filled the room that startled the pair. "The secrets that were unlocked on the peaks of Kilimanjaro were much more than treasures. But we all wanted to believe and were led to believe, led throughout history." "Dad?" called Katie to the man who stood in the shadows. Stepping into the light, the elderly black gentleman stretched out his arms to embrace his daughter. "Kathryn, my dear child, it's been so long." Lou and Troy watched the heart-warming reunion as Katie cried tears of joy. After a few moments Katie gained her composure and turned to introduce her friends. "Dad, these are my friends, Louis Stryker and Troy Bishop. This is my father, Dr. Robinson." Each of the men greeted the other with warm regards as they shook hands. Dr. Robinson smiled, "Well Louis, we finally get a chance to meet. I've heard so much about you." The look of surprise showed on his face, "Sir, it's an honor to meet you." Dr. Robinson turned to Troy, "Son, if you're not a chip off the old block! What a fine young man you've grown to be, Ben and Mary would be proud." It felt good to meet someone that knew his parents, inside Troy had so many questions. "Dr. Robinson, as you can see you've taken us all by surprise, I thought our meeting would be later?" A look of seriousness crossed Dr. Robinson's face, "I would not be here today, if I did the expected. From this point on you must remember that nothing is as it may seem. Come, let's go somewhere we can speak in private."

The wall seemed to open before Dr. Robinson could walk into it. Standing at the entrance were the two men Troy remembered from the restaurant last night. The inner room was a command center. There were computer terminals showing worldwide locations and weapons of all kinds. They walked into a boardroom and Dr. Robinson gestured for them to have a seat. A screen slowly descended from the ceiling. "In all honesty I wasn't expecting our meeting to be so soon, but due to my daughter's taste for fine art this unscheduled visit could just as well serve our purpose. For many years, I've lived a life in the shadows. Always on the fringes of society, watching those I love from a distance and trying to uncover a long hidden secret. My daughter has never known her father, not the way that she should have. I have lost everything dear to me because of that night so long ago. I have many regrets about my family and their sacrifices, but I will never forget the miracle of that evening or the chaos that followed and even if I could, I wouldn't go back and change any of it. The night air was filled with excitement and the preparations for the arrival of the alien contingent were in their final stages. The group I belonged with was being briefed and re-briefed for our role in the historic event. We were mostly religious leaders and activists for human rights. The "welcome wagon", I guess you could say. The tension and expectation was heavy in the air. Everyone was anxious to see the aliens, myself included. Can you imagine the wonder that was felt by all as the craft carrying beings from another world landed right before our eyes? It was the most amazing sight! But nothing could prepare me for the shock that was to come! As the aliens descended, no that isn't the right word, as they floated towards us from their ship, I was struck in my very soul at what I beheld. They were like us! They looked very human with the most mystical, beautiful eyes you can imagine! And their skin, it was as black as the night sky. It was lit from within so as to appear to have a midnight blue sheen. The thought of touching them overcame me and I knew their skin would feel like the softest silk. I began to weep in my heart as I realized they must be my ancestors, all of humanity came from them! You should have seen the looks on some of the faces in the crowd! It really blew a lot of people away that the aliens were black! I will never forget their Queen and her deep understanding of us as humans. She picked up on the shock instantly and confirmed that humanity still divided itself in such a trivial manner. She was going to give us the cure for the plague that to this day is still with us. I'm still not sure exactly what caused the shooting to start, but I do know that the aliens did not fire on anyone. They were prepared for such a thing to occur, but still their Queen was wounded. They hurried her to their ship and left. That's when a massacre began on the ground. There were bullets flying everywhere. Someone wanted all of us to be eliminated. I knew this was a cover-up of some kind and later when ICON released that doctored videotape of the incident, I knew who that someone was. I stand here today before you by the grace of God. My life has come at a high price, one that my family and I have been forced to pay time and again. When I think of all the secrets I now know, sometimes it just wears me down. There is a war going on that is invisible to all, except those of the inner circles and those of us who have been pulled into the vortex by accident or against our will." Troy walked over to Katie and comforted her as silent tears marred her beautiful face at her father's words. "How ironic that the two of you have grown so close. My daughter has had to hide her true identity to be able to live without the intrusion of ICON. It is the same with you Troy. Your parents were killed because your father was getting too close to the truth of ICON's plans. How you escaped their notice is baffling! I dare say if they ever find out you are alive there will be no hesitation on their part to destroy you. You have to be very careful, young man. These people play for keeps. That is why we have organized ourselves. It's the only way to protect our people and try to uncover the ugly truth about the last 20 years. We've learned so much about the Ancient Ones and their time upon this Earth, but I feel it is only the tip of a very large iceberg. If you direct your attention to the screen you will see that on Kilamanjaro their temples were revealed after a massive avalanche. The existence of this museum is proof enough that they established the tribes of Earth. Somehow, we've lost our knowledge of them over time. These aliens must be their direct descendants and our guardians. The government of that country completely shut down the mountain and NATO intervened implying world security issues, without disclosing the extent of the discoveries to the world. Out of the blue, they drafted acts to return treasured artifacts to the people of Africa. Man's destructive greed and disregard for our planet has poisoned our world, somehow contributing to this horrible plague. We formed the Brotherhood to combat the evil that is murdering millions of our people. At first we thought it was only isolated cases of kidnapping to obtain the blood of blacks by a few paranoid whites, but after we became organized and more determined in our methods, our intelligence sources revealed we were the harvest for the world." Troy, Katie and Lou looked to one another, unable to deny what was happening. Dr. Robinson gently took the hand of his daughter, "I'm not saying that the government as a whole or white people in general are killing us. As little as 25% of whites were slave owners during the 1800s, but the rest of the country accepted it as the better good for the nation. The attack on the aliens wasn't the work of the white race but that of a few. Just the thought of a superior race shook their very foundation. During my years fighting for civil rights it wasn't always the violence, but the systematic undermining of blacks, that proved most deadly." The screen came alive with the towering spacecraft of the Cape bringing the trio to the edge of their seats. "They say the decline in murder rates is due to the advancement of space medicine they are now developing on moon colonies. The space serum produced to fight the plague can only be extracted from the blood of sickle cell donors. Here on Earth, our agents are very successful in their underground efforts. For the last ten years all developments there have been Top Secret and ten of our agents have lost their lives for what I'm about to show you. At no other time in history have our people been in such demand other than slavery, still they have come forward in good faith to help the world fight this plague. Systematically, the government recruited people of color from all walks of life. Lawyers, doctors, pilots, scientists, technicians and even astronauts, most of which have never been heard from again. The inquiries of the families have gone unanswered due to national security. The footage you're seeing, our last agent was able to get out before he was killed. Notice the thousands of black personnel at the colony. The next segment was taken two months later, if you look closely no blacks. We've monitored every historic mission and the only ones that have returned were of course the astronauts. So you can see why I needed to meet with you, not in an effort of recruitment for the Brotherhood, your lives and that of our children are in grave danger." The eyes of the trio were as much alive as the bright lights that came on. Katie searched for words, "Maybe there's a reasonable explanation. After all, this is our government we're talking about." Dr. Robinson calmly responded, "During drastic times, men take drastic measures. Mankind has polluted this world to the point that Mother Nature is only protecting herself. If history repeats itself so does the plague." Lou replied, "It may not be the actual government but more of a controlling power, like ICON." Troy broke his silence, "Well one thing is for sure, the answers we're looking for aren't down here. Dr. Robinson it's been an honor meeting you and I'm sure we'll meet again." Katie embraced her father as they all departed, "Be careful and don't underestimate ICON, they wouldn't hesitate in eliminating any of you. I love you sweetie," he whispered.

As the three stood out front, Lou tried to flag a cab, "Man, what have we gotten ourselves into? As together as your pops and those guys are, they're still searching for answers. Just what do they think we can do about this mess?" Katie pushed him aside and with a single gesture a cab came to a screeching halt. "I'm not so sure about you, but when the situation presents itself at least one of us will know," she laughed. Troy opened the door smiling, "She might have a point." "Don't even go there." Lou waved off the comment. During the ride back to the hotel they continued the humor all the while trying to suppress the thoughts of genocide. Troy watched the faces that passed in the tinted windows. He now wanted to believe his dreams and inner feelings were a hoax, the years of pain and being different. In this city he felt a presence like no other, the dreadful dreams now brought peace, strength and unity. The lovebirds were lip locked when the cab stopped, "Since you two can't get enough I hope you guys don't mind getting the fare, see ya tomorrow at the Cape."

When Troy reached the hotel elevator he only thought of sleep. Even though it was early, this time he welcomed the dreams. He watched the floor numbers light one after the other, feeling for once he wasn't a nut. Entering the doors of his room he could see the launch pads of the Cape through the windows. The smell of the cool ocean breeze relaxed Troy as he sat on the bed to undress. Soon after laying back he felt himself drifting to sleep. Yes that's want he wanted, a deep sleep. The burning image of a Brotherhood member at his college jumped into his thoughts, proud and determined. Troy remembered the young man speaking to passing students on his bullhorn. "How can you say you love this nation? How can your nation love you when it takes your blood and tears for granted, forcing you to live in fear and poverty? We have to die because the plague doesn't care who's right or who's wrong. Look around you, look at the thing that's killing us. All the pollution and disease, drugs being handed out like candy, white men in the night taking our babies! I'm not looking at Capitol Hill! I'm not looking around the corner or across the sea. I'm looking at you, right here and right now. This plague can be beat, if we all fight it together, but we're not going to stand by while our people are slaughtered again. We don't have time to figure out who's behind the mask, standing in the shadows of the night, killing and bleeding our women and children. If it's blood they want, then it's blood they'll get! Watching eyes will be on Capitol Hill, and on every dark street corner and if more blood flows, it just might be theirs." The image melted back into his subconscious as he fell deeper into slumber.

That night, across the way at the cape, Zenani opened her eyes and sighed as the security cameras whirred all around her. Her every movement was news, as she rarely ever gave any sign that she was alive and alert. The guards escorted the messenger to the outer chamber where he would contact Kehoe immediately.

CHAPTER NINE

The next day dawned bright and clear, a perfect day to begin the finishing touches to his life-long dream. Troy sat up in bed, nearly blinded by the sun reflecting off the waves crashing to shore. "What a place to train" he thought as he stumbled to the bathroom. In the massaging jets of the shower, he came fully awake and excited about the day ahead. There were a few butterflies flitting around his stomach. After all, this was the Cape. The pressure would be on as soon as he stepped through the doors. For a moment, he thought of his parents. This wasn't just about what he wanted, it was their strength that had nurtured him and taught him to believe in himself. He let his emotions wash over him like the shower he stood beneath. A feeling of resolve and determination filled him and he knew no matter what happened, he'd make it through somehow. This thing with the Brotherhood was a different matter, though. The thought of some sinister forces at work made him feel uneasy. His whole life was tied into this mystery but he was damned if he knew any of the answers! He stepped from the shower, trying to leave behind his last train of thought. He focused on the days ahead and finished his morning routine just as Katie and Lou arrived at his door. After some small talk and coffee, the trio set out for the Cape.

They were all nerves on the ride over and scarcely spoke, as each was lost in thoughts about their journeys to this time and place. When the cab pulled up, they looked at each other and smiled. The three friends walked inside full of wonder and excitement, like kids in the candy store. There were tables lined up across the lobby with packets and information about orientation. Troy, Lou and Katie gathered their paperwork and were instructed to go directly to the main hall for an introduction by the commander of flight operations. The hall was nearly full and they chose seats near the back. The low murmur of voices throughout the hall came to an abrupt halt as several men came on stage before them and took seats in a semi-circle around the podium. An elderly gentleman, dressed in civilian clothes, arose from one of the seats near the center of the circle. He was very well dressed and appeared quite virile for his age. He shook hands with each of his colleagues on stage and approached the podium. Every eye was on this man as he began to speak. He introduced himself as Arthur Kehoe and was rewarded with a round of applause from the eager young audience. Most already knew he was ICON, those who didn't may as well have been living on another planet. Space exploration and study had grown immensely since his involvement began with NASA nearly 20 years before.

Troy listened as Kehoe spoke at length of his pride and patriotism. Something kept nagging him, though. Something in the shadows of his memory floated effortlessly to the surface of his conscious mind. He flashed back to a scene from his childhood. He was skipping down the street, oblivious to his surroundings, when he bumped hard against two men dressed like government agents. At first he was frightened, they were so much bigger than he was, and his mother seemed to have vanished. Just as he was about to turn and run from the imposing figures, his mother arrived. She gently restrained Troy in mid-flight and offered apologies for her rambunctious son. The older of the two men spoke up, waving his hand as if to dismiss his mother's apology, "Please, Mrs. Bishop, there is no need for an apology. It's great to see this young man so full of energy." He ruffled Troy's hair and winked at Mary. Clearly confused by a stranger's familiarity with her and her son, Mary had stepped back unconsciously and pulled Troy closer to her body, "Excuse me, but how on earth do you now my name?" Kehoe had nodded to his friend, a younger man with shockingly white hair, and then gave him

157

instructions to continue on without him. He then turned to Mary and smiled graciously, "I'm sorry, ma'am. I never meant to alarm you. My name is Arthur Kehoe. My corporation funded your husband's research. We like to familiarize ourselves with our employees' families and naturally I could never forget the face of such a lovely woman as yourself." Mary still felt uneasy, but she smiled at the man's comment and excused herself and Troy with more shopping to be done. Troy flashed back to the man on stage, something boiled inside at the thought of this man, standing there spouting off about his nobility while his parents lay beneath the ground, taken from him at this man's command! Katie noticed Troy's expression and leaned over, squeezing his arm, "Not here, Troy, not now. We'll handle this together, I promise. We've both got a lot of payback in store for him, but now is not the time." Troy returned her gaze and found his tears mirrored in her eyes. "You're right, sweetie. I'm O.K. Thanks for talking some sense into me." As he turned to look back to the stage, Kehoe returned to his seat and the commander of flight operations took the floor and prepared to address the crowd. Moments passed before the cheers for Arthur Kehoe began to subside.

The commander attempted to regain his audience, "Ladies and gentlemen, astronauts, never in our history have the countries of the world joined together for a more noble cause than that we face today. The barriers of race and prejudice were set aside so that we may face the future as one, the human race. The plague that grips our world can only be beaten when we work as one. We know that we are not alone in the universe. The future of our children and the safety of this planet are in your hands. You're the best, the smartest, the strongest; our last line of defense. Never has man's will to survive been so severely tested. In the following weeks the training you'll receive is all you've been preparing for most of your lives. The administrators will brief you and assign your teams. Let's go people. The count-down has begun."

Troy looked out among the faces, recognizing many, seeing the sparkle in all their eyes. He had arrived. Memories of his parents filled his thoughts. Thinking how proud grandpa would be, inside it felt as if they were with him. All the military brass was enough to blind him, never had he seen so many professionals assembled like this before and most were minorities. Above the noise of shuffling bodies, the clang of bells over the public address system sounded, "Attention, all G-14 personnel to the observatory, all G-14s report to the observatory." Troy knew instantly this was the call for the astronauts and rocket scientists as groups of people headed to their respective areas. The observatory was simply amazing. Troy was in awe of the technology that surrounded him. Galaxy holograms sparkled above his head. Silently they stood on stage, men in black suits. "No security briefing would be complete without them," Troy mused. "Ladies and gentlemen, please be seated," boomed a voice from among the men on stage. "You have all received top secret clearances and have given DNA samples which will assist the identification process here at the Cape. Security agencies from around the globe have unified their efforts and have allied to form the International Intelligence Agency. For the last twenty years the IIA has compiled intelligence that is instrumental in the development of Magma Fusion technology. At the beginning of the 21st century we saw the end of the Fossil Fuel Age. The world's scientific communities searched for years to the question of cold versus hot fusion due to Einstein's famous formula. ICON research facilities bridged the gap by introducing the first Magma Fusion reactor system enabling the Cape's technology to spring light years ahead. Instead of concentrating on standard theories of deuterium-tritium conversions, ICON ruled this out and discovered the purest plasma energy, volcanic magma. The most abundant, free flowing natural resource never questioned by man. The power of Magma Fusion was unimaginable. Many scientists sought only one, cold or hot fusion; not knowing magma combined them both. The magma here on Earth produced energy beyond our wildest dreams. The minds of ICON took it a step further using lunar rocks rich in iron and titanium oxide minerals. We have now harnessed the power of the stars. Twenty-five years ago the question was finally answered that we were not alone. Visitors came from another world. Samples of the landing and launch area baffled scientists who tested the scorched ground finding traces of minerals found only in moon dust of earlier Apollo missions. They worked to solve the mystery of the alien spacecraft's flight capabilities but the connection wasn't made until the Kilamanjaro Incident. Now Magma technology has reshaped our future and has taken us to unbelievable accomplishments. No longer will space travel be hampered by gravity. Laser weapons of the future will no longer have less power than the sun. Mankind is faced with the grave task of saving itself from the plague and you are the astronauts that will blaze the way. Taking you amongst the stars, I give you the Mantaray!" All eyes in the room fought for night vision as the hall was engulfed in sudden darkness and the brilliant lights of a huge three-dimensional hologram appeared before them. Troy's first thought was of a stingray he had often seen diving off the coast. Make no mistake, they had taken Stealth fighter technology to new heights, and maybe that's why they recruited fighter pilots so fervently. Awesome! The hologram displayed all angles of the fighter craft and softened to reveal the inner compartments. It was as if the craft came alive with hatches opening and instrument consoles glowing into action. Troy couldn't believe his eyes when an outer hull on each side slid back revealing some type of laser cannons. The voice proudly boasted,

"These beauties come standard with the Mantaray. The magma laser can pop a pimple on a mosquito's ass within a five-mile radius. Gone are the days of rocket boosters and shuttle piggybacks. Take-offs and landings are now done from a hover mode, similar to the old Marine Corps fighters of the 20th century. The next few months, your training will be rigorous and demanding, pushing each of you to the brink of human expectations. Before it's all said and done, you'll be flying the Mantaray in your sleep. The people of Earth are faced with the deadliest plague ever known and our best hope of a cure lies in developing advanced space medicine. The bonding of our nations is essential for success. Our young people are our future and the true soldiers in the fight against this deadly disease. It is your mission to transport these soldiers to the moon colonies to assist in finding a cure before man is wiped from the face of the Earth." Troy felt uneasy as his mind drifted to a time when he felt so proud just to see another black face on campus or flying along his wing in combat. In the sea of minorities he counted maybe seven Caucasians if that many. This was affirmative action to the power of ten, the chance of a lifetime with no turning back. But somehow, just for a moment he felt the hair on his neck rise as if warning him. The words he'd heard from other blacks all his life came back in that instant, "If white folks get a bunch of us together and talk like we gonna do them some good, you can bet it ain't gonna be good for us."

The rest of the day was filled with back-to-back briefings, from experiments to proposed space flight training. Everyone was filled with excitement when they left the Cape looking forward to what tomorrow would bring. Many of the astronaut hopefuls resided at the same hotel, which now seemed to take on a circus-like atmosphere. The lobby was a maze as Troy excused his way toward the elevator. He heard rapping on the glass of the lounge's window. Stepping closer, he recognized Lou and Katie waving him to come in. The place was packed as he squeezed his way through to greet his friends. He sat and they all held each other's eyes during a moment of silence. Lou leaned back grinning, "What's wrong with this picture, everyone's partying like it's 2099, but we're sitting here like we've been shot from a cannon." Katie looked into her wine glass as she swirled it around, "That's because they don't have a clue, there's no way such technology could have been kept secret this long" "I agree, we've flown everything in the arsenal and there hasn't been a hint of Magma fusion, I have a feeling your father was right about Kilamanjaro. Let's see what we can dig up," said Troy. Lou motioned for the waitress, "Speaking of fathers, I think we need to go back over your Dad's notes, maybe some of this madness ties together." Troy rose to depart, "You've got a point there, and ICON is smack dead in the middle! You guys enjoy, I'll see you later."

Stepping into the tinted glass elevator, Troy felt as protected as the cloaked figures he saw below. Soon the cloaks would drop, welcoming the darkness as dusk now embraced the city. Children dotted the doorways awaiting the relief that complete darkness would bring. A time to play for some and go to school for others. The little children brought a smile. He remembered his own school days. The innocence that the adult world corrupted unknowingly. The thought of a child being harmed was unimaginable to Troy. How another human being could fathom the acts being committed towards children of color. Even in the worst ghettos, rarely were there crimes against children, least of all white ones. Black community leaders were the first to introduce the Parents for Peace program that spearheaded the much-needed gift of blood to children that became afflicted with the plague. Troy rubbed his arm thinking of all the blood he gave, but nothing could erase from his memory the sight of children sick with the plague. The program was such a success they began calling them the children of the gift, soon the dreadful murders and kidnappings started to decline. Sadly they never completely stopped. Troy easily spotted members of the Brotherhood at almost every corner, standing ever vigilant. Deep inside he felt their pain and understood the watchful eyes of a people that couldn't rest, knowing the wrong that never slept. The days' events had measured up to his highest expectations and maybe Lou was right about everything tying in, but where did he fit? His whole life was like a puzzle with so many missing pieces, feeling so in tune at times, then like an outcast at others. When he reached his room his head felt like it was spinning; his parents, aliens, ICON, how did all this connect? He watched the lights of the Cape in the distance feeling a peace he hadn't known in so long, was this just a dream come true? In his thoughts this feeling had nothing to do with being an astronaut. He just couldn't put his finger on it but there was something about this place that gave him a warm feeling. He normally felt relaxed like this when he went home to visit his grandfather, remembering his childhood and Zoë. What ever it was made Troy slowly close his eyes to savor the moment. His left hand clenched involuntary, not from pain. He felt a surge of energy. Troy struggled to open it, noticing the outline of veins in the shape of some kind of star that grew brighter with each pulse beat. Troy had long ago accepted these occurrences. Though he never thought of them as gifts, they often enlightened him and on a few occasions actually saved his life. Since he had arrived at the Cape they were quite different, more real and visual. He felt stronger. Since arriving at the Cape, he had experienced weird feelings of oneness with the animals he came across on walks or at the ocean. The birds and squirrels at the park always flocked to sing their praises of life. He felt their presence and shared their life trials of joy and sorrow. He thought maybe the mammals of the ocean had a closer connection with man and should commune more intensely.

Hadn't science always said that we came from the ocean? So what was it now that beat within his very soul? He breathed heavily and sweat dripped from his forehead as he watched his glowing palm.

Far across town, deep within the confines of the Cape's most guarded silo, another star appeared. The deafening sound of the alarms echoed as the technicians and scientists scrambled to their stations. The substation could withstand a nuclear attack and utilized the most modern advances of Magma-technology, it made Arthur Kehoe proud. Technicians ran this way and that, scurrying to man their stations before Mr. Kehoe descended from his penthouse office high above the crashing waves of the Cape. The beautiful alien girl inside the chamber had risen from her bed and began pacing the room, holding her hand and chanting some message. The word "Hatari!" was repeated over and over as she floated to and fro in her confines. Just then Kehoe stepped from the elevator and stood silently watching the girl lost in her own world. He barked out orders for the technicians and donned a bio suit to enter the chamber. As he entered, he saw her palm pulsating with the blue light he remembered from the landing of her mother's ship so many years ago. He feared that now the time had come for her return. Maybe the girl was answering a message of some sort that only she could hear. Judging from the level of her activity, he was sure that something beyond his control would happen if he kept her here. Where could he take her, though? The only other place with enough security and cloaking technology was the moon base. Kehoe strode quickly out of the chamber and called upstairs and ordered a Mantaray, A.S.A.P. There were no questions asked as the girl was quickly bound and escorted to the waiting craft. She had quieted considerably, but the star in her palm still pulsated as blue tears traced their way down her velvet cheeks. Her face was a mask of indifference; only Troy knew how she felt inside, as he too felt her pain. He looked into the night sky and saw a streak, almost undetectable, race from the Cape towards the black universe above. He wondered why he suddenly felt as if he had lost a piece of himself.

CHAPTER TEN

Troys' life became the Cape in the months to follow. He thought about that night many times afterwards, but the feeling of loss had become bearable as his rigorous training became the daily norm. His friends, Lou and Katie, still spent a lot of time together, but their training schedules kept them from getting together as they had in the past. Whenever they did get a chance to hang out, it always became an investigative session. They were convinced that the puzzle was coming together. They were more frightened than ever that the events of the past were the key to understanding this mystery. For Troy and Katie it became an obsession. They both needed to understand what was going on. Their lives had been shattered as children and now ICON was once again involved with their well being. Lou, believe it or not, became the cool head among the group. He cautioned his two friends about becoming too wrapped up in figuring out the past and its ties to the present. He reminded them of the sacrifices to reach this point and by putting their dreams in jeopardy they would only place themselves farther from the truths they sought. So it was that the trio began to focus earnestly on training and Troy, most of all, began to forget the past, if only for the time being.

The intensity of training was everything he could ask for and more, the scientific developments of Magma-technology revolutionized everything from computers to space travel. Troy absorbed the knowledge like a sponge as ICON continued to change all aspects of power conversions and lunar mining increased by 80 percent. The exploratory mining had made some major breakthroughs of new mineral deposits called Puma ore. The new ore soon boosted advances in the medical community. With its' many advantages, ICON's space medicine came closer to a cure for the plague. All indications showed destruction of plague cells with the blood of sickle-cell anemia patients. The drugs proved most effective with freshly drawn blood. The countries of the world recruited and employed the assistance of minority patients. Soon with the help of Parents of Peace, this accounted for the Top Secret programs that were soon adopted by ICON to contract the services of the patients at the moon base. The mission was to deploy these badly needed patients to the moon with the new astronaut corps. The flight training tested the very imagination of all the astronauts. The capabilities of the Mantaray were remarkable. No longer was space travel being shot off in a rocket and destroying the ozone in the process, but rather harnessing the power of a star without dangerous emissions. Troy found himself sitting for hours at a time in the hangar staring at all the angles and running every vital stat through his mind. When the day arrived, he felt like a small boy on Christmas day. With all the astronauts assembled, they filed into an area where they found the Mantaray hovering.

Troy would never forget the hum of the reactors as the gigantic craft appeared suspended about six feet off the ground. The first few days, the instrument drills were mind-boggling and most of the commands were hand pressurized or voice activated within the helmets. The astronauts were in a state of confusion even though they understood the concept. It wasn't until they saw the Mantaray in flight and watched hours of film that they could they grasp the flight theory. Once inside the simulators the confusion continued, error after error, crash after crash. Troy battled with himself to put it all together. Never had he sat in a cockpit that completely moved, conforming to his flight pattern. What was almost unbelievable was at speeds beyond that of sound it could dart sideways, come to a complete stop and reverse flight. Each day the names of the active astronauts were taken off the board. Some were unable to withstand the Gs, most merely couldn't get past the chair. The chair was an extension of the commander and the controller of the reactors. At first glance it made Troy think of an easy chair. The space suit and helmet aligned as virtual skin interlinked with the console surrounding the chair. Day after day the instructors bombarded the astronauts with more data and requirements. Little wonder now why there were few qualified crews. With each passing day the class members were falling by the wayside. It still made Troy proud to be surrounded by such outstanding black talent and intellect, although the majority of the instructors were white. They were commonly referred to as Moles, and it was rumored that a mole crew had been flying the Top Secret missions. The mole crew flew the scientists and volunteers up to the moon base.

Troy rarely saw Katie or Lou. The study of Magma science involved each professional in extensive training in remote parts of the world concealed by a web of governmental secrecy. Though Troy was making progress with his training in the simulator, he thought it only a matter of time before he too would be a washout. Troy pounded away at the bag in the gym daily. One day during an intense workout, a rather small dark man spoke to him in a strange foreign tongue, "You must bend more before each strike." The thought of this guy correcting his form briefly irritated him, thinking of all his martial arts training but he tried it anyway. The bag snapped with more authority. Troy turned to find the stranger had vanished. "Now that's odd," he thought. Of all the brothers he'd met since arriving, he hadn't seen this guy. It wasn't surprising, until now he hadn't known that brothers came in so many flavors. The more he thought about it as he headed to the showers, with that British accent the man must have been of Aboriginal heritage. Dismissing the thought, Troy finished his shower and got dressed heading for morning training.

Approaching the training site, he noticed everyone standing outside the facility laughing and giving high fives.

"Hey, what's all the excitement about?" he asked. "They just posted the new axe report," someone replied trying to peer over the wave of bodies. A sudden case of nerves hit Troy knowing this could mean the duffle bag drag and seeing the disappointed looks on a lot of faces. "I thought they weren't going to make any determinations until the end of the month?" Troy said. The guy shouted back, "The word is Kehoe himself ordered the program moved up, something about them hitting a mother lode of the ore, and you know the old man, time is money and money is time." Troy hesitated when he finally got close enough to see the board and tried to swallow as he scanned down the list. The butterflies in his stomach fluttered as he read the list. Scanning again to make sure his name wasn't there, Troy sighed and shouted, "Yes!" and felt some pats on the back from his peers. "No class today fellows, it's time to celebrate! The party is on the beach!" yelled a voice from the crowd. Troy thought about how some of the guys were probably feeling. It had been tough with more in store. They were still the best in the world, and would go on to be commanders of space shuttles. Just thinking of the Mantaray made him feel humble.

It didn't take long before things got into full swing. Soon the beach area blasted with soulful music as the smell of BBQ made mouths water. The sunset and festivities soon brought partygoers of all sorts ready, willing and able. The cool ocean breeze sprayed the desire of twilight on those that welcomed the night's embrace. Troy had almost forgotten the kick that alcohol had when he tasted the home brew in the punch, "No wonder everyone was so happy," he thought. A small hand pulled him into the middle of the crowd of beach dancers, "All work and no play will make Troy a dull boy!" said a woman displaying some sexy moves. All the dancing made Troy think of his parents and how they loved to carry-on. The old man was always talking about them being on some show called Soul Train.

"Pops was always the life of the party," Troy thought for a second, "maybe that's where I get all my skills." "Watch out! You asked for it!" he laughed. It wasn't long before they had a train line of their own with sand and butts flying all over the place. You know the party is good until you hear that sound, "SLAP!" Somebody somewhere has gotten out of line. The shouts of the woman broke the sudden silence, "Fool! I know your mama taught you not to be grabbing on people's asses!" The guy stood holding his cheek in shock as his friends pointed and laughed. His face changed to rage as he cocked back to hit the girl. "SWOOSH" went his hand. Suddenly he stopped in mid-swing. A small man caught his hand. "It's not nice to hit ladies," he smiled. Troy remembered the face. It was the guy from the gym! This should be interesting! The laughing friends of the guy slowly encircled the small man, "Oh my God! It's Midget man to the rescue. You have got to be joking me!" Troy moved closer in hopes of helping the guy because it didn't look good for the home team. Like a pack of wolves they closed in, as they taunted, "Look Aussie man, you shouldn't put your nose where it doesn't belong! Now I've got to hurt you!" said the big bully. The expression on the little man's face was as if he didn't speak English. Troy sensed he wouldn't make it through the crowd in time. The blow came from St Louis, "Smack!" The little man moved like lightning as the big man missed and knocked out his own friend. Wasting no time, the little man struck with precision, clothes lining the second guy across the throat. While doing a split, big man lost his manhood. Springing high off the ground he caught one guy charging with a front snap in the head. He then turned as the big man groaned, getting off the ground. Troy knew instantly what he meant by snapping your wrist. The blow was so fast big man wouldn't remember what hit him. The crowd loved it as they stepped over the downed warriors like they weren't even there as the beat and the party went on.

Troy began to walk away from the music and laughter and head down the beach. The night was so clear. The stars above shone brighter than he had seen them in a quite a while. As he searched the sky above, he wondered how Katie was doing tonight. Lou had given her a hard time about the congressional fundraiser she was attending. It was easier for Troy to understand that Katie fit into two worlds, but Lou was still having difficulty with the whole stupid color issue. Troy wondered sometimes whether Lou would ever really forgive Katie for having a white mother. It wasn't that Lou hated white people; it was just that he had always been very proud of his race. Troy thought that with all the madness in the world over this plague epidemic, Lou had every reason to be wary of the establishment. Maybe that was what he was really worried about. Maybe he was scared that Katie would begin to melt into that way of life and be lost to him. Troy decided to have a talk with Lou later about what was really bothering him, Katie's skin color or the thought of losing her. He glanced at the ritzy building Katie was in right now. The towering glass structure twinkled with lights from within. He hoped she was having a good time at the very least. She was under as much pressure as he and Lou, maybe even more.

As Troy walked back to the party, Katie looked around again for some way out of this boring affair. She walked to an open balcony and stared at the ocean below her. Lou was right, she didn't belong here. But if her career was going to take off, she had to mingle. Being invited to a congressional cocktail party was just one of the ways to promote herself and get in some much needed networking. Lou would just have to understand. As she turned to go back inside, a perky, petite blond walked up beside her. "You must be thinking the same thing I am!" she smiled. Katie placed her hand against the base of her throat and smiled back at the woman. "Oh, yes, I just needed a breath of fresh air. All these powerful people in one room is quite overwhelming!" The woman laughed as she took Katie's arm and guided her to a corner of the ornately decorated room. She waved a young man over with a serving tray full of champagne glasses. "Here, dear. Have one of these. My name is Melanie Borden, of the Massachusetts Bordens. I have been attending these gatherings ever since my father decided that my brother should run for his senate seat next year." Katie's eyes flashed in recognition. "I am so sorry, I didn't recognize you Miss Borden! Your family is practically legendary in the political world as well as the business world. Excuse me, I don't mean to babble, it's just been such a long evening already!" Miss Borden giggled as she patted Katie's arm, "Oh my heavens, don't apologize. You wouldn't recognize me! I have been out of the country for many years. I was educated in Paris and have only recently returned to the United States. My family, as you say, they are the legends! I am just beginning to make my way in the world. It's so nice to meet someone my own age, though. What is you do, Miss? I'm sorry I didn't catch your name!" "My name is Katie Kimball, and I'm a student at the Cape, flight control and computer operations." The charming young woman smiled broadly at Katie, "My dear, it is an honor to meet one of the Cape's students and a female as well! How wonderful that you are so talented and beautiful! We must get to know one another better. My father wants me to head up his new computer applications company and I'd love to have you as a consultant, if you have any spare time that is! Of course you'd be handsomely compensated." Katie smiled at the thought of how much progress she was making after all. An inroad with the Borden family, this evening might be exciting after all! She followed Miss Borden across the room and was promptly introduced to Senator Borden and several other graying senators as well. She chatted briefly with them and then she and Miss Borden strolled around the room mingling with all the lawmakers and their staff. Before long, they had arrived back at the balcony where they had met earlier. As the two reached for another round of the expensive champagne, Katie laughed to herself about the evening she was enjoying. Wouldn't Lou be surprised? More likely he'd hate it that she had made a friend among the upper crust. Melanie laughed with her and began to talk about all the people she had just met. "Katie, you would be astounded if you knew some of the things I know about these old guys!" Katie went into another round of giggles as the champagne tickled her nose, "Umm, juicy gossip about the country's premier leaders, who could resist?" Melanie inched closer to Katie and pointed out several of the older senators. "Would you believe that Senator Raymond is seventy-six?" "No way! He only looks fifty-two at the outside!" " Yes, Katie dear, that's the idea! But I swear he's seventy-six. And Senator Alton, he's a ripe old seventy!" Katie nearly choked on her champagne, "What on Earth are they doing to look so much younger? I know plastic surgery can do wonders, but they seem so lively!" Melanie tilted her head and spoke in a whisper, "Katie, those men look twenty years younger than they are and they are physically in the shape of men much younger than that!" Katie looked at Melanie and shook her head, "This might be a personal question, but how do you know that?" Melanie really got a kick out of this question! When she finally stopped laughing she answered Katie's puzzled look, "Let's just say that some of my close personal friends have been close and personal with these Senators! Women our age can't even keep up with these guys, if you know what I mean!" Katie still looked puzzled, "How can that be though? I mean plastic surgery can do a lot, but it can't turn back time!" Melanie decided to spill the beans. "A lot, and I mean a lot, of these guys have had cancer, diabetes, coronary problems and a host of diseases that cripple most people as they age. From what I gather from their mistresses, my girlfriends, most of these men have been getting injections of some kind for years! I'm not sure what it is, but one girl told me she saw her guy being injected. She wasn't supposed to see it, but she did. She said it was some kind of red fluid. It looked like blood to her. But that is just crazy, it makes them sound like vampires! The thought of it makes me sick!" Katie trembled all over and felt like she would throw up. It couldn't be! Not these people! "My God!" her mind screamed as the room full of well-heeled monsters swam before her eyes. Calm down! she ordered herself as she began to ask Melanie more questions. "What on Earth do you think they are being injected with then?" Melanie shrugged her shoulders, "I really have no idea. Whatever it is, they aren't sharing with the general public! They must have some kind of under the table relationship with the FDA. Lord knows someone had to approve whatever it is that they are taking. I am beginning to wonder if my father is getting these "injections". I hope its just good genes!" Katie wanted to get out of this whole charade as quickly as possible, but she couldn't just bolt out of there. Melanie might get suspicious. She had to have a moment to herself, so she excused herself to the powder room.

As she made her way across the ballroom floor, she forced herself not to look anyone in the eye. Her mind was turning on all that Melanie had told her tonight. It couldn't possibly be what she was thinking! But then again, if anyone were to do such a thing, these people would probably be front and center to embrace injections that would keep them in their prime. Power was like an aphrodisiac to the men in this room. It was the very thing that defined who they were. You can't hold on to the reins of power if you're old and ill. What a terrible price people were paying to keep the wealthy in the bloom of health! Katie decided to try and keep her rapport with Melanie open. Maybe that consulting job could help her in more ways than one. It certainly wouldn't hurt to get computer access at Borden headquarters. She entered the powder room and sat before the mirror looking at her reflection. No wonder Lou was having a hard time with her life and responsibilities. Sometimes she wondered who she was as well. Lou might never get a handle on the issue of loving a biracial person. She braced herself for the fact that he would probably end their relationship instead of dealing with all the problems that seemed to crop up between them. How many times had it happened before? She wasn't white enough or she wasn't black enough. At times she thought it would be best to be on her own and focus all her attention on her career. That was one place where she shined. No one really cared about your skin color when their system crashed and you were the only one who could bring it back up. She sighed as she powdered her nose and reapplied her lipstick. Whatever happened with Lou, she'd still have her work. Right now that seemed like a port in the storm. She rose to leave the powder room and overheard two female voices in the lounge area. "Whatever those Senators are using, it works. Who cares where they get it? I just wish I knew where to get some myself!" Katie hurried out the door and returned to the balcony once more, knowing she was going to have to get out of this party soon. As luck would have it, Melanie reappeared just as she was about to make her getaway. "Katie! Katie! I'm so glad you're still here. I have to leave soon myself, but I wanted to give you my business card. I am serious about the consulting job. I do hope you will consider my offer. And besides, I'd like for us to get together whenever you have some free time!" Katie smiled and took the ivory card from Melanie's well-manicured hand. "You are too kind, Melanie. It's been a pleasure meeting you. Of course I will consider your generous offer. It may be just what I need to break the monotony of my studies. I'll be sure to call you Monday and let you know how my schedule is going." "Katie dear, I will be waiting for your call. I have to be going now, thank you so much for making this evening more exciting." She took Katie's hand and smiled brightly before turning to leave with one of her fathers' staffers. Katie wasted no time in taking leave of the soiree, herself. As she drove through the darkened streets, she knew she had to find Troy as soon as possible. He would be the first person she told about this bizarre evening.

The moonlight glistened on the waves as Troy walked along the beach. Looking up at the stars he heard someone calling "Yo, Troy hold up." It was Lou in a jog to catch up with him. "Man that is some party! Did you score my man?" Troy smiled, "Naw, but I had a great time. How bout you?" "Did I? The honeys were all over me! But it just didn't feel the same, you know, like the old days." Troy could tell by Lou's expression that he was serious, "Thinking about Katie I suppose, must be love." Lou pushed Troy in the back, "What do you know about love? Matter of fact, when was the last time you dated?" Troy scooped up some sand and watched it sift through his hand, "Hey man, we were talking about you, not me. I'm not talking body counts here, but what you feel deep inside your heart for someone you love. In those rare times when two people come together and you just know it, nothing can change what you feel. It just happens, regardless of the differences. Lou either you're blind or stupid to deny the love that you and Katie have for each other. My brother, with all that's going on in the world today, you can't even see what's right in front of you." Lou took a deep breath, "You're right, I know. But this love stuff kinda makes me nervous, and besides when are you going to take your own advice?" They both began to laugh, "Well, it's like I said, I guess I'll know it when it happens."

Upon reaching their building they noticed the shadowy figure of a woman pacing at the entrance. Katie's soft voice broke the night silence, "Well, if it isn't the terrible twosome, kind of late to be out picking fruit don't you think?" Lou attempted to kiss Katie on the cheek, but she wasn't in the mood. She pushed him away with her words, "And you, smelling like a perfume factory! No telling where your pocket rocket has been." Troy tried hard to hold back the laughter as Lou stared angrily, "Hey bro, what's so funny? This woman must be out of her damn mind and you around here playing Dr. Love. I must've been crazy to listen to you. I knew this could never work. I might as well head back down to the strange fruit!" Katie put her arm in Troy's and gave Lou a look that could kill, "Yeah Lou, you know the saying, the darker the berry, the sweeter the juice. I can't offer you anything but a complex. So go on down to the beach and find a woman who's dark enough to ease your conscience!" Lou's face was a mask of anger as he turned and stalked off down the beach. Troy called after him, but that only made Lou pick up his step and soon he disappeared into the darkness. Katie sniffed back the tears that shimmered in her eyes. Troy pulled her closer and whispered words to comfort her as the ocean breeze whipped stronger along the coastline. Katie pulled her coat tighter around her as she looked up at Troy. "I shouldn't have said those things to him, but lately he's made it more than obvious that I'm just not going to fit into his "world", not with this skin." Troy took Katie's hand and tried to explain the actions of his friend, "Katie, Lou is so confused right now, he doesn't know up from down. Truth be told, you are the first woman to steal his heart and he's just trippin'. He is using this color thing to put some distance between the two of you. Not a smart thing to do, but this is Lou we're talking about! He'll come around sooner or later, and you'll be just fine. I do hope that no matter what happens, the two of you can at least be civil to each other, I mean we're a team, right? I can't have my two best friends at each others throats, can I?" Katie smiled as she touched Troy's face, "Maybe I picked the wrong friend to fall in love with." Troy gently took her hand and pulled it from his face, "You'll always have my friendship, Katie, and you know that. But this thing with you and Lou is a good thing. Sometimes people have to face their demons to be able to let go and truly love. Lou will figure it out. He's no "rocket scientist", at least not yet! But mark my words, he'll get over whatever is bothering him and when he does, I know you'll be there to give him the love he needs." Katie sighed and hugged Troy closer, "I know you're right. It's just that Lou was the last person I thought would go there over my color. It just hurts so much, Troy. It's hard being biracial. Nobody claims you and everybody blames you. I'm lucky to have a friend like you, though." Troy smiled and hugged her back, "You're alright with me Katie-lady, even if you were orange with green polka dots!" The two friends smiled at each other and began to walk towards Troy's building.

"Hey, what brought you out here anyway, get bored at your cocktail party?" Katie stiffened at the mention of the party. "Troy you wouldn't believe that place! It was so elegant and formal. So many powerful people, it was overwhelming at first. I was trying to find a way out when one of the Bordens came across me standing on the balcony." Troy raised his eyebrows, "Bordens, eh? Don't they own just about everything?" Katie laughed, "You got it! And of course you know their political history. Well, this Borden was a young woman by the name of Melanie. She's been away in Paris getting her education. She was so friendly and charming, not at all what I expected. To make a long story short, she took me under her wing and introduced me around as a gifted young computer genius and ultimately offered me a consulting position at her father's new computer applications division!" Troy whistled low, "Wow, maybe I should start going to your parties instead of these hedonistic beach blowouts!" Katie laughed at her friend and strolled over to a park bench along the edge of the emerald lawn. Troy followed her, gazing above at the stars and velvet expanse of night sky. He sat beside her and noticed a lone tear tracing its way along her cheek. "Katie, what's wrong?" Katie shook her head and tried to speak, but her voice caught in her throat. Troy moved closer and put one arm around her shoulders. "It's not this little argument with Lou, is it?" Katie shook her head no and began to speak, "Troy, I heard some really strange things tonight and if they are true, then we are all in more trouble than anything we could have imagined before. I mean this makes ICON look like a bedtime story!" Troy turned her around to face him, "Katie, come on, what are you talking about?" She took a deep breath, but Troy could still feel her trembling like a scared rabbit, and he didn't think it was because of the chill night air. "Melanie told me about some of the senators at the party tonight. She went on and on about how they had beaten cancer and heart disease and all this other stuff that should be ailing them to this day. I remarked about how young they all looked, and that of course they should be in good health and she informed me that most of them were seventy or more. Troy there is no way a seventy-year-old man can look that good! Maybe one of them, but not the whole group! She also informed me that they have these young mistresses who can't hold a candle to them in the bedroom. Of course I kept exclaiming that plastic surgery could do a lot, but not that much. That's when she told me something that really tripped me out!" Troy's face went from disbelief to fear as he listened to the rest of Katie's story. "She said that one of her friends, a mistress to one senator, saw her guy being injected with a strange fluid. Troy, the girl said it looked like blood! You don't think it could be, do you?" Troy looked like he might be sick. "I knew it, I just knew it!" Katie jumped up and began pacing around, mumbling over and over. Troy got to his feet and grabbed Katie hard. He forced her to stop pacing and look at him. "Katie, we don't know what it was!

179

I hope to God it wasn't blood! But if it was, we have to keep this to ourselves, do you understand? You cannot be flipping out over this! We need a way to find out what's going on and you are in the right place at the wrong time, here." Katie tried to control herself and suddenly she understood what Troy was saying. "You're right, Troy! If I take Melanie up on her offer, maybe I can get in with the in-crowd and find out what the hell is really going on! I bet everything I have that ICON is involved somehow. ICON's practically another branch of the government as it is." "That's my girl. Now you're using your head. If we are going to make it here and figure out this whole mess with ICON, I need you to think with your head, Katie, and not your heart, okay?"

Katie's hazel eyes flashed their usual fire "My heart is obviously defective at the moment, my friend. My head is usually my best bet anyway!" She smiled as they began to walk to her building in the Cape complex. As Troy and Katie disappeared in the growing darkness, Lou partied late into the night, trying to forget the angry words that passed between Katie and him earlier in the evening. He knew she'd only spoken the truth about what was really bothering him and he felt ashamed for having hurt her as he had. "Either I get my shit together, or I leave her alone and stop hurting both of us!" he thought as he drifted back to the Cape housing area. He stared at the waves lapping gently on the beach and thought of Katie's tender caresses. She was so good to him, but was she good for him? "That's what you've got to figure out for yourself, dog." he whispered to himself across the stillness of the night.

The next morning came early into Katie's room as the telephone rang loudly in her ear. "Hello?" she yawned into the mouthpiece. "Darling, I'm sorry, did I wake my sweet baby girl?" Katie sat up in bed and smiled at the love in her father's voice. "Yeah, dad. I had a pretty late night last night." She stifled another yawn as she fumbled on the bedside table for her watch. "Well, I sure hope you are not making a habit of partying into the wee hours with all those rowdy Cape cadets!" She laughed into the receiver and promptly informed her father about her "exciting" cocktail party with the nation's top political leaders. She left out the part about the injections, discussing such a controversial and potentially deadly subject over the phone would not be a good idea. So when her father invited her to lunch later in the conversation, she gladly accepted. She asked if she could bring Troy along, she wanted him to be with her when the subject was broached, and of course her father agreed, but then ruined her good mood by asking if Lou could come along as well. Katie grudgingly agreed and if her father noticed her reluctance, he failed to question her about it.

Troy was trotting along the beach when he came upon Lou stretching. The eye contact between the two was brief, as each extended an arm and their fists touched. Lou looked down the beach, "We need to talk, you mind if I join you?" Troy smiled, "Sure, let's do it." The two began to jog and talk. "I guess I kinda blew it. I just hate to be accused of something I haven't done. Man, you talking bout pissed, I couldn't believe how mad she made me! I've never had a woman get under my skin like she has, and the big trip is, after I left you guys I went back to the party with the sole intention of getting my groove on. I had this honey all lined up, then blam! All I could think about was Katie!" Lou hadn't realized how much he was talking and finally looked at Troy who was wiping tears from his face, dying with laughter. Lou pushed him as they ran, "Oh, Oh, so it's like that! Man, ain't nothing funny, I'm going crazy, and you up here laughing!" Waving his hand as he tried to catch his breath, "Naw, my brother it's not like that," cried Troy racing to catch up with him. "Seriously Lou, you're in love! Hey look, I'm sorry about laughing, but Katie really cares for you, she told me herself. You guys need to talk things out, is all. But I don't know if she would take you

back if she saw you with that puppy-dog look on your face."
Lou's expression changed like Missouri weather as he threw
a left hook that just missed Troy's head. "I've got your
puppy-dog!" he yelled as he began chasing Troy down the
beach. The two sprinted along splashing in the surf. Lou
finally tackled Troy with a last ditch effort. They lay
exhausted still unable to hold back the laughter. "Sooner or
later you're going to have to tell her," Troy grinned. "Tell
her what?" asked Lou as he leaned back on his elbows.
"That you love her, you big dummy." Rolling over to one
knee Lou jokingly pronounced, "My darling Katie, I love
you." Troy motioned, "Yeah, but cut to the chase, and say
it with more feeling." Lou tried again, "Katie, I love you."
Filled with excitement, Troy encouraged him more, "That's
it, but this time shout it with some soul, so the whole world
can hear." Flinging his arms out, Lou shouted, " I love you,
Katie!" They looked into each others eyes and playfully
raced together to embrace, "Oh Lou, I love you too," said
Troy, as they stumbled and fell back on to the sand. Their
fun and games were cut short when they heard a real
woman's voice, "And all this time, I thought it was another
woman!" Lou abruptly pushed Troy away, "Get off me,
fool!" Katie tossed a couple of towels at the pair, "If you
two are finished, we have a engagement with my father,
meet me at the pier in thirty minutes." They stared at Katie
as she walked away. "Now, that's a woman!" shouted
Troy. Lou grabbed his towel, "Just shut up! "Katie, I love
you!'' he mocked. Troy shouted to Lou, "Look at the bright
side, at least now she knows!"

Once upstairs Troy hurried to make the thirty-minute
deadline, quickly showering and changing. This meeting
with Dr. Robinson might be helpful in his search for the
truth. The bits and pieces of his father's work were the key,
but how? As he walked to the pier, he could already see
Lou and Katie standing on the dock holding hands. Lou
must have taken a "monkey shower." He remembered how

his grandfather would jest when he was young, "Boy, what you do? Throw the water in the air and run before it hits you?" Just thinking of home made Troy remember the taste of Miss Molly's home cooked breakfast. He sure was hungry all of a sudden! He hoped Katie's plans included something to eat! Approaching the lovebirds, he noticed Lou pointing at a fast moving boat piercing effortlessly through the waves. The Hydrofoil lowered into the water as it slowed and crept to dock for the waiting passengers. The serious stares of the Brotherhood seemed always the same, distrustful. One of the beefy men assisted Katie as she stepped aboard and nodded to Troy and Lou as they all took their seats. Shortly after pushing off, the high speeds of the boat could be felt as it bucked like a LA low rider. Soon the ride smoothed out as the hydrofoil elevated and seemed to take flight. Far out into the open sea they went without a word from the men. Troy and Lou both noticed the bulge of weapons on the men. Katie continued to stare ahead as one of them pointed and began talking into the mic of his radio. Katie turned and smiled, "There ahead, we're almost there." Troy could see a yacht in the distance, but for the moment he was more delighted with the dolphins that playfully raced alongside them. The boat lowered down into the water as it slowed to dock beside the super yacht. Dr. Robinson stood on deck smiling as his bodyguards carefully parted only long enough to let Katie embrace her father. His voice always so serious, "You look more like your mother every time I see you. Gentlemen, thank you for coming, please make yourselves comfortable." He extended his arm and motioned for them to enter the luxurious cabin. The bodyguards quickly scanned the room and instinctively posted themselves outside each door and near the windows, all except the two Lou called Lurch and Igor. Katie was already cutting her eyes at Lou before the horseplay could start. Ignoring Katie, Lou whispered to Troy, "You rang." Troy managed to contain his laughter. The two bodyguards said nothing. If they heard Lou, they made no acknowledgement of the fact. Katie and her father talked as he led them on a tour through the rest of the yacht. The now lone bodyguard Igor carefully watched Troy as he walked over to get a closer look at Dr. Robinson's library. His eyes gazed across the many wonderful works. He smiled when he saw photos of the doctor in his youth. Lou had joined the prowl, "Hey, check this out, the old man was a Black Panther, fist held high, black power to the bone, baby!" They both laughed as they pointed to the huge Afros. The girlish smile in one of the photos caught Troy's eye. His eyes widened as he recognized the old college backdrop. In the sea of faces, his mother smiled out at him! "Mother," he whispered. The distinguished voice of Dr. Robinson broke his trance, "Now, that was taken years before the Panther movement. That's your father and I in the back. I guess we both wanted to save the world, him with medicine and me with the movement. We all marched with Dr. King. An amazing woman, your mother! Those were trying times! Your father and I were like most young black men in those days, big ideas with fire in our hearts. Your mother understood better than anyone the importance of being organized. I remember after Dr. King's death we were at a rally and the brothers were about explode when this little sister took the mike and roared. The hall was quiet as a church as she spoke, reminding us of continuing Dr. King's dream. Needless to say calmer heads prevailed, but it was strong black women like your mother that kept the focus on the struggle to survive." Dr. Robinson walked over to the desk globe and gave it a spin and stopped it with the other hand. "Africa, the motherland! By the turn of the century more than 90% of South Africa's population was infected with the HIV virus. That same year the top five economic countries of the world committed over 50 billion dollars to the space program. Barely a few million and some outdated medicine were collectively acquired for those suffering in sub-Saharan Africa. In less than two years 15 million were dead. Millions more were orphaned with no plans made for their care. In 5 years the borders were reopened and the white population was 4 to 1 and back in control of South Africa and the diamond mines. Coincidence or design?" Shaking his head, Dr. Robinson sighed. Realizing how emotional he had become he nodded to the chef to begin serving lunch. "Excuse me, I digress, this was to be an afternoon to dine and spend with family." Lou slid Katie's chair back for her to be seated, "Dr. Robinson, so much secrecy surrounds the AIDS cure. Why doesn't it work with this plague we face now?" After passing the cream, the doctor leaned back in his chair, "Up until now that secret has protected the lives of all people of color. The secret was a flower, a flower that grows in the lush tropical forest of Mount Kilamanjaro. Its growth couldn't be duplicated. It grew wild only on Kilamanjaro. The world didn't care about the death of our people, closing all ways out with no help coming in. But as you know, just as many whites were dying and needed the cure as much as we, the latter was fate. Only a hand full of leaders assembled and Ben Bishop was there as well, front and center. Death came quick and in huge waves. It wasn't clear in the news reports when the avalanche on Kilamanjaro happened how many had died, but for some unforeseen reason Ben insisted that we go. Rebels had complete control of the territory but allowed our humanitarian journey. Thousand of locals were injured and killed in the devastation. We did as much as we could in the hospitals and your father wanted to travel farther up the mountain to help the tribal people caught in the mountain's wrath. Working around the clock we saved as many lives as possible. Treating injuries was one thing, and then we learned that members of our team were seriously ill and dying with the virus. Again we found ourselves helpless. I remember we were all so weary! We had taken shelter in this hut. Our own people were dying and this old medicine man quietly walked in and looked at each of the men. He barked some orders to one of the women of his group. She raced to his hut and returned with an animal skin bag. We all thought, "What the hell?" We had tried everything at our disposal. The old man grabbed a bowl and took some dried herbs out of the bag. He ground the dried flowers down to a fine powder and mixed it with water and made each of the men drink the potion. The women began chanting and wailing as the medicine man danced around them. Within minutes the men went into convulsions and began to vomit. The women helped them as the medicine man poured more of the liquid down their throats as the night wore on. By morning the men were sleeping peacefully and were kept cool with wet cloths as the ritual continued for two days. The hours seemed endless as we waited. Finally the old man and the women walked out and allowed us to enter. I could see the immediate difference in the men. They were trying to sit up and speak. I saw the wonder in Ben's eyes. I knew he was thinking the same thing as myself. We dropped to our knees and rejoiced in prayer. In the days that followed, the women returned daily with the strange potion. Soon the men were able to stand and take solid food. We continued our work with the tribes and helped to bury their dead. Before long our men had regained their strength. It wasn't until then that we saw the medicine man again. We had our interpreter ask about the powerful potion. The old man smiled and knelt to the ground and plucked a few of the flowers that covered the forest floor. We could only shake our heads in disbelief. The sunset across the Ngorongoro crater reflected the miracle before us. This enchanted land had bestowed its gift to man."

It suddenly dawned on Troy his parent's passion for flowers! He remembered their greenhouse and how exotic the plants were, nothing like the ones around the house.

Katie interrupted, "There was never any indication that the cure was discovered in Africa, I thought that," Lou interrupted, waving his toast. "Yeah, what's his name? Sir Gregory, you know, the British dude. The one that received the Nobel Peace Prize for discovering the cure for AIDS." Reaching over to stop the flying toast Katie hissed at Lou, "Will you stop that?" She regained her composure and continued speaking to her father, "Father, what I don't understand is how Magma Fusion is connected to Tanzania?" Dr. Robinson's expression completely changed in that moment. "That was the second miracle." Dr. Robinson looked as though he had aged ten years. Troy watched as Lou pushed away from the table upset, "Hold up! First they bottled up the cure and then walked away with Magma Fusion? How could you let them get away with all the goods?" Looking at the frustrated young man the doctor roared, "Have you ever seen a million people dying before your eyes! Have you? The smell of rotting corpses, children too sick to cry, unable even to blink away the flies! Mr. Stryker, our duty was to a dying nation, shepherds trying to protect the sheep! Well it isn't the flock on Earth we have too worry about anymore." Troy watched as the two men stared. Lou's head dropped as Katie eyed him and stepped over to stand beside her father. Troy tried to ease the tension, "Sir, that's why we're here, to learn the truth and understand what happened on that mountain." Dr. Robinson walked quietly to his desk and reached for his bible. "My whole life I've lived by the word, offering the other cheek. When you showed me the hieroglyphs I knew your father had completed the bible, their bible. All these years, I asked myself why? Why Ben and Mary? My attempted assassination, I understood. But as Mr. Stryker stated, they had it all. Ben's secret struck at the very core of the beliefs of mankind, challenging everything we've been taught to believe. There was no chance they would leave him alive to uncover their betrayal and manipulation."

Katie went to the computer and quickly brought up the files. "Father, most of them are just primitive drawings. Surely an intelligent life form's text would have been more complex." Troy wearily jested, "That's it, your father is right. It wasn't for them. It was for us...mankind." While pointing at the screen, Dr. Robinson continued. "You're all scientists. Think! The writings are of the periods of man, what we were and could comprehend. Who wrote the bible as we know it? No mention of dinosaurs, just Adam and Eve with no other indications of the humble beginnings of man. Where did we lose history or how did it really start, evolution from apes?" Dr. Robinson rubbed his temples as he thought of all the propaganda released to make people believe a lie. He spoke softly to his daughter and her friends. "What I am telling you today I have not repeated since we left Mount Kilamanjaro." He paused and looked about the room.

"From sun up to sun down with the help of hundreds of the tribesmen, we picked as many of the healing flowers as possible. Late one evening there came a terrible rumble, the ground shook beneath us. The workers ran scrambling for their lives. Suddenly all was still again. After several minutes passed without any further rumbling, we thought it was probably aftershocks of some kind. The next morning the medicine man was standing at the edge of our camp, several warriors encircled him. In those nervous moments the medicine man spoke as our interpreter translated, "The gods have opened the mountain." Confused as to what these words implied, we could only follow him as he disappeared into the thick jungle undergrowth. The warriors formed a perimeter around him and led the way. We quickly grabbed our medical supply packs and struggled to keep up with them, traveling all day to reach the base of the mountain. At dusk the medicine man began a ritual dance around the campfire. High above at the mountain's peak, a brilliant array of lights sparkled in the dark. We were amazed by the display and began discussing what could be causing such a magnificent glow in the night. The next mornings' climb was with feverish anticipation of reaching the glorious summit. The closer we got, a deep inner peace overcame our traveling party. All dreams of riches and greed dissipated, gone was fear. For the first time in my life I knew peace and love, this was truly a holy place. Soon we could see a large crack in the side of the mountain that twinkled in the sunlight, wet from a small stream. The waterfall's rainbow shone brightly within the gentle mist, a welcoming sight for all. The men cooled themselves with the crystalline water and within the falls our eyes did feast. I reached out and touched a wall covered in diamonds! As I stepped through the falls I beheld Paradise! Inside the mountain was a valley more beautiful than I could have imagined. Fruit filled trees and the soft sounds of birds warmed my heart. Animals of all kinds grazed in peace. It was like the bible says, the lamb lying down with the lion. Slowly we walked deeper into this lost, unknown world. Along a wall we first noticed the engraved hieroglyphs. Your father began taking pictures of all that we saw. Then down a path the stream did flow. We followed, pushing aside the lush foliage. The stream emptied into a lake. The vessel before us didn't even register! It was so large, it was seconds before our eyes reached it's covered top. What was this place? This land within the bowels of the mountain. The medicine man stood at the water's edge his voice piercing the peaceful land. "What is he saying?" we asked. Our native guide responded, "The Halls of Man." Ben and I stared at one another in amazement! The name implied so much to both of us. We were being shown the history of man from the dawn of the ages! We walked around the water's edge to view the enormous vessel. It wasn't until we stood facing the giant gangplank that it sunk in, Noah's Ark! A chill ran up my spine as we walked the gangplank. Each step echoed in the heavenly silence of the valley. My heart raced when we reached the main deck. Wide stood the doors to the ark, animals still graced the stalls and paced peacefully about the ship. It took us hours to explore. Tools and different artifacts were in perfect condition and more strange hieroglyphs were found carved into the walls about the ark. The secret history of man enchanted this lost world. Green pastures with stone alcoves revealing hidden truths and lost treasures. We saw the Ark of Covenant containing the Holy Grail, chariots of gold, and beheld the very tablets of the Ten Commandments! At times I couldn't stop weeping. The alcoves always shrouded us in this warm glowing light, and the feeling of peace never left us. It was almost a week before any of us realized that we hadn't slept or ate. Filled only with the spirit, no hunger or tiring was felt. We were surrounded by perfect peace and the truth of the ages. Finally, we entered a temple of sorts unlike any of the others. I marveled at the technology before my eyes. It was the first time I had ever seen holograms. Images of worlds, formulas, data codes and languages danced in the air around us. None could understand what we were seeing. In the middle of the room stood statues of robed men in a circle bowed in prayer. At their feet was a partial rounded carving of the faces of mankind. When I stepped closer a bright light briefly blinded me, and then appeared the hologram of a man not of this Earth. Everyone stared in disbelief, not because he was an alien, he was a black man like us. His pearl black eyes brought us back to reality as his voice filled the temple, "My brothers of mother Earth, I am Balimar, the unspoken one. Chosen are you to walk this land of the holy. So weak is the mother. Used up by those she has given life. The ways of the Ancient Ones are that of the Father and the Holy Ghost. His son is the light. Along the path, the children, his gift to you. Across time those that bear witness, repent this hour and all eyes will see the glory." The image suddenly disappeared. None of us understood what we had witnessed. It was like a dream. Then I heard Ben yelling with excitement, "Hey, over here! Get a load of this!" Sitting on a platform was a metallic chariot. No way it could have been Roman. Its design was futuristic, without wheels. When Ben stepped on it, the control panel lit-up. Two hand depressions sat atop the panel and when he touched one the darn thing rose off the ground. You should have seen Ben's face! When he took his hand off, it tilted and dropped like a rock. We all laughed as he stood and dusted himself off. Actually he got pretty good after a few tries. Before we knew it he was flying out the front of the temple. We were like kids with a new toy. Then all hell broke loose. "Earthquake!" someone shouted. It wasn't a good time to be inside of a mountain. Stones were falling from the ceiling. Across the valley you could see the natives running out of the entrance. There wasn't time for us to make a run for it; we would be stoned to death before getting half way to the mountainside. Suddenly Ben shouted, "Hurry, get on!" It was our only chance. Everyone squeezed on board. Clearly the thing wasn't built to carry seven people. It was a shaky take-off and being pelted by falling rocks didn't help. We took a beating, bleeding and barely hanging on to the damaged craft. We flew out of the side of the mountain seconds before it completely collapsed. Smoke came from the sides of the craft now high above the jungle. Ben did his best to control the chariot but it went into a nosedive. Thankfully no one was killed in the crash. When I came to, the Army had surrounded the area and government agents were questioning us. Needless to say we never saw that chariot again! To my knowledge that's where ICON first got Magma technology." Tears filled Dr. Robinson's eyes as Katie spoke softly, "If these actual hieroglyphs were compiled from the photos Dr. Bishop took, it must have taken years of research to figure out the meanings and put them in order. Then to convert them to discs." Katie continued to study the screen in front of her.

Troy spoke, "My mother was an historian. One of her many passions was photography. I remember as a child helping in the photo lab of my grandfather's drugstore." Dr. Robinson snapped his fingers, "Of course, your father had worked years to help find a cure for the plague. Why kill them when he was so close? They wanted the bible. They must have thought it was in the house, when Mary was working on it at your grandfather's store." Katie broke into the conversation, "Well that's odd," she said as she pointed at the images flickering on the monitor. "See this priest-like figure represented in hieroglyphs? I didn't catch it at first, but if these drawings were written in the tongues and documented the different periods of man, that guy sure got around." "What do you mean?" asked Lou. Katie began clicking with the mouse, "See how the drawings and the languages are different but this guy is always the same. Look at this sketch of the universe. It shows some kind of space travel. Then come the early cave drawings of him protecting his group. Here Moses is preparing to cross the Red Sea. There's the figure on the other side. This is the Crucifixion of Christ, next is the burial site. There he is, standing beside the open stone door. Whew!" Katie clapped in excitement. "They've been with us all along." Dr. Robinson looked at his old college friends and set the photo back in its place. He mumbled, "Divide and conquer. Even now they keep people rambling about with all these different religions, unable to unite. This would shatter their very foundations and for this everyone I've loved had to die." He sat and lowered his head, no longer able to speak. Katie rose from the computer desk and went to her father. "Oh daddy, you've suffered so much over the years! You lost everyone and everything that you ever loved." She wept softly as she held her father's hand. Troy began to speak, but his voice caught on the words and the tears forced them back down his throat. Lou walked quietly out to the deck and paced about like a caged animal. Katie slowly raised her head and spoke as the tears stained her face. "You've seen a lot of things that we can only imagine, things that would have broken a lesser man. You've known people who were taken from us just as we were beginning to grow up. All this time, I've felt sorry for myself! I never knew that my happy, secure life was bought and paid for with yours. Troy and I came here today to tell you about something I learned last night and now I can barely think of what it was! There has to be a way to bring all the secrets and lies out into the open. ICON has ruined so many lives, and God only knows what they are capable of if they ever find out that we know part of what they are up to! But I promise you this, I will not rest until the truth is told." Dr. Robinson grabbed his daughter and shook her, "You will stay out of this! I have lived my whole life in fear of what ICON would do to you and your mother if the connections were ever made. I can't lose you now! You're all I have left!" Troy stepped toward the pair and spoke, "Katie, your father is right. This is my fight. I'll handle it from here, I couldn't bear it if you were caught up in ICON's web." Katie started to disagree, but she remembered the tears in her father's eyes and decided to remain quiet. Troy exhaled as he sat on the sofa, "What Katie is trying to say is that ICON has developed some kind of wonder drug that's like the fountain of youth. So far it's been their best weapon against the plague. The scientists at the moon base feel as though their research with space medicine is almost complete."

Dr. Robinson tossed a newspaper at Troy's feet. The headlines read, "Band of Brothers join Crusade against Plague." The anger in his voice flowed, "There's your missing ingredient! Why do you think they've been killing our people for all these years? Their blood! Some of the brothers are only concerned about their own political gains and through their stupidity they are going to lead our people to slaughter. As God is my witness, I will fight this evil with my last breath." When he hugged Katie Troy knew their meeting was at its end. "Take care of my baby girl. You won't have to look far because the Brotherhood will be there." Lou and Troy shook Dr. Robinson's hand. He gave Troy the photo, "I thought you would like to have this." Accepting the photo Troy whispered, "So now I know where I got my madd flying skills. Thank you doctor." The ride back was a silent one, somehow the Cape looked quite different as they approached. After returning to his room, Troy sat and stared at the photo. His childhood memories of his parents were very vague but after today he felt he knew them better. He squeezed the picture close to his heart as he drifted to sleep.

CHAPTER ELEVEN

It was always strange seeing the changing of the guard in the early morning hours. The minority scientists were arriving for duty and the Caucasians leaving. Most of those that did work day hours always worked in the filtered lights of the sub-levels. The morning briefings began without a hitch and then came the hours of medical examinations. The astronaut's moods changed when they were filed into a hangar filled with ICON's security agents. The suited agents were equipped with the latest Magma weapons. The Space Director led them on to a platform in the center of the room. The men braced themselves as the platform began descending underground. A warning horn sounded and level lights blinked as they dropped. Troy checked his watch and in minutes they had reached solid ground. Several men in chemical suits stood outside the glass encased room. The space director announced, "Gentlemen, welcome to Mantaray City, this will be your home for the next few months. Before we enter, certain precautionary measures must be taken." Beyond the glass they could see a world of activity with workers zooming past on electrical carts. The men in the chemical suits had gone through the air lock decon room and came in to collect their belongings. Troy and the others stood nude in the warm mist of the decon room. After carefully donning their chemical suits they entered the mysterious underworld of ICON. A female voice blared status reports over a PA system as they toured the complex. Troy touched the dark cool wall. It was remarkable. The surface was rough like the place had been carved out. The director turned and smiled, "Our Magma-mining technology allows us to conceive all kinds of possibilities, wait until you see our mining operations." The group was still trying to comprehend what they were seeing. At almost one mile in diameter it wasn't until they saw a flash that they noticed a hole in the ceiling and ground. Walking toward the center of the complex they could better see the glass that surrounded it. Troy estimated that it was about 500 meters across. From here they were able to look down and see other levels. In the blink of an eye, SWOOSH!!, a blurry figure raced past. The men were shocked, then curiously pressed against the glass to get a better look. "What the hell was that?" someone shouted. The director laughed, "Ah, that would be your instructor, Commander Solomon. Gentleman, here we have been able to duplicate the weightless atmosphere of space, and as you have just witnessed we're not space-walking." By the look of the stunned faces his point was well taken. "The greatest thing about Magma technology is that we only have to be concerned about how it's applied, miniature computer chips do the rest. No more pollution, explosive mixtures, or costly engines and in this case; no bulky space-suits." The director smiled at the sea of faces that were mesmerized by their first glimpse of this Top Secret area. It took hours to tour the first few levels of this new world. Troy could only imagine the full extent of the place. He was amazed by all the new wonders, scientific equipment he had never heard of and experiments of unbelievable proportions being conducted. The one thing that didn't slip his notice was that there were no minorities, except for his group. The medical level was the most impressive of all, with hundreds of doctors and nurses attending to plague patients. The director's expression changed, seeing the plague ridden patients. He managed a faint smile "We are so close to beating this damned plague, the space medicine so far has been our only salvation. Each day, thousands die waiting for the small amounts to come to Earth, but soon all that will change. You've only seen a small portion of our facilities and before I exhaust you further, let me show you to your quarters." The group turned and followed the director down the aisles of sick patients and Troy wondered about all the people who lay dying before him. He stood motionless as the rest of the group filed out, remembering all his days in the hospital. Troy finally snapped out of his reverie and began following the group. As he moved past the beds, he noticed the transfusion bags of blood. But what caught his eye were the markings on the bags, the same ones he remembered as a child, HbSA. A twist of fate, natures own cruel joke on man? How could something that once took lives now preserve them? This place felt so unnatural, like some kind of ant colony or something, Troy thought. So many people running around, busy at all times, a world that never slept. The sector they were taken to seemed very isolated from the rest of the population. The director advised them of their pass codes and that they would be changing over to the flight suits they would find in their quarters. Their quarters were far more than anyone expected with state of the art accommodations. Everything was voice operated, from opening the doors to flushing the toilets. Inside the main closet hung different uniforms and flight suits with names already emblazoned on the chest. After changing, everyone met the director out on the main deck in formation. He stood silently facing the anti-gravity tunnel when suddenly there appeared someone descending like superman. Once he landed on the dock everyone waited in anticipation for the airlocks to open. The director snapped, "ATTENTION! THE MANTARAY COMMANDER, GEN. DUKE SOLOMON!" The group standing before him froze at the sight of their commander as he removed his helmet. They had all heard this commander's name whispered around the Cape. They hadn't believed the rumors, and now here he stood before them. Troy was in awe as General Solomon began to speak. He couldn't believe that this was the same guy he'd run across on several occasions, the aborigine from Australia! His voice boomed warmly around them. "Men, you are all here because of your expertise in your chosen fields. Your color may also have played a part, but your character is what brought you to this historic moment. We are going to train in ways you've never imagined and I promise you before we're through, you will positively hate the ground I walk on!" As all heads began to signal no, he continued speaking, "Yes, you will, and that's fine with me. It means that I have done my best to prepare your entire being for the challenge that lies ahead. Leave your skepticism and your beliefs here and follow me to the next level. You are about to become the first and finest commanders of the Mantaray fleet!"

The men followed their new commander into a lecture hall. Awaiting them were teams of scientists as Duke Solomon assumed center stage. "This is were it starts. Day 1 of the rest of your lives, some of you won't make it or will fail to comprehend the magnitude of Magma technology. These gentlemen before me are some of the brightest minds of our time. They've assisted me in the development of the chair and the construction of the Mantaray. The principals of the Mantaray aren't much different than those of the human body, the brain and the nervous system leading through the body. The chair being the brain, the control system of all activity of the Mantaray. You will be broken into groups and go through round-robin training and evaluation. I don't have to remind you of the importance of such an undertaking as this and the impact it will have on the world. So sit back and enjoy the ride." At that time all eyes watched the men in white smocks that began typing into computers as the hall became dark and computer consoles came to life in front of the men. They could hear Solomon's voice over the miniature earphone they were instructed to insert. "First, let's look at what you're dealing with, from conception to some of the evolutionary progressions that have taken place." The men studied the diagrams and data for hours as the scientists provided the explanations and theories behind them. This process went on for days with extensive studies and briefings in all areas of Magma-fusion and related experiments. Troy found himself mesmerized by the Mantaray. Even with his aerospace engineering background nothing had prepared him for this. It was like unlearning. All the principals of the 20th century somehow seemed twisted. The science team force-fed them every fact and capability of Magma-technology. Troy thought about Dr. Robinson's story, "The chariot, the chariot, the chariot!" His thoughts drifted back to the story of the mountain and them crashing in the chariot. He stared at the hologram and finally realized, "They've duplicated the reactors of the chariot!"

Duke Solomon was never far from the group, like a mother hen. He took extreme pride in the specialized training, carefully taking notes of the men's performance. Everything started to make sense, Troy immersed himself deeper into all facets of the Mantaray. What at first appeared so complicated soon began to make sense. The slender spine extended ovally into a triangular pattern completing the stealthiest configuration he had ever seen. The microcomputer systems responded as independent brains adjusting wingspan and shape to firing multiple-target phaser weapons. The round-tip edges surrounding the craft revealed miniature fuselages to compensate for evasive maneuvers. Almost giving it a life-like quality of a Stringray gliding in the sea, its wings able to almost flap, adjust and flex as a bird in flight. The one thought that crossed Troy's mind as he tapped his pencil on his console, "So how in the hell are you supposed to fly this damn thing?" he mumbled. The sudden slap of a heavy hand on his shoulder shook the cobwebs, "It's quite easy actually, once you've mastered the Chair." Troy sat straight in his seat after realizing it was the Commander walking past. He wasted no time pulling up the diagrams of the Chair on the computer. Tap, tap a hologram appeared above the console. It looked more like a leisure chair with a lot of bells and whistles. He laughed to himself as he smirked at the fancy suit and helmet next to it. After a few more taps all the gadgets and data flooded the screen. Looking more like scuba gear than anything else, skin with a bunch of wiring. The crazy chair, upon closer examination, wasn't sat in but rode like a super bike. This was getting stranger by the minute, with highly evolved virtual reality being the foundation for the works. The helmet and the suit working as one, the brain and the nervous system running through the suit.

The morning they saw Duke Solomon in the space suit smiles came across their faces. The training area they stood in was similar to that of an aircraft hangar as the commander's voice echoed, "I hope you ladies have enjoyed your time with the eggheads because today you start the chair. Your suits have been designed to your exact dimensions. As commanders, you are the lifeline of the Mantaray. Samples of your voices have been taken over the last few months and have been programmed into the computer for command activations. Here in these simulators we'll test and help develop your skills to ready you for actual missions. The Mantaray is the only spacecraft of its kind with capabilities man, until recently, has only dreamed about." As he turned around in the seemingly empty hangar several of the floor panels opened as the simulators came up. Assistants led the astronauts to their assigned simulators and helped them into their suits. Using a pressurized gun to apply the electrodes to their temples the assistants met some resistance, "Hey my man, is all this necessary? I thought you guys just stuck those things on," said one of the astronauts. "Relax gentlemen, you'll feel a slight prick. We just want to make sure you're well grounded" chuckled the general. "I can't see! Oh Lord, my eyes!" Duke Solomon laughed, "Stay calm, it'll pass in a few seconds. The electrodes are patching into the mainframe. There, you see, almost better than new." After getting the okay nod that everyone was fine, the general continued. "The journey has just begun, using this technology and virtual reality allows you to become the ship. There are no reflexes faster than the blink of the eye or the origin of a thought. I told you I'll push you to your limits and I wasn't lying but first let's take a little ride. So buckle up and leave the driving to Mother, it's her way of letting you know what the Mantaray can really do." The area began to clear of personnel as Duke Solomon found his way into a glass enclosed control room. Upon pressing one of the instrument buttons, the astronauts all jumped as if they were jolted. Their eyes adjusted to the panoramic scene with digital figures flying before them at light speed. The voice they heard next was that of Mother, addressing each by name. The virtual helmet shield allowed only the computer images to be seen, "Hello Commander Bishop, Magma reactor checks complete, weapons charging, system is one hundred percent, beginning hover sequence in 5,4,3,2 1." Troy blinked as the virtual shield changed to sky blue and he could see the surrounding landscape a few hundred feet below him. Hearing the voice of Duke Solomon snapped him back. "During this part of the program Mother will allow you the opportunity to adjust your senses to the controls before we begin. If you tilt to your left, you'll notice the adjustments the Mantaray makes, voice commands for views front, side, rear and the same for reactor thrusts, and weapon firing. Different wing shapes are accomplished with the flexing or out-stretching of your arms that you'll find necessary during evasive maneuvers. The computers feed updates instantly as they occur from sections of the craft which we feel will give you the edge of its capabilities at all times." Each of the astronauts began their commands and adjustments in their virtual worlds. All were astounded and laughed with glee as the crafts turned and flipped from their movements. Solomon's voice came over their systems, "I hate to interrupt your fun gentlemen, but Mother wants to take you for a little ride. Don't attempt to adjust your televisions, you are now in a dimension most dare not enter. Okay Mother, they're all yours." The soothing voice of Mother came over the system. Everyone felt the controls start to move on their own. Visual images were relayed of the landscape as they felt the hum of the reactors. Mother's animated voice sounded most human, "Reactor thrusters on, elevation 1000 meters and climbing." A second of fear gripped the men as on their screens they saw the ground beneath begin to disappear. In a matter of seconds they were miles above Earth, "15000 and holding, activating RR units now, sector sweep in progress." Troy felt a slight shift as his craft lunged forward at a high rate of speed, his hands and arms making involuntary movement with each motion of the craft. Suddenly swooping back down toward Earth at an alarming rate, the craft bellied out and flew between some mountains at a ninety-degree angle. He hung on for dear life at the exit as Mother expertly preformed a barrel roll as if to impress him. Troy felt like coming out of the chair but knew he had to somehow understand all the quick commands Mother was giving, not to mention the controls themselves. His body reacted so weirdly as his feet shifted and clicked devices. All the while out the corner of his eyes he saw all the wing formations the Mantaray was going through. So all those years of playing video games as a kid would finally pay off, he thought. He was amazed at the small maps and charts that appeared and disappeared in a second with each change of the landscape. Then Mother "Climbing to Earth's outer atmosphere." In a flash the Mantaray darted toward the heavens, he saw the world getting smaller and smaller. It seemed as though he was in a dream as he reached the outer edge of space. The Mantaray's reactors sounded as if they exhaled when he penetrated the quiet darkness of the stars. The virtual display now showed different types of planetary formations and meteor clusters. If this was space, Troy liked it. The colors were more than he ever imagined. Honk! Honk! Honk! An alarm sounded, "What's happening Mother?" Troy called, startled by the loud noise. His screen showed four missiles cruising in his direction, "Danger, missile launch, taking evasive action, impact estimation 20 seconds." Troy shouted, "Where did they come from?" The Mantaray tumbled and rolled as one missile zoomed past, "Deploying plasma flares, weapon systems on line." The second missile exploded upon impact with one of the plasma flares. The third, Mother took out with laser cannons. Troy blew a sigh of relief, "Nice shooting Mother, but have you tracked the location of the source?" "Roger, heat footprints originated from an asteroid located in Alpha sector, scanning shows one star fighter on the dark side," Mother said. As they approached the asteroid, the star fighter appeared from behind the asteroid, "Mother, watch out there's two of them!" Troy shouted. The laser cannons of the Mantaray blasted in both directions hitting both targets. Mother swung the Mantaray around, "Mission complete. Thank you Commander Bishop, we make a good team." Troy smiled as he saw the blue marble coming into view and the descent through the clouds made him feel like a bird in flight. When he landed on the launch pad his virtual screen went blank, "Welcome back gentlemen. I hope you enjoyed the ride. As you can see we have a lot of work to do," said General Solomon. The astronauts sat up as they tried to adjust their eyes to the room's light. "Oh baby! I've got to have one of these!" laughed one of the guys. Duke Solomon watched as the men filed out. He turned and spoke to the empty room, "So Mother, how did they fair?" The computer replied "Very well actually. Their brainwaves and heart rates remained within the required spectrum of human tolerance. Subconscious guidance abilities were detected in one member of this group." "Who?" Solomon asked, visibly surprised. "Commander Bishop" came the reply. General

Solomon chuckled, "Mother, this is unlike you to jump to such conclusions. It had to have been a one-in-a-million chance that Bishop saw the second fighter before your sensors did. So the kid has quick reflexes, what makes you so sure it wasn't luck?" After a short pause the soft voice answered, "He not only acquired its location, he took the shot." The general could only stare at the monitor as it replayed.

Slumping into his chair back at his room, Troy let out a sigh of relief. The Mantaray demanded total concentration and it surprised Troy how drained he suddenly felt. This was far and away the most grueling training he'd ever encountered. He was tired to the core of his being. He knew he would give his right arm for just one night of sweet, deep slumber. Since that wasn't going to happen anytime soon, he waved his hand and on came his computer. In an instant, his nightly dose of Mantaray began from the rooter to the tooter. Today's ride in the Chair was wild, he thought as he watched the screen flashing before him. Something like hang gliding and wishing. You want to go left and your body seems to flow as one with the Chair. It's like the instant you think of going left, you are. This was like food for the brain that just kept on coming. Old computer chips were now replaced with Magma-chips that surpassed voice commands and evolved to thought activation. Troy felt his eyes getting heavier as he fought against sleep. Data and diagrams all became a blur as he gave in to dreamland. Always the same dream, running and bright lights, so tired, can't run any more, the loud voices, "They're over here, close to the river!" Splash! The cold water, got to get away, can't breath. Troy woke up gasping for air and sweating as though he had a fever. "Computer, display the time," he said. Troy jumped up in amazement as the computer flashed 4 am into his brain. "Got to get rolling!" he thought as he jumped into the shower.

All the astronauts stood in silence as Duke Solomon and his staff filed into the training bay, "Good morning, I trust you slept well. You all did so well yesterday that we decided to reward you with a new wardrobe." Instead of looking excited, the group seemed to hold their breath in a collective wait-and-see mode. The General's voice boomed throughout the room. "These flight suits are unlike anything you've known. Temperature controlled sensors readily adapt to the most extreme conditions. The material is much like latex but more comfortable, almost a "second skin", so to speak. This design allows for total body synchronization and extracts body heat as a source of energy. The result of this process is "parchment". We combine the finest metals with space-age linens. They are pressed together like gold leafing. This enables you to withstand temperatures from arctic colds to a burning furnace. Pay particular attention to the accessories, gentlemen. The jet pack also produces your oxygen supply. Observe the soles of the boots, the smallest engines known to man. In zero gravity and with the use of the Magma-chip, the possibilities are endless. Last but not least, your firepower. These may seem to be gloves that go along with your suits, but they are really the best application of Magma technology. Laser pulses generate with your very thought of firing on a target. Watch as I demonstrate the capabilities of Surgenomics." Raising one closed fist and with a quick extension he released what appeared to be a bolt of lightning. The smell of burning metal filled the room as they stared in amazement at the hole burnt into the wall. Duke Solomon cleared his throat, "Now that I have your attention, this is why your space walk training is so important. You are going to have to move like you never have before. The kill zone is about twenty-five meters, anything more than that is only a meager jolt. Are there any questions before we get started?" "Yes sir. Why all the fire power if our missions are for exploration and peace?" sounded a voice from the crowd. The general's short pause was noted by all in the room, "It should be no surprise to anyone that we are not alone in this universe. Judging from our last encounter, we are dealing with superior beings. Reports from Mars are revealing possible life forms beneath the surface. As well as we might wish for peaceful encounters, we must prepare for any situation."

Duke Solomon stepped into the glass encasement away from the men. A second door slowly opened as an extending platform carried the general out, high above the empty space. Looking like a diver standing on his board, the general gave an effortless thrust and soared into the air. The men could hear his voice over their systems as he turned to speak, suspended in the air like the cartoon characters from their youth. The looks of amazement lingered on their faces although the fancy of flight had been the driving force in all their lives. But here before their very eyes the moves they witnessed were done with the body alone and not an aircraft. The general commanded attention with each bold maneuver and topped it off by using one of the many stationary asteroids to bounce off with a tuck and roll. After a few buzz passes, he effortlessly hovered down in front of the group. Tapping the side of his helmet, "The thought activation system is very complex, but once you've mastered it, it is the same as your brain telling which body part to move. As you can see our space environment is complete with all the trappings. Stay alert gentlemen, don't be fooled by the silence that surrounds you. There is no room for error. Ah! I almost forgot, in the event your suit is ripped, blasted or torn," he slid a blade from the side of his boot and cut an opening in his sleeve. They stared curiously as the material's edges seemed to melt resealing the ragged ends. Duke Solomon smiled, "Though the hole is left exposed at least the rest of your suit is sealed. The most you can expect is a little space radiation. Like most games, the rules change. There is no 911 out here and no second chances. For training purposes your gloves have been modified to stun only, that's until you can safely play with the toys we provide. Are there any questions?" he paused, "I didn't think so. Prepare to enter the air-lock and wait for my command."

Timidly the men entered as someone whispered, "How the hell did he say you turn this thing on?" "Just say, flame on fool!" another jested. The sound of the air lock halted all chatter and the general hovered watching the indicator light above the door. A smile crossed his face when the light changed, "Release the hounds!" he commanded. The men tumbled out like a herd of wildebeest, some hitting the asteroids others flipping out of control. In less than a minute the training crews were out retrieving those knocked out cold by either walls or running into each other. Troy felt himself flying upside-down talking to himself, "Left, left, I mean right. Got to slow down and think. Think Troy" "Whoa!" he shouted before he belly flopped onto one of the asteroids. The impact knocked the air out of him as his vision began to blur before passing out. Troy began smiling for some reason as he shook his head to clear the cobwebs. He then remembered looking through the tall grass and watching them float. How serene and graceful they moved, but she was the most wonderful of all. Troy thought, "She's little like me." He hadn't ever thought much about girls after all. She's a girl but nothing like he's ever seen. She must be a princess but now she's floating this way! "Got to get away!" Troy gasped for air and awakened to find himself tumbling helplessly. "The dreams!" he thought. "Maybe I can glide like them. Gen Solomon said this thing is thought-activated, might as well give it a shot. First I've got to stop this damn tumbling, got to relax." Troy began to recall studying the schematics of the suit's system. "Just relax" Troy he kept saying to himself, "this is no different than the old nitrogen maneuvering units, Y-X-Z-axes, that allowed pitching, rolling, and yawning. So with 14 jets on the back and 2 on each boot, got to be careful of what I wish for. Boots activate 10% thrust, center back jets stabilize at 20% thrust." To his own surprise he felt the vibration of the jets as he leveled off to a standing position and hovered. He watched as his classmates continued to bonk all over the place, "Increase centers by 20, let's glide baby." Troy began soaring about the room with ease, trying different turns and power levels. Soon he was flying like superman pushing his flights to the limit. Most of his classmate hung on to asteroids as Troy began to coach them on and soon more joined in flight. The voice of Duke Solomon boomed through the helmets, "Very good teamwork, let's see how you perform with a little cut-throat. Gentlemen your gloves are now activated and to make it interesting allow me present your OPFOR." The opposing astronauts jetted in with fire in their eyes and blasting faster than the cadets could move. Troy shouted, "All systems full thrust!" as he flew into the heart of the attack, splitting the group like a bowling ball. The shock of the attack sent many wheeling out of control allowing for easy pickings. Troy and a few of the more advanced cadets held their own in the warfare as the effects of the pulses from the gloves rendered victims unconscious. A feeling of rage came over Troy seeing his peers being brutalized. The dazzling speed with which he moved tripled. His commands were automatic, sensing the urgency of his dilemma, now alone and outnumbered twenty to one. The general glared at the determined trooper, "It will soon be over sir," sneered the OPFOR commander at his side. Troy took a blast from his blindside that hurled him onto a jagged asteroid. Lunging off seconds before the next blast, Troy punch blasted a pair end over end. He zoomed past another group that missed and blasted their own. Flying and fighting so close, his blasts became punches and the numbers became smaller. The general nudged the commander, "You better get in there tiger. I'm sure you don't want to miss the fun." The fury in his eyes fueled his assault toward the combatants. Reaching the smoke-filled airspace, he zeroed in and blasted the only figure he saw directly in the back. The man contorted in agony spinning lifelessly out of control. As he hovered closer to confirm his kill, he heard, "Oooh! That had to have hurt." Turning quickly he spied Troy standing on a nearby asteroid. He pushed the crumpled body aside in frustration. The two locked eyes and screamed as they flew through open space and commenced blasting. Troy began twirling as he increased his speed and steadied for his target. The OPFOR commander tried to pull up to avoid the collision but then Troy pulsated into his chest with both fists. BLAAM!!! The general watched the scorched figure cartwheel past his view, "Those were pretty extreme measures, son." Troy looked into his eyes as he waited for the air lock to clear then pressed the release panel. He took off his helmet, "There's no pity for anyone that would shoot a man in the back." Joining his fellow astronauts in the medical ward, he was greeted by cheers that sounded more like moans and groans. The doctors assisted Troy in removing his suit to treat his wounds. He could only imagine the outcome if the gloves were not set to stun.

After receiving clean dressings, Troy limped back to his quarters and eased onto his bed to rest. He stared at the ceiling and tried to keep his eyes open when he heard the soft "ding!" of his computer, "You have mail, " a voice sounded. Troy slowly got up and walked over to the console, "Computer, display mail file." His spirits were uplifted when he saw that the message was from Katie. "Hi Troy, I hope you can see this feed. I've been around the world in eight days, it seems. I had a few weeks of down time, if you can call it that, here in Puerto Rico. I am working day and night with the radio astronomy antenna here and trying to write a program that will enable our personnel to better track the signals sent out by what they think is an actual black hole! I never thought I would get this opportunity, but here I am. I also have found out that our funding is from ICON, small world or just a coincidence? Something tells me it's neither. I sure miss you guys and wish you could fly down and we could catch up, but I know you are tied up with your training. I know it has got to be really tough. Lou is a shuttle commander! Can you believe it? He made several trips to the space station and seems really excited about his position. It was months before I heard from Lou and we still pray that we hear from you soon. Just be careful, I have to go now." Katie blew a kiss as the screen went blank. Troy leaned back smiling on his bed, "Computer, shut down." "Lou, a shuttle commander," he thought drifting asleep.

The path was barely visible she had taken up the mountain to view the crater. Looking across Katie wondered how Troy was doing. It was so unlike him not to contact her. So many things didn't make sense with all that was going on, why was a black hole so important? What could be more important than the extinction of mankind? Her thoughts raced to one of the security briefings that most of the world's most brilliant minds attended. The keynote speaker was none other than Arthur Kehoe himself. For several minutes he addressed the leaps and bounds of ICON Industries and their goals toward deep space exploration. All eyes were glued on him in a moment of silence, "The issue before us today is how to monitor our neighborhood. I commend the outstanding work you've accomplished with our deep space probes. For centuries we've watched the stars. We now know we are not alone. Still we must extend our interest in hopes of future communications. In the effort to better understand the galaxy in which we live, probes have been lost. What isn't clear is if this is the result of mechanical failure or the gravitational pull of a black hole. Einstein's theory confirmed nothing could escape once entering a black hole. Although we stand committed to continue deep space exploration, at fifty million dollars per probe we need answers and soon. So the challenge that we face is locating the black hole. I now open the floor for any comments or questions." The puzzled look of the crowd drew a flood of questions instead of solutions. "How can we find something we can't see? No physical evidence exists as of yet that proves they even exist." "Where do we start looking and with what?" Dr. Fairchild, the designer of ICON's computer systems stood, "Mr. Kehoe, surely you don't expect answers right now when scientists for ages have been baffled with this possibility." Kehoe's face blushed with anger, "The line has been drawn in the sand, and failure is not an option nor is it acceptable. My fine doctor, for what I am paying you, all of you, either provide us kindly with a solution or sit down and shut up!" The doctor's glasses fogged up as he struggled to find his seat. The hush that came over the crowd was of mutual agreement to find a hole to crawl into rather than face the daggers in Kehoe's eyes. The subtle attempt of someone trying to clear their voice could be heard over PA system. The soft voice finally broke through, "Doppler. I mean use a Doppler type system." Katie couldn't believe she had spoken. Every eye in the hall closed in on her. Dr Fairchild bolted up out his chair, "Dear child, you were only invited here to observe, so do keep your hideous remarks to yourself!" "Doctor Fairchild!" boomed Kehoe, "Sir, you are trying my patience. Now unless you want to head my research facilities in the Antarctic, I highly suggest that you let the young lady continue. Please, as you were saying." Katie adjusted the microphone at her station, "As a child I grew up in a part of the country they called Tornado Alley. So little was known about tornados until they started to use Doppler radar." Dr. Fairchild bounced out of his seat again, "Doppler radar to find a ...I've never heard such a stupid idea in my life!" No one was surprised when the nod came from Mr. Kehoe and his men in black escorted the fine doctor out of the hall. "I must apologize for such rude behavior, Ms. uh?" Kehoe snapped his fingers at an assistant who whispered, "Dr. Kathryn Kimball." " Ah yes, Dr. Kimball, we must hear more."

Feeling more relaxed with Fairchild gone, Katie breathed easier, "Sir, most of the concerns you've heard should be taken into account. The principal that I was addressing wasn't for us to find a black hole but for it to find us. The Doppler radar was just a means of compiling data on the vortex of a tornado. There were many ways of retrieving this information. One common way was to release these small metallic balls into a tornado for better readings of what was happening in and around it. Then with the use of two or more Doppler's, they were able to get three-dimensional images of the tornado. Now, keeping Einstein's theory in mind that nothing, even light could escape it's pull, we must turn our attention to modifying the ball just to transmit it's location back to our satellites. Since the first probe in 1999 all have disappeared in this sector, near the planet Mars. If we release thousands of these balls in different parts of this sector the only thing left to do is wait and let the black star do what it does best. I also recommend that we build another telescope and antenna system on the surface of the moon for better triangulation. When any of the balls come up missing, we concentrate our search from the last transmissions." Kehoe stood and approached the podium, "I like it. Young lady, there's nothing worse than standing still. In this room you'll find the most talented people in the world and they're at your disposal. If at anytime you have a problem or lack of cooperation, please contact my staff." Katie was mobbed by well-wishers and those wanting to make appointments after Arthur Kehoe and his staff departed. Unknown to Katie, Delores Bates whispered to Kehoe as they entered the elevator. "Do you think they bought it?" Kehoe smiled, "It doesn't really matter whether they did or didn't. All that really matters is that we find that hole before our alien friends decide to pay us another visit. Besides, we masked this entire system. One thing that we are sure of is that they didn't fly out."

Katie felt the warm sun on her face as she thought of poor Dr Fairchild freezing his buns off in the Antarctic. The ringing cell phone in her backpack was startling as she fumbled to answer it. She flicked it out in one motion, "Dr Kimball" she answered placing it to her ear. The music and high-pitched voice forced her to hold the phone some distance away. "Katie, Katie can you hear me? Darling it's Melanie, I'm at one of mother's dreadful garden parties. Let me step into the parlor, how about now?" "Yes, that's much better," Katie replied. "I have such wonderful news" she squealed. "The research and development department have completed the final prototypes of the balls and they work just as you said. The board of directors of ICON Industries was so impressed they've already rushed us into full production. Equipment and parts for your telescope are flying in from around the world as we speak. This deal has to be worth at least fifty million dollars! I don't know what you did but Arthur Kehoe himself requested that you personally oversee the project. He has even sent down his own helicopter for you. It should be there within the hour, so don't delay. Chow." Before Katie could get a word in edge wise the connection was dead.

The scramble to gain some type of advantage had begun. In the following weeks the intense secret training would open their eyes to technologies never known. Mankind wasn't about to take the plague or the aliens lying down and certainly not without a fight.

CHAPTER TWELVE

It started like any other day in the life of an Astronaut, 0300 hours but with only a few hours of sleep. Lou felt more focused and confident than ever; test after test, rechecking all the double checks. As Mission Commander of the transport fleet, many lives depended on his actions and judgment. Never had a mission of this magnitude been attempted. The newest generation of XL-500 space shuttles was only recently revealed, and he felt honored to command this historic mission. The Cape was a zoo with all the news crews, politicians and activists milling around waiting for the perfect photo-op. The eyes of the world watched and waited. All hopes of a cure seemed possible with the new space medicines and some very special kids, the children of the gift. Blessed with a gift to save a world, bestowed with an equality that those of the past never realized. Here and now they stood, willing to share their life essence. Despite all the obstacles, their numbers professed that they had turned the other cheek. Lou's eyes burned with tears as the thousands began the careful boarding of the space shuttles. A wave of black fists protruded atop the crowd, proud and defiant symbolizing the salute of the Brotherhood. The true champions, sworn protectors of the afflicted were now unable to stand at the side of those they had served since birth. He felt in his gut what he saw in their eyes, something just didn't feel right. A small hand embraced his. It was Katie's. "Commander, it's time" she smiled as she squeezed his hand. They turned and joined their crew with camera lights flashing as they readied to board the craft.

The XL-500's compared to the old space shuttles was like comparing a small twin-engine plane with a 747 jumbo jet. Upon boarding, the crew went straight to work conducting systems checks. All systems were go and the transports were secure and confirmed with mission control. Lou felt satisfied and began his last-minute tour of the vessel. When he reached the transport compartment, he saw Katie standing on the platform. He rested his hand on her shoulder. "I should have known I would find you here," he smiled. "Come on, I was just about to make a final check." They walked down the aisle looking at the small smiling faces as the medical staff prepared them for take-off. The comfort and space afforded each little guest their own medical personnel. Still the sight of IVs' and kids just didn't mix. Lou could sense that Katie was feeling the same when they heard a wee voice. "Uncle Louis, over here," waved the little hand. Lou recognized the bright smile immediately, "Tina? Hello sweetheart. I didn't know, I mean your mom and dad didn't tell me. Are you okay?" The perky child laughed, "Oh yes, I'm having so much fun, mommy said she has been trying to reach you for weeks. Uncle Louis I knew I would see you. I'm a big girl now." Lou kissed his niece's forehead and Katie saw his expression change, "Believe me I didn't know either, all files on the children have been highly confidential" she whispered. Lou's eyes narrowed, "They knew, but it's all good. Let's get this show on the road, at least she's with us and I'll protect these kids with my dying breath." Katie embraced Lou more fiercely than she had intended. A voice came over the intercom system, "Launch sequence to begin in T minus 60 minutes." Lou whispered to Tina, "It's show time. See you at our next stop." The technicians and medical staff made final confirmations and started to exit the craft. Lou and Katie both returned to their stations and began the final checks.

Miles below the surface, unknown to the watching world, Duke Solomon turned to the attentive pilots gazing at the hologram. Their focus shifted to him as he began to speak, "Gentlemen, today we embark upon the stairway to heaven. It has been said, "to see the soul of man, you only have to look into the eyes of a child." Today we witness the bright promise our children bring to mankind. The whole world prays for the glory that only these children can produce. Here on Earth many have guarded and shielded them from those that could not understand, but out there you will be their protectors. The vast frontier of space is unknown. If ever a group of warriors was up to the task it would be the men of the Mantaray fleet. For the last few weeks you've trained leagues beneath the sea for maneuver purposes. You've jumped to light speeds to leave Earth's atmosphere without a hint of your presence. The primary mission of the XL-500 is to safely deliver the children to the space station before they are shuttled to the moon's surface. Their mission will then be to orbit the planet Mars and conduct a series of experiments. Our present weapon capabilities do not extend to such lengths and that's where you come in. It is believed that a black hole exists somewhere in the sector of Mars. Since the 20th century, countless satellites and unmanned probes have been lost to this "hole". It is our belief that if the hole is located, future missions could easily avert the same fate. The universe is getting smaller by the day and now with other known life forms out there by no means are we willing to risk the lives of our people on another chance encounter. As they used to say in the wild, wild, west; it's your job to ride shotgun and make sure they get home safely. Colonel Bishop, you have been appointed as mission commander. Are there any questions?" A quiet hush filled the room, "If not, your next briefing is at 0200 hours, so get some rest." Suddenly the men surrounded Troy to shake his hand as they headed back to their quarters. Duke Solomon stood silently watching news coverage of the launch when the dusting of the old janitor disturbed his thoughts. Without a glance he whispered, "Are you sure he's the one?" "So it is written," replied Dr. Robinson cautiously as he dusted his way out the room.

Troy's eyes were glued to the ominous jet crafts preparing for their historic journey. He slowly dressed wishing not to miss a moment as the countdown began. "Cape Control, this is Exodus, all systems are green." "Roger Exodus, begin launch sequence on my mark, T minus 10, 9, 8." Lou and the other commanders punched codes and data into the onboard computers bringing their consoles to life. In the distance, the crowd of on-lookers rejoiced when the reactors of the XL-500s flamed blue. The high-pitched hum emitting from the flared fuselages only served to spark the celebration. The jet crafts began to taxi as each pilot checked their reactors, swirling heat waves on the runway. "3, 2,1 Ignite!!!" The distinct booms of the reactors briefly awed the crowd and brought about cheers of exultation. The thunderous jet crafts zoomed down the runway and into flight, vibrating the souls of all those present. Lou leaned back with the G-forces as he guided his fleet into the heavens. "Cape Control, this is Exodus, beam counts are sufficient, switching reactors over to Magma-wave sound four. We are now leaving Earth's atmosphere." "Roger Exodus, all instrument readings are a go, your delta vee is normal, enjoy the ride and good luck." The sinuous band of colorful airglow encircled the Earth's atmosphere as the vessels entered space's embrace. Lou watched the big blue marble with astonishment, "Computer, calculate orbiting approach for the space station and activate the ship's gravity unit." Satisfied with their safe departure, Lou couldn't wait any longer to check on the children's well being. The monitors still showed the excitement that was taking place back at mission control.

In the soundproof room above mission control, Arthur Kehoe surveyed the spectacle as one of his executives entered and waited for a sign to approach. Kehoe snapped his finger, "Yes, what is it Delores?" "Sir, we've just received a transmission report from the moon base. At their present site and depth they're recovering high levels of the ore in its purest form." "Wonderful and with the payload en route, the fresh blood supplies will prove to be the missing ingredient. Inform them I want no delays and to double the transports down to the surface. Thank you." Sinking back into the firm tightness of his leather chair, Kehoe sibilated watching the fleet enter deep space. "In the interest of saving the world these foolish people are serving allelon agnoia, and with them I will defeat the saviors they dream of! Computer, connect video link with space station ASAP." The artificial voice replied, "Video link complete in 3,2,1." The camera scans of the space station were breath-taking as the enormous colony rotated slowly around its axis. Brilliant flashes of light reflected on the surrounding solar panels. Kehoe smiled at the site and shifted his thoughts on the celebration in the control room. "How stupid, he thought, "could they be?" For over two decades they had been building the moon base and space station from hard-earned tax dollars. Now all control by ICON Industries was disguised in the cloak of national security. National security, just the mention of those words and heads would not only turn but also virtually swivel, the other way. His prize jewel was the moon base. How could a people spend trillions of dollars to reach a planet and never return? No one ever questioned the world leaders and now he ruled even them. He inhaled slowly as if to ingest his own power. To gaze upon the station made him feel humble. It was truly a futuristic vision beyond anyone's imagination, more than 8 miles in diameter suspended 300,000 miles from Earth, a small country nestled secretly in space. The computer scans provided Kehoe with an inner peace as he watched the busy bodies preparing to make history. The space villages appeared as small malls or shopping centers, offering all the trappings of home, surrounded with plush green gardens with trees. "Computer, so much for Mayberry. Are the landing docks prepared?" "Confirmed and the Mantaray Force is nearing launch stage." "Outstanding, advise the commander to proceed as planned," Kehoe sighed. His thoughts drifted back to that fateful day in Africa, who would believe retrieving that ancient chariot would somehow reveal the secrets of the pyramids? These dark secrets held in a people that bore no mark in the eyes of the soul. He breathed once more for his secret.

Duke Solomon stood above the aqua docks carefully watching as Troy and the others boarded the Mantarays. His voice sounded almost regretful as it came over the intercom, "Gentlemen, we've been cleared for launch, it's show time. The future of our planet and finding a cure for the plague rests with these children. It's a big universe out there with some new players, so stay alert and Godspeed." The men all saluted and began instrument checks as the lids to the Mantarays hissed shut. Troy felt a tingle as the floodgates opened and water soon started to fill the cavern. It was hard at first to accept all that the Mantaray was capable of, but nothing made sense anymore, reactors powered by magma able to energize under water and to top it all, beings from another planet. When he thought again, a few months ago he was ready to commit himself to a loony bin. His mind raced back to the many conversations with Dr. Robinson. Looking down as he straddled the chair in the Mantaray with night vision panels aglow he knew in his heart, this was nothing conceived on Earth. What really puzzled him was the strange feeling of knowing the answer he sought wasn't down here. The crackling noise of the water completely submerging his craft brought his thoughts back into focus. The Mantaray's reactor hummed faintly when he guided the craft forward after the cavern's wall descended revealing the ocean deep. One by one they departed in formation then accelerated in speed until they burst through the caliginous surface, already breaking the sound barrier without a sound, no traceable heat exhaust, no flutter or flame just ocean spray. Within minutes they reached the boundary of space. They watched the blue Earth suspended in black space. Troy began to pray. Hearing the Lord's prayer over the secure net touched them equally as they all joined in. After a moment of silence, Troy announced, "Manta-force, prepare for hyper-jump to sector 5 of the moons orbit, let's keep tight posture until we can confirm we're alone out here." The silent surge of their reactors propelled them deeper into space. Gliding peacefully as a feather afloat but at speeds never before known, each pilot stretched his wings performing barrel roles and twists feeling the limits of their own skills as the Mantarays tempted them to be more daring. Troy smiled at the joyful glee of his squadron then thought, "What the hell?" and did a few himself. Being in a Mantaray was a virtual experience connecting the mind with technology of a third kind. Thoughts were constantly scanned and updated with data in minds eye performing motions of flight through thought. Troy was glancing to see Mother Earth in all her bluish glory beaming proudly of all the life she harbored. Nothing like a rear-view mirror, Troy thought noticing his world getting smaller and smaller. The holograms of the moon's surrounding space and surface glowed within the Mantarays as the pilots carefully studied the flow of in-coming data. "Manta-force this is squadron leader, at this time lock in region grids. This dark side is leaving us no other choice than to break orbit and to get up close and personal. All we need is a clean sweep before the Exodus completes it's unloading, prepare for sector sweep on my mark 3,2,1, mark." The fanning of the Mantarays was like birds of old, banking left and right in sequence with Col. Bishop continuing dead ahead. The security of the dark side was a necessity in his eyes and everyone could sleep a little bit better knowing there were no bogeymen lurking. The vexatious light of the moon sent chills up Troy's spine reminding him of how long he had waited for this day. Reports from other squadron members came across the air identifying their patrol sectors. His computer screen gleamed exposing the alignment of his men descending toward the moon's surface. It was only the radio contact that allowed a Mantaray to observe the other but once that was cut, it would disappear like a thief into the night. The outline of the rocky surface looked like the icing on a cake. Troy remembered waiting on his mom to finish her final touches so he could lick the spoon. None of the scientific photos he had studied could compare to what he was seeing with his own eyes. He banked gently toward what seemed to be a mountain but actually was an immense crater. Unable to resist the temptation that gnawed at him, Troy slowed to a standstill. Slowly he rotated the vessel in a complete circle to take in the view. Although the pitch darkness captured the quite desolation that surrounded him a few stars provided all the light he needed. Clouds of dust rose lazily upon his approach to land. Thinking of how the first men who landed on the moon felt suddenly crossed his mind, "This looks like a good place to park," he chuckled. He reviewed his instrument panels and secured his helmet when the computer's female voice cracked, "Opening docking platform, awaiting detonation codes." This was one feature Troy didn't like. It was necessary in the event that a pilot was compromised to ensure that no Mantarays wound up in enemy hands. Troy sadly typed on his wrist pad "Ben and Mary". In matter of seconds his body began to float. "Activate gravity soles" he sighed as his boots sought the anchor of the ground.

His first thoughts as he stared into the dark horizon were of some empty desert but nothing like the void he's tried to fill his whole life. "Driven by a desire all this time to do what?" he thought, "Just to walk around the moon." The long step from the craft felt like it took a lifetime to strike dirt and then he was bounding with the next step. The soft dust bellowed with each step until Troy found himself prancing like a ballerina. Bringing his feet and knees together he bounced off and engaged the suit's built-in jetpacks. Soaring ever so free, the open space allowed for some fancy flying. His voice command disengaged his flight and slowly he sank back to the surface. "Might as well use the new toys," he joked. Even if he was on the moon, it was nice to be on solid ground although movement was rather slow.

The rough landscape and potholes didn't help matters nor did it stop the only high ground in the area from attracting him like a beacon. It was the same crater he flew over before he landed. In the sheer exhilaration of moon walking, he hadn't noticed how far he had ventured. The crater took on the appearance of a mountain as he approached the rim. Troy studied the structure with admiration and began deciding where to start his climb. All the photo studies had led him to believe the moon was flat. It wasn't until he reached a level area of his climb that he saw what seemed to be several cave-like openings. In the distance he could barely see the Mantaray, "Commander Bishop, my scanners are showing an atmospheric disturbance in our present location. I'm unable to receive complete satellite feeds." "Mother I copy your last transmission, transfer your readings to my waist monitor, over." Troy knew that being on the dark side would limit signal strength as he looked at the monitor. The image outline extended maybe only a few miles from the surface and revealed a mass of illuminating spots of all sizes. Although the Manta-suit kept his body temperature constant, beads of sweat formed on his forehead. Troy felt the hair stand on his neck recognizing the screens shift.

The first thud struck at the base of the crater and bounced gently in the dust. At first glance Troy thought of a baked potato as more and more debris began to hit ground and the crater. "Meteors!" he yelled. He quickly looked around for a way down and back to the Mantaray. The air was filled with hot streaming rocks. Troy knew his chances of making it to the Mantaray were near impossible. If he was hit by just one of these projectiles it would be like being shot by a cannon. "Mother!" he shouted over the popcorn sound. "Yes Commander," "There's no time for me to make it to your location, activate your energy shields, I have spotted what appears to be a cave opening in the rock. Hopefully it is large enough for me to seek shelter, Bishop out." As he looked up the crater he knew this was no time to do it the old fashion way, he would take his chances flying. "Activate suit thrusters," he snapped. He lifted up from the ledge and headed up as one of the meteors bounced several times off the side of the crater and hit him in the side. Troy felt like he had been hit by a truck and was twirling away from the crater. "Got to get control," he thought while fighting off the pain. Spreading his arms like wings he redirected his thrusters and blasted toward the opening. After dodging a few of the streamers, Troy stumbled as he landed in the cave and came to rest on his elbows. A pinkish glow surrounded the Mantaray with occasional sparks flying from its force field from being struck. Troy breathed a sigh of relief, "Mother, I'm inside the cave and safe for the time being, how are you holding up?" The soft voice responded, "Shield strength is 98% and holding well. All indicators show a huge mass following these fragments." Troy stood to get a better look, it now sounded like a battlefield as portions of the entrance crumbled. Some of the meteors were the size of a house leaving imprints as they smashed into the surface. Troy thought better of standing at the entrance and backed further into the cave. The one thing any astronaut could least afford to do was to think the worst. But Troy knew the Mantaray couldn't withstand the hit of a large meteor. Even as advanced as his suit was it could only sustain him for about 12 hours. This meteor shower could last hours or maybe even days and Mother was his only lifeline. Troy looked around wondering how deep the cave ran, thinking that part of the crater's ridgeline was closer to the Mantaray and could have an entrance he missed. He didn't have anything to lose by trying and he could always backtrack his footprints if he hit a dead-end. The night vision sensors automatically adjusted as he stepped into the bowels of the cavern. It reminded him of some of his adventures on the mountain as a kid. Although the moon was a completely different matter, a cave was still a cave. Troy was thankful he was still able to use his wrist navigator and plot points. The cave continued like a maze with some openings larger than others. If he could find an exit closer to the Mantaray he would have a better chance. He watched the navigator closely as he continued his journey hoping only that the meteor shower would subside. What seemed like hours of weaving in the endless maze came to an abrupt halt. Troy stared and sunk to his knees in disbelief at the rock wall that stood impregnably before him. In a fit of anger, grabbing a handful of small stones and dirt he hurled it into the stone face before collapsing from fatigue. He lay quietly in the dust circling around him before he noticed that it wasn't drifting back down as it normally did. Troy struggled to his knees with the rising dust, a draft? "That's impossible!" he thought. As his eyes followed the upward movement of the particles his night vision strained to peer to the height of the cavern. It baffled him when his wrist instrument found no sign of actual oxygen. But what was causing this unusual activity? "Mother, this is Bishop over." "Commander this is Mother," came the response. "I hear you loud and clear Mother, what is your status? Over." "The meteor shower has intensified; my shields are low but holding at 60 percent. These showers are only fragments of a larger asteroid heading into this sector." The televised images Mother sent were frightening. "If those are only fragments, how large is this thing?" A series of 2 scale estimates appeared, "About the size of the small island on Earth know as Maui, estimated time of impact is 15 minutes." Realizing his time was short, Troy looked toward the ceiling and activated his thrusters. In a few seconds he spied another hole within the upper wall and began to crawl through. After reaching a small intersection his night vision briefly blinded him, light. He closed his eyes to adjust his vision and continued to crawl, optimistic that he would get to the Mantaray in time. The light at the end of the tunnel became even brighter as Troy slowed his approach. He cautiously surveyed the outside, expecting a meteor bombardment. Instead he gazed upon a city. A domed base of some kind was carved from the inside of the crater. Just below, people bustled around in response to orders from a public announcement system. A quick survey of the area indicated it was a military operation. The PA blared, "This is not a test, I repeat this is not a test. Centurion tomogram sequence activated. All personnel proceed to level H. Commence movement of Sleeping Beauty." Troy stared in amazement as a coffin sized box appeared. The box levitated through the cavern below, guided by four soldiers. As he tried to make sense of what he had just seen and heard, his hand began to throb as it did when he was younger. He looked down and winced as the pulsation grew stronger. "What the devil?" he thought as the box drew closer to his side of the cavern. Just then he saw an image of the alien woman in his mind, it was though she were standing directly before him. The tears streamed unnoticed as he reached for her in the gloom. The memories flooded over him with amazing clarity. "How could this be?" These images had left him for over a year now. Here on the dark side of the moon in a meteor shower was the last place he expected to have them return. His mind couldn't be playing tricks! The box! Was she the "sleeping beauty" the announcer had just spoken of? As Troy began to grasp what was going on, she wavered in a blue mist and then disappeared. A flash of metal glinted in his eyes. He looked down just in time to see the titanium box disappear through a passage directly beneath him. Troy sat for what seemed an eternity when Mother's voice crackled like lightning in the air around him. "Commander Bishop, we are T minus 10 from impact. Please confirm your location immediately!" Troy began to respond as the dome above the crater whirred into motion. Below alarms sounded as a giant laser rose from the crater floor. Troy watched in stunned silence as the laser blasted into the darkness above. A deafening roar shook the entire crater as showers of the once huge meteor pelted the moons surface. It was raining gravel. Although he was relieved it was over, he couldn't get over the puissance of such a weapon. The whole experience was nerve racking and his gut feeling was telling him they wouldn't take kindly to him stumbling upon their little secret. It would only be a matter of time before they sent out patrols to assess the damage. Troy kept low while making his way to the opposite side of the ridge. Once he saw the Mantaray, he jettisoned fast and low to avoid detection. He felt his heart in his throat after touching ground, "Mother I'm home." "Welcome Commander." A compartment hatch slid open. After a very brief sigh of relief, Troy's fingers went to work on the controls, "Let's get out of here before they realize they've had a dinner guest, activate lift-off." It felt great to be in space again. Troy just wanted the whole episode behind him. The view screen showed the small dots of the other Mantarays. "Commander Bishop, we thought you were a goner, are you okay?" came a voice. Troy veered his craft toward the formation, "Yes. What is your status? Over." The pilot's face appeared on his screen, "We were able to avoid the shower thanks to some mad flying. What the hell happened down there? And what could turn a killer asteroid into dust particles like that?" Troy couldn't get the weapon out of his mind either, "I'm not sure but I have a feeling that ICON knows. Let's head on to the moon base, maybe there we can get some answers."

The silent glide of the XL-500 was better than Lou had expected. In the darkness of space the space station twinkled from the sun's reflections. The closer they got he couldn't believe what he was seeing, "Manta-fleet prepare for rendezvous and docking operations." The slow rotation reminded him of a Ferris wheel, a mass of technology once only dreamed about. The actual dimensions were nowhere close to all the briefings he had attended. This thing was at least a hundred times larger. Though he felt amazed at the leaps and bounds science was making with the new technology it seemed at every turn someone was left in the dark. After locking on his coordinates he flicked the vidcom, "Dr. Kimball, we'll be docking with the space station soon, is every thing secure?" The laughter of the children brought a smile to his face as he viewed Katie and her staff checking the medipods and giving a "thumbs up". Katie placed the last stuffed animal into a storage bin. "Sir, the last of the training aids all accounted for, Sir!" she playfully saluted. "Good, now that the fleet is secure, I thought you might want to see this." Their vidcom displayed the approaching space station as Lou listened to the delight of his crew. The busy activity became apparent with shuttles flying in and out, construction crews welding and the slow turning station revealing it's many stages. Katie fought to clear her voice, "My God, how could all this be possible?" Lou reappeared on the scene, "Those were my first impressions as well, but it's all possible in the name of secrecy which explains why we can't land directly at the moon base, too much shuttle activity as it is. First things first, let's get the children transferred then we'll talk home improvement." Lou began a series of control adjustments and soon a uniformed technician appeared on his screen. "International Space Station this is Exodus, request docking sequence over." "Exodus this is ISS, transmitting sequence, you're in range of a guidance beam, just relax and leave the driving to us." It was a strange sensation watching the instruments take on a life of their own, but Lou kept a watchful eye as the XL-500 eased into the docking bay. The feel of solid ground was unmistakable after any flight and as always he gave thanks. The cheers of the crowd could be heard through the glass windows that enclosed the docking bay. "Welcome to the International Space Station Exodus. Commander, preparations for your crew and the children are in order. A medical team is standing by to begin standard examinations before any personnel can be transferred to the moon base." The procession of medipods off the Exodus was met with jubilation but nothing was brighter than the tiny faces inside. Lou waited quietly as Katie walked alongside the last pod. Soon he heard his niece's amplified voice. "I'm a little teapot, short and stout. Here is my handle. Here is my spout. When I get all steamed up, hear me shout! Tip me over and pour me out." Lou bit his lip trying to hold back his feelings, "Well you could have fooled me. I thought it was angels singing." "No! Uncle Lou," giggled Tina "it was me and Katie." He touched the glass trying to connect with her small hand and they all began to sing together. Little Tina only sung a few more lines before she drifted back to sleep. The caravan of medipods was more than he cared to watch as the techs led them away. They all soon felt as though they were in another parade with all the well-wishers greeting them.

CHAPTER THIRTEEN

This space station was more than anyone expected, it seemed more like a settlement in free orbit. The rush of fresh oxygen could be felt as they entered the main sphere of the station. The glass enclosures afforded a full view of many of the station's artificial habitats. An abundance of sunlight bathed the astronauts in such a way they never felt before. The cylinders were miles in diameter and extended miles in length. All the cylinders had sufficient depth that provided perfect blue skies with cloudbanks. It came as no surprise that when they passed under a dark cloud they felt the cool rinse of rainfall. One of the technicians pointed out some of the agricultural areas of fresh fruits and vegetables and even one that was miles and miles of beachfront. They all smiled seeing the people surfing on generated waves. In another sphere they could see individuals in zero gravity enjoying personal flight. Katie smiled in delight and asked, "All this is wonderful but somewhat extreme don't you think?" The technician responded, "Indeed, but the world leaders decided if for any reason Earth had to be evacuated this station would serve as a platform until the moon and other planets could be developed for mankind's survival. Here are your quarters. Tonight's celebration will be in honor of your arrival. The units have already been updated with your DNA signatures so all you have to do is place your hand on the door consoles, if you have any other questions please feel free to use the com-links provided inside." As the rest of the crew searched for their names on the doors, Katie placed her hand on her console and the door slid open. Lou stood at her side as they both nodded with approval at the luxury appointments. "Not bad, not bad at all. Almost fit for a king," said Lou attempting to step inside. Katie held him at bay with one finger, "Or Queen, but I do believe your quarters are that way King

Louie," as she gently kissed him away. Lou stood steadfast with his eyes closed and lips puckered wanting more as the electronic doors slid closed. Katie's fading laughter brought his eyes suddenly open. He yelled through her door, "Girl, you know you ain't right!" before making his retreat down the hallway to his living quarters. Still mumbling to himself he stepped through the arched portal into his quarters. As he looked around he forgot, momentarily, his romantic woes. "Man, this place is laid out!" he thought. The beautiful plush surroundings were an interesting contrast against the stark otherworldly view. He heard the sound of water cascading and went to investigate. He followed the curved room to a glistening turquoise holographic wall and heard a female voice calling him into what was the most luxurious exotic bath he'd ever seen. Confused by the female voice beckoning him, Lou began to look around the room searching her out. "Commander Stryker, for your pleasure your bath awaits." Lou nearly jumped out of his skin as he realized it was a computer, and not a real female, "Damn! Just my luck." Lou tossed one of the fresh grapes into his mouth that set in a fruit bowl beside the bath and continued to undress and slid into the warm bath. After a few seconds of being submerged Lou wiped the water from his eyes only to behold a lovely figure within a hologram. Sliding up with his elbows Lou asked, "And who might you be?" "I am Fantasia, your personal attendant. Is the water okay? Might I suggest pleasure jets to help you relax?" Lou looked slowly around as the bath began to bubble from the jet spray. Just as he was beginning to lay back a sudden burst came from the bottom. "Hey! For Pete's sake, I feel violated," he shouted bobbing to an upright position. The image waved a hand halting the water action, "Excuse me commander, I assumed most men enjoyed that particular water feature." "Maybe if you have a little sugar in your tank." "Sugar in your tank? That is not in my data bank, to what does it refer?" Lou leaned back, "It's a long story, forget about it. Right now I just want to soak my worries away. So I guess you or attendants like you come with all the units," he sighed laying the warm washcloth across his eyes. "No," replied the image. "Generally alpha models are reserved for males and the Betas for women but there are many that prefer the same gender." "That's nice," said Lou slowly submerging under the water. After a few seconds of meditation he lunged up choking water, "You mean to tell me Katie is over there with some Denzel? Oh, hell naw!" Lou stormed through the hologram grabbing a towel and a small box on his way out. He fumbled adjusting the towel around his waist as the automatic doors slid open. In that instant he felt his shoulder bump into someone, as he looked up Troy grinned with amusement. "Whoa big fella! Where you racing off to with no drawers?" Lou braced the small box between his chin and chest and re-adjusted his towel. "Man, am I glad to see you! Give me second, got to bust computer boy upside the head," he said without breaking his stride. In front of Katie's room he impatiently pushed the Tele-com button as Troy smiled with a puzzled look. "Bucky, I know you in there, open up," he demanded. Katie's angelic face appeared on the screen surrounded by bubbles, "Boo, is that you, are we under attack?" "No! Just open up, we've got to talk." The quiet air locks on the doors whizzed open too slow for Lou while Troy chuckled, "Oh Boo! I would hate to ask why you call her Bucky." Lou just waved him off as he squeezed through the slow opening doors, "Where is he? I know he's in here." Katie stepped out wrapped in a towel drying her hair, "What's all the commotion about? Troy is that you?" she raced past Lou to embrace him. "It's so good to see you, come on in, when did you get in?" Troy couldn't get a word in edge wise with all the questions and Lou peeking in rooms and closets like a jealous schoolboy. He looked confused as his search came up empty, "Look Bucky! I know he's in here and I demand to know where he is!" The sweet smile melted as she turned like a Cobra ready to strike. Before Lou knew it a small index finger was poking him down to size. "Demand! How dare you come in here with all this drama, Mr. I'm not ready for a commitment! Besides, Cedric has been very helpful not to mention considerate." "Cedric! What the hell kinda name is Cedric?" Lou fumed as Troy stepped between the spatting lovers. Katie stalked back into the bath after giving Lou a look that could kill, and telling Troy he better save Lou's sorry ass. Troy tried hard to hide his amusement, but it was impossible. "Man, you are seriously trippin'!" Lou pushed Troy away and began to pace, glancing worriedly at the door Katie had disappeared behind. "This just ain't right, man," he mumbled to himself. Troy wiped the smile off his face and tried to reason with his friend. "Lou, what's up with you? I know some hologram ain't messin' with your head this bad. Just chill with the jealousy bit and ask the woman to marry you. First you need to do some major apologizing though. I haven't seen Katie this mad in a long time. Maybe now isn't a good time to propose, but its definitely time to kiss and make-up. I'm out, I'll see the two of you at dinner. Don't make me come looking for you either, man!" Troy bear-hugged Lou and left him standing in the middle of the room speechless, for once. Lou stared at the tiny box in his hand as one friend walked out and the other back in. "You're still here? I'm not in the mood for this Lou. Maybe you should just go and we can talk later after we've both cooled down. Otherwise it could get ugly up in here." Katie stood defiant with her hands on her hips. Lou started to say something, but instead he turned and quietly left. Katie stood rooted to the spot bewildered that the man who never shut up had just done so. She began to regret being angry with him. "Oh well," she thought, "a tiger can't change his stripes just like that. He's probably plotting how to piss me off again anyway. At least for now, I have some peace and quiet. Oh Cedric, did you say we have some moon dust body lotion in here? I'm ready to be pampered!"

Troy hesitated when his door slid open not sure of what to expect after all the commotion he had just witnessed. To his surprise there was silence, "Just my luck, everybody has remote-control gods and goddesses but my room is broke." He felt his eyes roll up in his head as soon as he lay down on the bed, "A nap will do me some good. Who needs a, a whatcha-call it anyway?" Unable to fight his need for sleep, he managed to slip off his boots. "Sir would you like a pillow?" echoed a soft voice. Troy fought to open one eye only to see the outline of a woman. "Say what?" he asked. "A pillow, commander would you like a pillow?" His attempts to wave past the haze failed, "No, I'm fine. Why is it I can't see you?" The image loomed as soft as her voice, "It is not of my doing, all personal attendants are generated from the mind's eye of those they serve." Troy was content to leave well enough alone, "Figures, even my deepest thoughts are a mystery. Just wake me for dinner, thank you." The welcomed embrace of sleep was one he looked forward to as he managed one last glance of the veiled woman.

The laboratory staff was in celebration, test tubes and flasks clinked now filled with champagne. All rejoicing, "We did it! It's a miracle. No more plague, no more plague!" they sung in one voice. The large looming face of Arthur Kehoe appeared above on the large vid-com bringing their roars to whispers. They all recognized his smile as that of a viper, and here they were the world's last hope, booty slapping and getting their groove-on. Many attempted to regain their composure by climbing off tables and taking bras from around their heads. The director of the Space station slowly made his way to front. Arthur Kehoe's expression changed little as his boardroom full of VIPs even held their breath. "Dr. Kensington, I take it that you're all in good spirits. Good news travels fast and I personally wanted to express my gratitude on a job well done." In a last ditch effort to wipe lipstick from his cheek, Kensington replied, "Mr. Kehoe. Sir needless to say, that's not necessary. We still have so much to do," all the while giving the behind the back signal to clear the house. The motion scattered them in seconds. "Our crews are now preparing to shuttle the children to the moon base where we expect even better results. The team and I were just having a little "before launch" celebration." "Indeed, just ensure that everything is online and provide me with all data as you get it. I'm sure you have pressing issues so we won't detain you any longer." Blink. The screen went blank as the good doctor wiped his sweaty brow.

Back on Earth, Arthur Kehoe sighed will relief, "Well ladies and gentlemen, phase one of our plan is complete and with remarkable results. The optimum results we hoped for will come at the labs on the moon base. The Exodus will then embark on its Mars mission to snare our dear alien adversaries. But for now we can ease the respective fears of our countrymen and put the plague behind us. Thank you for joining me in this momentous occasion and may our nations continue to unify our efforts to defeat the force that now threatens mankind. Delores, would you please be so kind as to escort our guests to the state room for refreshments while we await the President's news conference?" The flash within his eyes changed as the door closed behind his departing guests. "Idiots! Not to mention those lame brains at the space station. Ready my spacecraft and crew. This is no time for festivities when our very existence hangs in the balance. There's too much at stake to leave such matters in the hands of fools."

The hustle and bustle within the transport bay was at its peak as the space station crews prepared all pods for their historic transport. Lou and Katie stood hand in hand overlooking the vast bay as the medipods were carefully loaded. "I'm glad to see you two have kissed and made up," chided Troy as he walked up. The love struck couple greeted Troy with smiles and Katie extended her hand to show her ring. "That's only the half of it, Lou asked me to be his wife," she sighed. Lou cleared his throat, "We were hoping you would be the best man?" Troy embraced his friends, "It would be an honor." While the trio made last minute adjustments to their suits Lou gazed out at the moon glowing ever bright. "We've decided that fate has brought us to the moon and what better place to pledge our love. We were able to contact the minister at the moon base to perform the ceremony. So let's get this show on the road, Tina said she wants to be the flower girl and ring bearer."

The transport bays were alive with the buzz of engines while crews hurried to complete all loading. Lou made sure they were on the shuttlecraft with Tina who was in her usual cheerful singing mood. Katie and Tina belted out a happy melody as the engine surged upon lift-off. The opening of the bay brought in the bright starlight as the shuttlecrafts began easing out the bays. The slow descent of shuttlecrafts reminded Troy of a wagon train in a old western as they began to orbit before landing. The Earthly delight of the blue marble couldn't have been more marvelous than at this moment and why not, God's choice for his children. T he stream of shuttles came closer as the pitted surface loomed larger with each passing second. The vast moon base came into view like an ant colony. Troy could see the landing pad which was miles in diameter. Large domes dotted the landscape providing the controlled environment needed to sustain life. Upon approach, one of the large domes opened up as the shuttles neared touch down in one of the valley sized craters. The walls of the crater were lined with viewing ports that supported the idea of underground life. It was deemed necessary due to the constant bombardment of meteors. Soon they could make out the small figures waving with joy at their arrival and after the last shuttle touched down large doors opened as vehicles made their way out to greet them. The reception was even larger as the medipods were led into the swarm of well-wishers. If it weren't for the modern trappings, Troy would have thought he was inside the Grand Canyon. The astronauts welcomed the cheers that led them into the splendid banquet hall. The fuss was more than they could bear but the high spirits of the children eased the confusion. Amidst all the intros and speeches Troy, with Tina in hand, whispered to Lou, "Big guy, it's all set. The minister is waiting in the chapel. Let's do this before you get cold feet." Lou looked over at Tina. "Don't even think about it Uncle Lou," chuckled Tina. Lou got up and followed the fearsome two, "I heard of shotgun weddings, but this is ridiculous." Troy patted him on the shoulder, "Get used to it pal, it's all down hill from here." It seemed weird seeing Lou sweat compared to his usual confident self. He looked even more pitiful once they arrived at the chapel.

The chapel was backlit by the glow of numerous beeswax candles. The sweet, pure scent filled the air along with the heady fragrance of honeysuckle, Katie's favorite flower. Lou began to fidget as the minister entered the small intimate space. Troy laughed as he guided Lou to the altar. Tina slipped off toward a small door at the rear of the chapel. Inside Katie was fidgeting almost as bad as Lou. Tina giggled as she helped Katie thread a vine of small honeysuckle buds through her upswept hair. "Aunt Katie, Uncle Lou is just as nervous as you are!" Katie smiled at the term of endearment and stroked the child's hair as she wistfully watched the girl hold the small flowers in her delicate hands. "I guess we just want to be sure about this. It's a big step for both of us, especially for your uncle!" Tina pulled Katie close and whispered in her ear, "Uncle Lou is a great guy. He always kisses my boo-boos when I get hurt." Katie laughed and hugged the child tight. "Well I guess if you give him such high ratings, I better snatch him up while I still can!" Katie and Tina put the final touches to Katie's hair as the music began to swell outside. Finally they were ready to begin. Tina walked down the aisle first, carrying a small bouquet of honeysuckle. Troy and Lou stood at the altar with the minister. Katie came behind carrying her bouquet and looking lovelier than Lou could remember. The candlelight shimmered around her and enveloped her in a warm embrace. Lou knew in that moment that this was right. This woman was the one to share his life and have his children. The one to share his dreams and plans. The one who would follow life's path to the end in their golden years. He stood taller and squared his shoulders as he watched his bride drift towards him in the light of love. Katie noticed the change in Lou's posture and felt a surge of pride and adoration. No matter what life might show them, she knew this man would always love and protect her. How could she have doubted the decision to seal their bond? She quickened her step, no longer wishing to be far from her man. She longed for his embrace and the brush of his lips on hers. The closer she got, his heartbeat faster and as Lou looked into her eyes nothing else mattered. When the minister asked them to join hands, little Tina placed her hand in Troy's. In her face he remembered always looking up to his mother and asking why. It wasn't until now he understood her reply, "Baby, ask your Dad," and off to Dad he would go, "Daddy, how come the this do that or the that do this?" How he missed them so. Never a day went by that he didn't remember their love. His sweet Mama, giving her honey hugs saying, "Your Mama's love, mama's love." When the pastor told Lou he could kiss the bride, he knew they too were blessed. Now where little Tina got the rice is anybody's guess but her first handful busted up the kiss. She turned on Troy and the pastor was out the door first. Troy hid and caught Tina at the door as Lou and Katie ran for their lives. "Gotcha! Let's go get some cake and ice cream and let the newlyweds be alone." She spread her arms as wide as she could "Okay, Uncle Troy, but I want a piece this big!"

It was a relief to see the children out of the medipods after the long trip, even those in wheelchairs were fancy-free. This was a fun time for them. Troy tried to remember the last time he had so much fun, singing and dancing. It took quite a while before the happy little feet became sleepy and didn't mind being toted off for beddy-bye. Troy hadn't taken two steps before Tina had nodded off. "How sad," he thought, "it's taking babies to save the world." When Troy reached the nursery something inside him didn't want to put Tina back in the medipod. He stood holding her until one of the attendants asked if everything was alright. He nodded yes and eased her down. Tina whimpered without waking as the attendant reinserted her lines and sealed the pod. The thought of someday having a kid crossed his mind as he walked to his quarters. A boy or a girl, it didn't matter. He even tossed around the idea of having twins. As he entered his quarters a computerized voice asked if he would be requiring a personal attendant. Troy quickly replied, "No thank you please, no twilight zone for me tonight. I just want a good night's rest." He left a trail of clothes and flopped in his bed. "Children, heck I don't even have a wife. What I need now is some old fashioned sleep," he mumbled. The one thing he learned well in the military was how to sleep. Standing or sitting it didn't matter, you got your Zs' when and how you could and he could feel it coming on. The soft comfort of his bed allowed him to slip even faster. Sleep overtook Troy just as he was thinking how nice the wedding had been, a break from the stress and pressure of his latest mission. Troy shifted to his side and was soon in deep sleep. He could feel his mind turning even in slumber. The soft smell of cool night air seemed strange at first, but he was far into a night world of dreams and half remembered secrets before the scent had settled into his brain. He felt dry leaves beneath his feet as he ran through the woods, trying to find his way back home. Up ahead, voices rang loud and angry, shattering the stillness of the twilight. He could see the light from the porch just a few yards away. He hurried when he saw his mother and father in the yard with the man from town. Oh man was he in trouble! His parents were probably calling for help to find him. At first he didn't want to be caught outside, so he hid in some bushes just on the edge of the yard, but then he heard his father and the man arguing and his mother was crying! She turned to run to the house and had just opened the door when his father shouted and ran after her. The explosion lit up the night sky and threw Troy backwards in the brush. He screamed and jumped up in time to see the man run to a van parked on the edge of the driveway. He saw the back doors close and a small girl's tear streaked face in the rear window as the van pulled onto the road and sped off into the night. He couldn't tear his eyes away from the fading blue light that shone in the girl's hand as she tried to reach for him across the darkness. Troy bolted up in bed, shaking and crying out into the silent void of his quarters. He looked wildly around the darkened room, still half-rooted in the terrifying dream. He felt lost in the grief that haunted him all his life. How had he managed to bury this memory? His last sight of his parents as they were so brutally taken from him, leaving him cold, lost and alone in the world. He jumped as he looked at his shaking hands and felt a throbbing in his palm as the blue light glowed brightly in his eyes. What the hell was going on? He ran to the bathroom to splash water on his face in an attempt to wake up. He looked in the mirror and the face looking back at him was so raw with emotion that he was truly scared for the first time in his adult life. "Whoa, partner," he thought as he sat down hard on the edge of the tub. The cool tiles beneath him made him feel reconnected to the real world and he took every ounce of comfort he could from their solid surface. What had brought this on? He had been thinking of his parents at the wedding, the love they shared was always evident. They were always affectionate and made no attempt to hide their emotions from him. "I guess I've never really dealt with that night, I was too young to believe my eyes," he whispered softly to himself. "But what about the little girl?" That was too weird! And stranger still was the fact that his hand had done the same thing as he awakened from the dream. Oh God, was he having some sort of breakdown? He had dreamed of his space odyssey since childhood and now he was cracking up. "Hell no!," Troy shouted into the mirror. "I am not crazy and I can't ignore these dreams and memories anymore!" He paced around the small room and felt so confined that he had to get out and walk to think clearly. He stepped out of his door and headed for the garden pod just across the way. He was glad it was so late, no one else was around and he had the lovely setting to himself. It was amazing to have the flowers and trees of Earth in the vast depths of outer space. The sight of the lush greenery against the velvet darkness of space took his breath away. He sat in a small alcove surrounded by Greek statues and the calming sound of water in a fountain around the corner. "It's time to put two and two together, but somehow I doubt I'm gonna come up with four," he sighed as he leaned back and lost himself in the puzzle of his life. The reality of his memory now pierced his very soul, he could see them running back into the house, time and time again. He always knew how they died, but now he understood why...to save him. The sorrow in his heart brought him to his knees and unable to wipe the tears Troy pleaded toward the heavens for their forgiveness. He sobbed as never before, for their courage, for their love. How could he in his darkest rages question them for leaving him alone in the world? He cried so long he was sure the grass would always grow in that spot. Slowly he rolled over and could see the stars afar through misty eyes. Still he cried, "They came back for me." He wanted to embrace them both as he reached for the sky. Lying there in the cool grass with his eyes closed, he recalled a small child peering out the van's back window and her small palm glowing in the pane. Troy bumped his head several times on the grass, "She's alive," he stopped "this isn't about an alien invasion, they're coming back for her." He sprang up remembering, "The base on the dark side, even Fort Knox gold wouldn't require all that security to move it and certainly not when an asteroid is about to smash the place." Troy looked into his palm puzzled, knowing that he wasn't an alien but what connection did he have with her? He had no idea how long he had been in the garden, but deep inside he welcomed the memory of his parents. The silence of the garden was broken by the sound of voices, "Troy, are you okay? We've been looking all over for you." Lou repeated the question, "Dude, snap out of it, you okay? Troy stared past the hand Lou waved in front of him. "Katie he was right." "Who was right?" "Your father. I remember everything. It happened as he said, they tried to ambush the aliens and kill all the witnesses and my parents. But we were not the only ones to survive that night. The Princess lives." Katie sat on the bench in disbelief recalling the story her father had told. "He never said anything about an alien princess." "That's because they didn't see her sneak off the ship. I saw her playing with the animals when the attack began. After the Queen was shot the crew swept her away without realizing she was off the ship." Lou gave her hand a slight squeeze, "So they actually captured one of the aliens? Man, this is getting too weird!" The three sat silently watching the distant glow of Earth. "He tried to warn us but we still needed more proof," sighed Katie. "And we still do," sighed Troy. "Katie, after this mornings mission brief check the computer databases for anything about the moon base, something has to show up even if it's movement of supply parts to that other base. Lou and I will finish the pre-mission checks and check in on the kids."

Walking into the mission brief, the trio all had a different outlook on who the good guys were. Still in all their minds they couldn't forget the dying innocents of this plague, regardless of what kind of politics were being played out. Recognizing their respective stations they joined their crews when the moon base commander began the briefing. "If I may have your attention, so far we're well on schedule but regardless we are still at a disadvantage by not knowing when or how our enemy will strike. Some may consider our mission to Mars a long shot, but it may hold the answers to some age old questions." He flicked a remote and the dark room filled with a larger than life hologram of the universe. "The intelligence sectors have been compiling information to help us better understand the alien forces we're up against. Until the historic meeting some nineteen years ago, many thought aliens only existed in B-movies due mainly to governmental cover-ups since the 1950s'. It wasn't until this historic meeting that we dug into past records to piece together a particular pattern that went unnoticed. The planetary alignment we are fortunate to now witness only occurs every 26 months and at the end of the twenty year window. All data points to the asteroid field here on the other side of Mars. Most of the earlier astronomical data showed this unusual phenomenon that the scientific community is now sure was a black hole. But it was dismissed as an illusion due to poor imaging and the fact that no one could explain the disappearances of the images. This mission is the first of many to test the untapped truths of Magma technology. Already we're centuries ahead of previous space programs and with our newfound uses of the technology we will find the black star before they can come through our back door again. It is here that Dr. Kimball will release her neutron balls, but I'll let her give you the details." Katie stood nervously, "As the general was saying, all indications place the formation of the black hole in this sector. We are not able to pinpoint its exact location but if the neutron balls work as anticipated, that information will soon be in our hands. Each XL-500 will release over one million of these tiny balls in four areas of this sector that should provide sufficient coverage. This theory is used all the time to study tornadoes on Earth, but in this case we rely on the loss of data. In other words every ball will be accounted for and every satellite in space will be tracking them with their neutron detectors. The goal being that the black hole does exactly what we suspected all these years and that is to suck everything into it's black void. Once massive amounts are pulled into the void, the computers will respond to the lost data and we will have exact locations of the last transmitted data." Troy read Lou's lips across room as he proudly winked, "That's my baby!" The general resumed, "Thank you Dr. Kimball, for clearing up the theory aspects of the mission. Colonel Bishop, the following coordinates are security boundaries your Mantarays must cover. Now if there aren't any questions," he paused "this concludes your brief. Good luck to all." The chatter after the general left the room was mainly among the individual crews as each made last minute calculations and notes. Katie quietly stepped into the glass enclosed computer room to verify her data as the groups chatted down below. After carefully selecting the information for their mission, she sat back and began to scan the database. The screen was a blur of information, but her years of experience helped sort each file in an instant. The files contained everything from plumbing to the smallest detail of the mining operations but nothing unusual. Katie sat back mentally exhausted and about to shut down the program. The last file to flash onscreen was from the Cape. It was marked Top Secret. Katie watched as the upload came in. Although it was from the Cape this was different, Presidential and World Counsel seals. Atop them all ICON… Arthur Kehoe. Katie was puzzled as she watched the transfer, file after file as if he was downloading his complete files. "If I didn't know better Mr. Kehoe is taking a little trip and won't leave home without them. Bingo," she smiled. "There's nothing worse than hacking into your own program." She watched the screen while her fingers typed at light speed. Warning panels and Top Secret advisories popped up one after the other as she continued her quest, each time she typed the panels closed. It was like peeling an onion, layer after layer began to fall. The ICON logo finally appeared, she tried everything but she couldn't bypass it. "Damn it, slick bastard," she pounded on the console. "Running out of time, it will take hours at this rate. I'm so close, but I have no choice. If I had more time! I have to use my governmental access to override him." Katie didn't think twice before typing the final strokes. It fell. "I'm in," she sighed. The disc copying flowed as she waited until the download complete symbol appeared. Katie wasn't surprised when she quickly entered the program only to find more encryption. She ejected the disc and hid it in her secret place as she left.

Lou soared to the ledge of the crater and peered at the objects that dotted the barren landscape. "You have got to be joking, I thought those were satellites when we flew in," finally seeing Troy's location on the other side after a quick pass. "If you think that's something, wait until you see the ones underground. I just wanted you to see them up close and personal. Anything within a five mile radius will catch pure hell to the power of ten." Lou checked his watch, "It's about show time, let's head in. I just hope Katie was able to dig something up. We can't afford to be bumping around in the dark. Too many missing pieces to this puzzle if you ask me." "Roger that, meet you on the pad." The flight suits brought a whole new meaning to spacewalking or bunny hopping and with some serious gitty-up. Troy and Lou couldn't resist the temptation to bust a few moves on the way down. When they came through the air lock, Katie stood shaking her head. "Who taught you guys how to fly? Elroy Jetson?" Lou smiled back, "Why, was he one of those famous instructors at the Cape?" She just laughed revealing a portion of the disc before tapping it back down into her hiding place. She interlocked arms and began escorting them toward the ships. "When you hear who our benefactor is, we may want our knees in the breeze. So to speak." They both leaned toward her as she whispered two words. She wasn't surprised when they each lifted an elbow and carried her on to the shuttle. They both transmitted ahead to have their ships ready for take-off upon their arrival. Katie's feet didn't touch ground until she was aboard the shuttle. Both men eagerly awaited her explanation once they were alone in the craft. Turning her back to the two as she gingerly removed the disc from her secret hiding place, "First of all, they're going to know that I hacked Kehoe's program. I had no other choice. I had to use my access to bypass the final gates. I scanned the moon base and the Cape's databases and came up empty. Word is, Arthur Kehoe recently launched and is coming here and I guess he had to download all his files and programs in order to access them. Our other problem is that all the files are still encrypted which I should be able to decipher in a few days. I was just lucky that all the file names where not in code. There's even one called the Bishop experiments." Lou waved a hand across the blank stare on Troy's face, "Which is more reason for us to get moving and now. Hey buddy, I know all this isn't easy but you know as well as I do we have to get to the bottom of this. The more we know about what and who we're up against the better our chances." Troy gripped his hand in unity, "You're both right, let's get rolling. There's too much at stake. Let's hope we can make it to the space station." After strapping into their seats Troy hit the intercom. "Pilot, this is

Commander Bishop we're all secure back here." "Roger sir, we've been cleared, prepare for lift-off in 5,4,3,2,1." The surge of the reactors was music to their ears as Troy looked at the small disc in his hand. The moon base appeared smaller by the second then only craters could be seen. It wasn't long before the space station came into view, looming as man's wonder in space. The trio was strangely quiet on the trip back, all knowing there was no turning back. Instinctively, as the shuttle docked with the space station they sprung out and Troy passed Katie the disc. "Start working on this as soon as possible, we may not have much time." He tapped his wrist-com, "Mantarays prepare to roll." As he walked down the corridor to his dark gleaming fleet he could only wonder what other secrets the disc held. The Mantarays boldly fanned out of the bay followed by the XL-500s'.

A red light at the Cape flashed "Security Breach". The mad dash at the complex was quelled by Kehoe's voice, "I haven't been gone an hour. How could someone hack into our system, you get me answers and now! This program was supposed to be flawless, the best in the world and you mean to tell me some third world country just waltzed in and took it." The computer specialist shouted, "Got it. This was an inside job sir." "Damn it son, I have no time for fifty questions." The young man cleared his throat, "Sir it was downloaded by Dr. Kimball, she helped designed the program. I've contacted the space station and they've already departed on the Mars mission. Do you want me to request their immediate return?" The look in Kehoe's eyes was unmistakable. "No. Our Dr. Kimball and friends have just bought themselves a one way trip," he frowned. "Have Commander Randall dock. I need to speak to him in person." Arthur Kehoe watched the Mantarays as their leader broke formation. The download of his files were complete as Kehoe scanned his program to access the breach. He continued to type as the commander reported to his console. Rex Randall held his salute until Kehoe responded, "At ease commander. I'm sure you know why you're here. So let me cut to the chase. I couldn't afford this conservation being intercepted, I'm not sure of Dr Kimball's role in all this but it doesn't make any difference. There is no way for us to know who all is involved in this conspiracy so they all must be eliminated. Take your Red Force Team and intercept them. I need not remind you that no one, I mean no one, is to survive your attack." Randall didn't show any emotion until he completed his about face. "Finally Bishop, we'll meet under my conditions," he grinned.

The history between the two went back to their days at Top Gun training. It was a nightmare reliving Bishop edging him out during their last dogfight. Remembering the impossible tumble move that took him and his wingman out. "You won't be so lucky this time," he thought as mounted his Mantaray. Kehoe eased back into his captain's chair exhilarated that the hunt had begun. As his craft lifted off Kehoe instructed his pilots, "Notify the moon base of our arrival so those idiots don't mistake us for the aliens. Also have that so-called director and his staff standing ready. We have some things we must discuss." The Red Force Team blasted forward with a hundred strong. Kehoe pondered why men chose to fight, to leave their souls and gain power. Was power so intoxicating that it could bring many to death's door? The thirst for power had taken man to heights only dreamed of by predecessors. Kehoe knew he would never give his power to another. "Computer, pull up the Bishop file," as a small console unfolded before him. The changing light patterns reflected while he viewed page after page of ancient text. "Oh yes, dear doctor our little Nubian jewels are much more than the answer to the common cold," he said to himself. "If only you would have accepted my offer you might have been here to witness a true wonder. A chance of a lifetime I offered but you had to save the world, the determination of your son has been surprising and I must say he's full of the same fire. It's a pity he couldn't leave well enough alone. I'm sure they would have gone to the authorities if they had succeeded in breaking my encryption. Clever girl, that Doctor Kimball. When one is surrounded by thieves and cutthroats one must place locks on top of locks. It could be months or years before she comes close and that's enough time for my forces to reach and destroy them. How would the world accept another attack by the aliens?" he roared with laughter. The pitted surface of the moon came into view as the craft's computer sounded for landing preparations.

CHAPTER FOURTEEN

Dr. Simon fumed as he awaited the arrival of the founder of ICON Industries. Never since the conception of the moon base had landings of these kind been permitted. It made no sense for such breech of protocol and by the very person that instituted it. What really stirred him was that no personnel other than security staff were permitted within this area. The sky was filled with the intruders providing cover as the Mothership sought its approach. Although the landing was five miles away the monstrous vessel covered much of the area. All eyes were glued on the sleek dark tripod sled ship drifting down from the heavens. The design was more ominous than the Mantaray. Simon shuddered at the thought of its power. From his perch, Dr. Simon watched the dust storm that followed the mighty landing. It took almost an hour before it cleared. Kehoe's troops stood by the hundreds lining a path to the moon base, saluting when a platform began descending from beneath. The manta-suit allowed him the grace of a god as he passed through the ranks. When he reached the docking bay, Dr. Simon and his staff stepped forward only to be greeted by the bright red dots of laser cannons. Kehoe quickly waved off the added measures and remove his helmet. "Dr. Simon, please excuse the precautions but these are extreme times." The security team scanned Simon and his staff for weapons while he spoke. The whole episode left him nearly speechless. "Welcome to the moon base Mr. Kehoe, all has been prepared as you have requested. I'm sure you would like to freshen up before your tour of the base, if you would follow me I will take you to your quarters." "First things first, take me to the children," said Kehoe. The group wheeled past him in the opposite direction to the labs with Dr. Simon trailing behind. "Yes sir, right this way," he puffed to catch up. "I can't understand for the life of me how Dr. Kimball could have accessed your file by mistake, I could have had them return to get to the bottom of this." Through the vid ports they surveyed the outside activities of the mining operations and soon came to a halt when they reached the lab. "The mission they're on is too sensitive for delays and accidental or not she won't be able to access the files. But the last thing we need is intercepted transmissions, agreed? Ah, now for the mission at hand, here before us holding the very essence of life. The children are the hope for the world. We have no other choice than to increase production. You did receive the modifications I sent you?" smiled Kehoe. Dr. Simon shook nervously at the files as he viewed them. "Yes sir, but the course of action you are suggesting will have devastating affects on the children. These children are not a crop for harvest that we can just increase production. My God, within days they would be in comas." "Doctor please relax, the kids will have the very best medical attention to monitor their condition but understand me, this must be done. If these kids are the harvest for the world as you so vividly expressed there are more where these came from, so don't go soft on me now. Dr. Simon, your medical breakthrough has already made you a nominee for the Noble peace prize. It would be a sad day if one's life as a pedophile was revealed at such an inopportune moment. Do I need to remind you of your little friends in Atlanta lets say some thirty years ago?" Simon pondered. "OK! OK! You've made your point, what else do you want me to do?" Kehoe stepped close enough to kiss him before hissing. "Just follow my instructions to the letter and have the children ready for transfer to our second facility when I give the word." He continued to stroll through the medipods smiling at little faces inside. "Now that we understand one another, were you able to locate the CM3?" He clasped his hands in delight not because he had good news but because Kehoe had stopped talking about his mysterious past. "Oh yes, after an extensive search with spectrometers a crater was finally located, I must say it was like looking for a needle in a haystack. It's the primordial of meteorites with a metamorphic grade I would truly give a two. The rare carbonaceous chondrite fragments found on Earth were pieces of the asteroid that actually hit the moon's surface. It is my guess that the samples you sent from Egypt and South America were of this mother lode." He eagerly led Kehoe into the next glass enclosure for decontamination and a quick change into biohazard suits. "The staff and I thought it was very noble of you to name the bacteria found inside Tanta Carhua." "It was the least I could do to thank the people of Peru for their contributions in our research. Is this the Tanta Carhua?" asked Kehoe. Simon wondered if they were getting the same "thanks" he was getting for his contribution and smiled weakly. "Yes, this monitor will give you a closer look. All precautions have been taken to avoid any human contact. We have not yet been able to identify the origin of the bacteria or whether it is of this universe. It's something I've never seen," said Simon scratching his head. "Indeed, good work doctor, keep me posted. No need to escort me to my quarters I designed the place. Ensure that all command authority is routed to the command center within my office." The security team surrounded their leader and followed him out of the lab.

The presence of ICON was felt in every sector of the moon base. This made Kehoe feel better as he passed the alert security teams. When the doors slid open to his quarters, Rex Randall was already on the giant screen, "Red Team Leader this is Kehoe what is your status at this time?" "Mr. Kehoe this is Red Team Leader we have entered Omega sector and all signals are cloaked. Just give us the word and we will tighten the noose." "That's good news Red Team Leader, but have patience there have been no attempted transmissions to Earth so I'm sure they haven't decoded the files. Let them complete their mission and then their fate is in your hands." "Wilco, they won't know what hit them," he laughed. Kehoe tapped a key and the screen went blank and was replaced by a split screen of hieroglyphs and text of the Inca and ancient Egypt. Apart from the beautiful paintings the long shot had finally paid off. The Tanta Carhua was the same. If he were a religious man he would have said a prayer. All the years of stuffy libraries and museums and countless hours of restoring mummies had confirmed his theory. Why would ancient civilizations sacrifice their children? To escape the journey of death to be immortal. The one thing the Inca Emperors and the Pharaohs had in common was the Tanta Carhua bacteria. He looked at the many drawings with each awaiting something from the sky. This was the missing ingredient. Unknown to them this meteor held something unseen by the naked eye. The confusion that surrounded the drawings was the interpretation of the symbols. Rope knots represented sacrificed children, the sun god extended rays of light leading to each rope knot. The rope knots were then connected to a holy body that in turn connected ultimately to the pharaoh. Scholars always interpreted these rays of light as divine light. Kehoe had uncovered the true meaning, the lines were blood lines. It wasn't until Doctor Bishop's mishap in Africa that the pieces fell together. The outstretched holy body of both civilizations wore the same symbol found at the Africa dig, that of the Ancient Ones. Every potion associated with the mummies was identified except for one compound, the Tanta Carhua, and that was Kehoe's secret. When all the ingredients were combined they were toxic without the CM3. It was this that a priest offered to the pharaoh before his journey. Kehoe looked closely at the holy body thinking blood of my blood. Our sleeping beauty holds the key, no wonder that her blood always evaporated! Now the truth had been shown. The light from the holy body actually flowed from the base of the skull to the children collected by the priest for the pharaoh.

"So this is what my mad little scientist has been raving about, tapping the basilar artery at the cerebellum," he thought. For centuries his family had sought secrets of the Fountain of Youth, at one point as a teen he too thought his father was mad. The images of old photos were embedded in his mind of the labs in Germany and granddad standing proudly at Hitler's side. He knew now without the aid of today's technology they came no closer than the Mediterranean gene and the Master race would not hear of using blacks. The method to the madness was quite logical once he thought it through, an alien that no blood could be drawn from, children with a disease that prevents oxygen from reaching the brain, a little witch doctor brew and throw in the rock from hell. "So if we beef up a supply to keep everyone happy on Earth then I can direct all efforts toward the true prize of the ages," he laughed. "Copacocha, Copacocha!" he shouted for all to hear. When he turned to the white-haired assassin there was no hint of anything being funny. "Agent Hunt, Dr. Simon's service has been superb. See to it that he gets what he deserves." Hunt's stone cold expression never changed as he quietly left the room. Kehoe swung back around to his files, "Nothing personal, just business," he smiled.

The glide walk seemed much more pleasant than the ones on Earth. "Maybe it was the lack of distractions and pollution," Hunt thought. There was something about the show of force that made people just want to stay indoors, it felt like an empty airport. The sentries snapped to attention as he passed. Knowing he wasn't military made no difference, he was part of the food chain that put a bad taste in your mouth and then knocked it out. Most of the moon base personnel were either on shift or just didn't want to be seen. He stepped off at the gym entrance and carefully glanced for witnesses while reading the posted directory.

The musky smell of the gym brought back memories of his old rugby days at Yale, cracking skulls and collecting teeth. Convinced he was alone, he headed silently to the showers. The three doors at end of the hall were marked, "MEN, UNISEX, WOMEN." The loud singing of opera directed him through the UNISEX door. He undressed and wrapped a gym towel around his waist. The steam of the shower concealed his presence from the singing director as Agent Hunt took his position in the next stall. Dr. Simon gracefully conducted himself through broken notes until he turned and almost jumped out of his skin. "Oh my! You frightened me so, I didn't hear you come in," he patted his heart. "Why, Agent Hunt I would never have guessed, I mean, you know, you coming in here and all," fanning his bent wrist. Still without a word Hunt took off his towel and stepped into the water. Simon stared in awe, "Ooh myyy, you are so big, I mean, tall. How tall are you? Six five?" he bumbled. Hunt continued to wash with Simon's eyes glued below his waist until the soap popped out his hand like a cork. "Oh my. Look at me. I dropped the soap. My, my I'm so clumsy," he laughed getting on his knees. He searched the floor blindly unable to break his trance until he hit the soap across the floor into Hunt's foot. "Oh my, I'm sorry," he crawled across the floor. He looked up when Hunt turned facing him, "Ooh my! Why am I so bad? I'm a bad, bad boy," he spanked his own hand. His mouth dropped open when Hunt ran his finger through his hair, with the other hand he lifted his chin. "Oh my, I'm," CRACK! In one swift motion Hunt broke his neck and watched his eyes roll up in his head as he withered to the floor like a wet noodle. Agent Hunt began humming Simon's song on his way out. "Real catchy tune," he thought.

The whole universe seemed to unfold to the silent glide of the XL-500. Lou studied the hologram carefully. It floated in mid-air to his front side with numeric data flowing like water down a fountain. After making a few adjustments and calculations, he enhanced the planetary alignments he was viewing. Though his mind told him Earth was a thing of beauty, seeing the purple glory of Mars bathing in the reflective light of its moons was a close second. After verifying his data he tapped his communications console, "Space station this is Exodus over," and waited for the delayed response. "Exodus this is Space station over." "Roger, Space station we're now approaching our dispersion point and all systems are green. I'm sending the ships' orbital coordinates and return data, over." Lou smiled as he heard the cheers in the background of the incoming transmission. "Congratulations Exodus, we copy, all systems green, data verified and all coordinates are locked. You're half way home, how's it look up there, over?" "Space station this Exodus. The view is spectacular! Tell Dr. Simon it's just like he said, an opal surrounded by pearls. I'm sure he'll love the photos we're sending back, over." Even with the delayed open link Lou noticed the sudden quiet of the background noise and no response. "Space station this is Exodus, did you copy my last transmission, over?" "Roger Exodus, you've haven't heard, it's just that Dr. Simon is no longer with us, over." "Hey, don't tell me the guy took that West coast job offer and cut out on us," he joked. "Negative Exodus, the last report we got from moon base was that he died in an accident, over." Lou now understood the moment of silence and responded. "Accident! What accident? Are the kids alright, over?" "Yes, Exodus the children are fine. The report indicated that the accident was domestic but still under investigation, over." "Understand Space station, Dr. Simon was a good man, our hearts and prayers go out to his family, over." "Roger Exodus, he will be missed by us all. Mr. Kehoe has already contacted the Cape and his family, over." "Kehoe? Space station did you say Kehoe, over?" "Roger Exodus, Mr. Kehoe has assumed supreme command over all space operations, over." Lou leaned back as if not surprised, "Wilco Space station, thanks for the update and we'll continue data feeds as our mission progresses, over." "Roger Exodus, all systems are on line and tracking, good luck, Space station, out." The internal frequency broke the brief silence, "Exodus this is Blue team leader over," said Troy. "Go ahead team leader." "Roger Exodus, I monitored your transmission with Space station, is Katie on this push?" "Yes, I'm here." "Good, were you able to regenerate this internal station with new comsec?" "Affirmative Blue team leader, only our fleet will be able to monitor and use this frequency, over." "Great, because I'm not buying Simon's accident, the quicker we finish up this mission the better." Troy could see the concern on Lou's face over the vid-com, "Roger that, there hasn't been anything over the net about Kehoe's files and I'm sure they know by now." Troy nodded in agreement, "That's why we have to stay on high alert. Katie how are we coming along?" Katie just smiled, "Tough program, he modified a few areas but nothing I can't handle. It shouldn't be long now, I'll transmit it over as soon as I'm finished." "Exodus, that sounds good, well Lou are we ready to do this?" "Roger Team leader, all coordinates have been updated and we are a go, over." "All stations this is Blue Team leader, prepare for dispersion on my mark in 3,2, 1." The small fleet of XL-500s' and the Mantaray escort broke formation to span the outer orbit of Mars. Katie watched her monitor intensely to ensure that everyone was on their programmed course. She beamed with pride at the precision execution of their plan. "So far so good," she thought. "All stations this is Exodus, let's keep this simple and do it by the numbers just like we trained. Commanders once you reach your designated coordinates activate and release your payloads and it's bye-bye Red planet. Your Mantarays will secure your sectors so you don't have to worry about your back door. We'll rendezvous back at this location, so be careful and stay alert," she said. Her plan was simple, it was just all the other unknown factors she worried about, bad guys and aliens. All they had to do was to get to the North, South, East and West fringes of Mars release their detectors and wait for the big bad black hole to gobble them up, done deal. "Lou, everyone is locked, we can move to the East sector. I'm heading down to cargo to begin activation, over." "OK doll, just kick back and enjoy the ride." When the thrusters kicked in he smiled at the hum of the reactors and checked his vid-com to see his Mantaray escorts. "Blue Team Leader this is Exodus over." "Gotcha your signal loud and clear Exodus" "This puppy rolls like my pop's old Caddy, how you holding up in your VW?" Lou could hear Troy laughing and watched the Mantaray barrel roll with ease. "I know you mean Porsche," came the reply. They both watched Katie come up on the vid-com barking, "That's enough goofing off you two, what's our ETA?" "About three hours," said Lou. "Good, let me know when we are over Mars, Katie out!" After a few seconds they both roared with laughter, "I guess we know who wears the pants in your family," cheered Troy. "I heard that Commander," she blasted back "Matter of fact, both you guys clear this freq and that's an order!"

The closer they got to the planet it seemed to change in color revealing why it was called the Red planet. It had been over an hour since they had spoken when Katie came in, "Are we over Mars yet?" Lou answered, "Yes, you may want to come up and see this." "Alright, we're all settled down here. I'll be right up." Lou pulled up a panoramic view of the surface and talked to Troy in the background. "I'll tell you what, this place gives me the creeps. The sooner we're out of here the better." "That's a big ten-four good buddy," Troy agreed. "That Kehoe has got to be the Angel of Death in disguise. When he shows up you can start your body count." "Hey I'm feeling you, that's why I'm hoping those files of his will give us some evidence."

Katie came in and sat next to Lou, "Speaking of the devil, I have good new and I have bad news, which do you want first?" "The good news," they both said together. "OK, the good news is that I've hacked his program and the bad news is all I need now is his password." Lou grabbed his head in frustration, "That's just great! We might as well call back and ask him for it, you'll never figure that out." Lou then saw the familiar wave of the index finger, "I don't see why not, after we started dating it took me all of twenty minutes to figure out your little jive password. You with all your slutty little e-mails." Lou just arched one brow and jested he was turning the key to his brain, "Woman you're out of your mind! That's like guessing a pentagon secret or who shot JFK from the grassy knoll." Katie just threw up the hand. "Yeah right, Loverman," watching his mouth drop in disbelief. Then turning her attention back to the vid-com, "As I was saying, the problem with most males are their egos. They always associate their passwords with their prowess or foul parts of their anatomy. Regardless, I'm running a thesaurus type program to assist with any possibilities." "Well good luck, because Kehoe put the K in Kinky," Lou huffed. "All I know about the guy is that he likes to hunt and fish. The word is he fired half his staff for disturbing him on a hunting expedition," Troy said. "They say the fool was out hunting Bigfoot," added Lou. "Hhmm now that's interesting, Bigfoot," she pondered. "Damn, it does look like a face," Lou pointed. The aerial view exposed the face of Mars that brought a quiet hush over the crew. Signals from the other XL-500s' started coming in confirming their safe arrival to their destinations. Lou kissed Katie before she departed to complete her mission. After suiting up, she verified the data programs of the neutron balls and awaited the signal to discharge her cargo. Earth's encounter with the aliens made it necessary to have an early detection system to protect the human race. After the events of that day nothing had been the same, races turned against one another until this glimmer of hope to defeat the plague. Being an astronaut meant there were no sides to take, only the commitment to serve the world as one community. What ate at her was all suffering and dying while the truth about this whole ordeal remained in Kehoe's files. As much as she wanted to believe in the system, so much had went wrong before it would work. When she thought of her father and all the years he pretended to be dead, a chill went up her spine. "What could make a man with his credentials do such a thing?" she thought. Her instinct kicked in before her reasoning over ruled with logic, bam! She hit the eject button to open the cargo hole, the ceiling began sliding back causing the weightless drift of the balls into dark space. "Katie, Katie! What's happening down there? Are you alright?" shouted Lou. She turned quickly to vid-com, "I'm fine honey, but listen to me closely. Contact all the commanders and have them jettison their loads now," she snapped. "Hell, we're still over five hundred miles away from our release points," he argued. She pounded feverishly away at her computer "It doesn't matter, the Cape will get the same data results. Damn it Lou! It's a trap! Don't you get it? Now get those people the hell out of there!" Troy flashed in, "Exodus this Blue team leader, I copied last transmission. She's right! They could have stopped us before we got a thousand miles. If they ambush us out here who would be the wiser? Just blame it on the aliens, done deal." Lou jerked up his helmet, "You two are about to drive me crazy. So, where the hell are we supposed to go from here? Over!" "It doesn't matter right now, just get everyone to this coordinate since we're the farthest point from the avenue of approach," said Troy. Lou bellowed, "All Stations this is Exodus. This is not a drill! I repeat, this is not a drill. Jettison your payloads now, I say again eject payloads now! Reason? Expect enemy ambush at your locations. Listen up commanders this is not a drill. Dump those loads and haul ass to this location, over." Troy couldn't believe he didn't foresee this earlier, now he just hoped they had enough time. A faint smile was all Katie was able to manage as small dots blinked on her monitor at the four sectors surrounding the outer orbit. The space station will now be able to detect any black hole developments. It's time to rid the world of another monster, Kehoe.

"Exodus this is USS Nile, package is dropped, heading to your location. No enemy activity in Alpha sector, over." "Nile this is Exodus, that's good news, just continue to bring it in, over." "Break! Break! Break! This is Manta Zero two, I'm at the Nile's six o'clock and we have incoming! There's too many to count, over." Troy jumped into action bringing up everything in Mar's orbit on his vid-com. The USS Nile commander reexamined his data, "Where? Exodus my readings are negative, over." "Manta Zero two this is Exodus, I have nothing on my scans either, are you sure?" The nervous Manta pilot repeated, "Exodus, if the Nile don't get that rust bucket moving, we'll all be toast, over." Lou struggled to get confirmation when Troy appeared on his screen. "Exodus this is Blue team leader, Zero two is right, they have to be Mantarays! That's why you can't detect them. I'm downloading my last scan, you should be seeing them now, over." Lou's heart almost skipped a beat when he saw the wave of ships coming into orbit. "My God! Attention all stations this is Exodus. They're all over. You're gonna have to light boost to get out of there. Do it now!" he shouted. The crews all braced for the power surges to kick in. Tracking the incoming ships with Kehoe's forces in hot pursuit, Lou thought the future didn't look too bright. Troy's mind spun with all the data and digital displays of the solar system, knowing he would have only minutes to devise an escape. Looking at the hologram the options were few to none. His military training kicked in to rule out any attempt to fight through this attack. That would be suicide. If it came to outrunning them, the XL-500s' didn't stand a chance. He stared in a trance while the enemy dots engulfed his screen with the ultimate attack. Lights of danger glowed within the cockpit slipping Troy into a place filled not with fear but rather with glory. His hand slowly reached past the Mars hologram into the heavenly rock clusters that surrounded the four planets. The light of blue he feared in his darkest dreams flickered in his hand and he fought to close it. The cries of reality crashed in bringing the movement in space to a fast blur. Lou shouted, "Troy, they're coming in hot! What's the plan?" "Just fire up that Caddy and hang on to your hat, big guy. We have a little jump on them but when I tell you to, I want all ships to drop their force fields, over." Troy could hardly keep a straight face seeing Lou up on the camera thumbing backward. "Hello! Drop the force fields? Earth to Bishop, we're going the wrong way! There's no help on Jupiter, thank you very much, keep the change!" Troy tapped his keypad, "From my calculations and their rate of closure we wouldn't make it to Jupiter. That's why I need the shields down when we go in." Lou watched the Jupiter illustration zoom out as the swirling vastness of the asteroid belt came into focus. "Troy, not the asteroid belt, there's no way we'll survive that." Troy switched the screen back to the pursuing Mantarays. "No, there's no way they'll survive that. We got one shot at this, so listen up. This asteroid belt has been around since our universe was formed, circling our four planets without smashing and losing it's pattern. If my theory is correct it's like the atom's neutrons, protons and electrons free floating and repelling when need be but any other force of nature will attract their polarity. It's probably been our barrier of protection since the beginning of time. That's why we have to shut down all power, only use your thrusters for guidance. When I give the word shut down all reactors. Ready! Now!" The sudden darkness was ghostly, the crews felt helpless entering the field of projectiles. Smash!

Already they were catching small fragments that shook even the big XL-500s'. "Steady, just remain calm," Troy reassured them.

At the moon base, Arthur Kehoe took joy in the unfolding mayhem. "Moon base we're under attack!" "Indeed you are," laughed Kehoe as he shut off the communication link. "Commander Randall this is moon base. Don't be worried about their pleas for help. I'm jamming all signals to Earth. Everything is going according to plan, call me once the job is finished, over." Kehoe took pleasure in the devilish grin on the vid-com. "Wilco moon base. I've got them in my crosshairs. This should be a breeze, time to finally punch Bishop's ticket, Red Team leader out."

The three scientists that waited for Kehoe at his door argued over who was to tell him. His quick hand gesture brought the trio forward, "Sir, you wanted us to report to you personally if there was any change in the kids conditions. We tried to warn you they couldn't withstand such transfusions, they lapsed into comas and we placed them on life support," one of the scientists said sadly. They waited for his response as he finished his data input on his console. "Such a pity. Did we achieve the quota I gave you?" he blandly stated. "Yes sir and then some." "Excellent, prepare them for transfer to Base Two. Then notify the Cape of our unfortunate loss, have them send replacements on the next shuttles. Be sure they compensate the families. We don't want any legal problems, now do we?" The three totally agreed leaving as quickly as they came. Kehoe calmly returned to his computer and awaited his selection. Information had come at a price unknown to many, countless bribes of government officials, dark alley deals and secrets taken from the lips of dying men. Knowledge was power and his was endless, spanning the globe turning brother against brother, reaching into the ancient chambers for forbidden whispers. His eyes gleamed upon viewing the Egyptian text, the ancient tongues divulged truths religion dared not. A lifetime spent seeking those things unspoken. Parables of young pharaoh's ruthless leadership for two hundred years but a modern autopsy showing they died before sixteen and what of the long lives of biblical figures? The only intelligent civilization documenting the worship of gods of other worlds, testaments of balls of fire from the heavens, scroll accounts of miracles and curses of and by man. Regardless if fable or truth, from tribes to temples, one mark appeared in all the ancient works, that of the Unspoken One. The dumb luck of some do-good doctors stumbling upon the greatest find of the ages then to lose it to an earthquake. If it weren't for government red tape he would have mowed that mountain down to an anthill. Fortunately for him, his agents were tracking Dr. Bishop's activities and were able to smuggle his findings out of the country. A flying chariot, no doubt coming from the babbling mouths of bush men and medical rejects. The intelligence community didn't buy into the hoax even with the pay-offs, and due to the biblical artifacts that did surface the security lid slammed so hard even the Pope stood guard. The turn of events in his quest came in the scrolls of Ramses Pharaoh of Egypt, he wrote, "It is the fourth season of the plague that has swept through my land. To the pleas of my people I have no answer as death grips us. Mercy on wings of fire lights the night sky, descending from the mountains were holy men of blackest skin. Their touch of light heals the plague sores. The priests were given medicines of the rocks from the sky joined with the blood of the chosen. When the people of Egypt began their healing they worshipped the visitors more than I. The priest brought before me these men of treason, their life's blood a token to Ramses, Ruler and Living God of Egypt. This entrusted secret of four lifetimes known only to the priest that searched the vast lands for the Ancient bearers, that their light eternal be known only to me." At first he thought

263

these were ramblings of a madman but many of the unidentifiable contents of Ramses's potions later identified by the Cape were found to contain compounds similar to that of lunar samples. Just as in the prophecies, Bishop's work held true to the plague's cure. Why not the secret known only to Ramses and his priest? Life eternal. Kehoe looked at the ancient drawings, "The two combined," he whispered. Agent Hunt entered and announced that the last medipod had been loaded. Kehoe smiled when he entered the transport looking at almost lifeless tiny faces. "My precious darlings once united with Sleeping Beauty your light will unlock the mysteries of the Unspoken One." Kehoe's expression turned serious when saw a red indicator light flash on one of the medipods. "Mr. Hunt, ensure the captain has the proper security codes to clear the laser fields, time is of the essence and we can't afford delays. Also have the medical staff prepare the Princess, I want to begin as soon as we arrive." Hunt departed noticing another pod light blinking, another one dead. This whole kid business wasn't his style, why keep them on life support? He watched the excitement on Kehoe's face as another light flashed and he smiled when the life supports kicked on. "Sick puppy," he mumbled closing the hatch.

CHAPTER FIFTEEN

Lou and all the pilots struggled to maintain their crafts within the turbulent rout of stone. The usually quiet ships now shrieked as if they were being dragged down a gravel road. He dared not think about the consequences of taking a direct hit from one of these baby mountains. Katie managed the bumpy trip to the co-pilot seat when Troy showed up on the vid-com. They could tell he was fairing no better. Katie spoke to Troy, "I've been trying to raise the moon base but they won't respond and all the walls are down on the program. I still don't have the stupid password." Troy flew upside down to avoid doom. "It's no wonder with Kehoe running the show. All stations, listen up. Some of these asteroids have gorges large enough to set down in, use your reactors only when you have to. If my hunch is right all hell is going to break loose when they enter this energy field so we need to take cover quickly, over." "Wilco, over," they sounded off. The seconds felt like minutes as they drifted into gaps and caves with their Mantarays taking defensive postures. Troy's comms link flashed indicating traffic on the moon base frequency. "Bishop, I know you can hear me. You can run but can't hide!" Randell boasted. Troy recognized the voice but didn't say a word. He thought how he never liked the guy anyway, rotten to the core. He would never forget the first day of Top Gun training. While everyone was standing on a class break, Randell found a kitten in one of the corners of the hangar. All the guys were mad at how cruel he was to bring the kitten so close to the deafening jet engines. He had just waved them off smiling and innocently tossed the kitten into the monstrous engines. The next thing Troy remembered, his classmates were pulling him off Randell. Randy the Raccoon was his name in school from the two black eyes Troy gave him, beginning the bad blood between the two.

When the wave of Mantarays entered the field, the dark space was streaked with lightning. Swirls like the aurora borealis whipped the asteroids into a frenzy. Rex Randall shouted his charge, "Nothing can save your sorry ass now, Bishop!" The Mantarays lashed out, the might of their lasers blasting at the core of the asteroids. The dance of the stones no one could have envisioned as the flow of their motion halted and struck at the foreigners with the vengeance of the heavens. From inside the asteroids the crews watched in amazement, the space around them came alive bursting through the enemy Mantarays like missiles of stone. With no escape, the enemy Mantarays were pounded from all directions. The asteroid field sought out its intruders like the fury of a tornado, penetrating their hulls like hot coals dropped in snow. The ones that got even close to the hidden crews were picked off from defensive positions. The bright orange explosions could be seen across the vastness of the field, signaling the end of Randall's Raiders. Troy's ship faced out firing at the incoming ships. Those he didn't get were knocked off by the hurling asteroids. There was no escape. The small asteroids beat at them until larger asteroids finished them off. The screams of the doomed fleet could be heard when Troy observed a flaming Mantaray heading straight toward his location, "I've got a lock on you now Bishop, your voodoo can't stop me, I'm gonna get you, Bishop!" he watched the bloodied face of Randall on his screen. Watching the tracking indicator as Randall tried to get a lock to fire, Troy's face appeared on his vid-com, "Same old Rex, you know it don't have to be like this." Randall got Troy on target, "Enough talk, now you die!" He saw Troy smiling, pointing as if to say, you better watch out, right before he fired his lasers. Out of the corner of his eye he finally saw it, SMASH!!! The gigantic asteroid zonked him out like a Mack truck taking out a dragonfly trying to cross the road. It swept across so fast Troy only saw a bright flash and a tiny puff of smoke in the blur. He saw no other surviving Mantarays on his screen. Troy closed his eyes at the thought of all the senseless deaths. Suddenly his memories swept him to his childhood, his mother reading the bible to him before bed. He loved the stories, though many were so sad, the one that stood out was the story of Moses. What this asteroid field and the Red Sea had in common didn't matter, he just thanked the Lord for seeing them through. He sat watching the wreckage float past as space returned to normal. Troy scanned his instruments and called out to his fleet, "All stations this is Blue team leader, is everyone ok, over?" All stations answered in sequence that they were fine until it got to Lou. "Well this is Exodus, would somebody please tell me what the hell just happened? Is this the twilight zone or something?" he yelled. "If I had to say, we just got a hand from the big guy, if you know what I mean," Troy replied. Lou shook his head in disbelief, "When I get my hands on that Kehoe, all this crap because he's pissed off because he didn't bag Big Foot! I'll give him big foot, right where the sun don't shine." Troy was glad to hear the laughter of the crews. At least he knew their spirits were still up. "What did you just say?" Katie asked. Lou began repeating, "I said I'm gonna kick his," "No, the part about Big Foot? Wait, let me try something," she began typing. "SASQUATCH" "That's it! Troy we did it," she screamed. "I told you, the typical male ego, in full effect. Just figure out his fantasy and bingo, the firewall is down," she rejoiced. "Troy I'm sending you a copy as it downloads," she said as Lou butted in, "You mean the boy fantasizes about Big Foot, now that's nasty!" So it came down to this Troy thought watching Kehoe's files materialize before his eyes. Maybe now they could get at the truth. "I'm getting them, great job and Katie," he paused, "thanks." His voice trembled. She knew the sadness was the same as what she was feeling. Maybe airing Kehoe's dirty laundry would shed some light and bring about some closure. All the things her Dad had revealed were so unreal that it was hard to comprehend a human being committing such hideous acts. He was able to crawl away after being left for dead and even hearing the story on the ship she didn't want to believe it. Kehoe represented the Institution of the civilized world, the American way, mom's apple pie but anyway you sliced it he was just another thug in a suit. Inside she felt so stupid and used, like she had turned her back on her father that day. All the years feeling sorry for herself and there her father, limping riddled with scars from the gun shots and she still dared to question his integrity. It stood to reason that they would need more evidence. After almost being murdered themselves and having the files, she could understand the plea in her father's eyes for her to believe him. The tears began to flow as the impact sunk in. If she didn't believe him, she could only image him trying to go to the police. She didn't want to think about what poor Troy was going through, with both parents gone. In a breath she realized this struggle had brought them all together cementing the bond that she had always felt for Troy, one like that of a sister for a brother. So after hearing his thanks, her only reply was, "No Troy, thank you." Lou stuck his mug to the screen, "Can we get a group hug and get the hell out of here!" Lazily the asteroids drifted as if nothing had happened, the calm after the storm. One burst was all it took to lift off from their rock havens and this time no one questioned having their reactors off. The Mantarays swayed between the asteroids like feathers in the wind, so peaceful was this place that no question or doubt crossed his mind of whose glory he had been blessed to witness.

Just as instructed, Kehoe's staff of doctors stood in a circle waiting in a glass enclosure. They did not turn to look when the pressure locks released upon his entry, fixated in a reverie speechless. The soft hiss of the medipods did not disturb them, only Kehoe's steps on the stainless floor gave notice for them to part. "Ah my beauty! The life of the party aren't you?" The delicate silhouette hung in a balance of air inches above the surgical table enveloped in an angelic mist of purple and blue. Slowly Kehoe walked her length, barely tracing her exquisiteness with one hand causing twinkles like pixie dust to sparkle and float revealing the eloquent nakedness of her skin. He bent close as if to kiss her lips, "My darling princess, they know not what you are but I know the miracle that can be. Unlocking the secrets of the Unspoken One is my crowning achievement, with your life fluid and the blood of the children of the gift, eternal life will be mine!" His eyes flashed wildly. Filled with pleasure, he turned shouting, "Bring the children and start the procedure." The medipods were moved closer forming a circle around the alien princess. The floor rose in a pyramid with Zenani above, the connecting tubes already flowed red with blood of the children. A panel opened on the surgeon's table beneath the girl shining a light on the back of her neck, from a hidden section slowly came the sinister hypodermic needle aiming toward her nape. The complex filtration system trapped the trickling blood from the medipods, extracting the wanted amino acid Valine. A hush came over the room as the needle entered the base of her skull, expecting screams of pain when her eyes and mouth opened they all shivered at what sounded liked cries of a whale. Blue tears dropped from the pearl black eyes while the clear fluid oozed down the tube. Sadly the moan lasted moments after the needle came out and her eyes closed again. Kehoe stood transfixed when the fluid finally united with the blood and swirled into a wonderful emerald green. "Run the test, quickly you fools," he shouted. He had already begun to roll up his sleeve in anticipation of his injection. "Sir, you can't be serious. It will take months of testing before we can confirm it's outcome," one doctor argued. "Is it compatible to that of the tomb?" Kehoe continued to swab his arm. "Yes sir, but there's no certainty!" he plead. Kehoe yanked the serum from his hand and held it up to measure his draw. They all looked to Agent Hunt to be the voice of reason, but he stood steadfast with his usual emotionless glare as they all stared in horror. Arthur Kehoe didn't blink as he stabbed into the basilar vein and squeezed down until the deed was done. "Moon base this the Cape, come in, moon base this is the Cape over," blared the signal. Agent Hunt answered the call keeping his eyes on Kehoe. "Cape this is moon base, over." "Thank God. Is everything okay up there? Our sensors picked up a massive sound wave, we thought it was some type of explosion, over." Hunt's eyes stay glued to Kehoe as he began stumbling and convulsing in pain. "Moon base, you wouldn't believe what's happening down here, it's a zoo! Birds have flocked to the sky by the thousands, wild animals are running throughout cities and reports are coming in from sea captains of dolphins and other sea life going berserk. Are you experiencing any problems on your end, over." The doctors surrounded Kehoe as he reeled and flopped about as if he was on fire. "Cape this is moon base, everything is good on our end, we'll contact you if we have any problems, out." Hunt went over and pushed the doctors out of the way as they stood and watched. "Don't just stand around, give him mouth to mouth or something. What kind of doctors are you? Get out my way!" Kehoe lay balled in the fetal position when Hunt rolled him over. What they saw made them all stand back. The old man began transforming before their eyes, the wrinkles dissolved from his face, his gray turned to blonde and before them was a blue-eyed young man. "Agent Hunt, you look as though you've seen a ghost," said Kehoe. Hunt took his arm and turned him to the glass to see his reflection. Kehoe touched his face in amazement, "Holy

Secrets of the Pharaohs, it worked! Hunt, it worked," he celebrated. The staff and guards all shook hands and cheered as Agent Hunt watched silently. Young Kehoe laughed with the group until he spied Hunt unshaken, "Agent Hunt, is there a problem?" he asked. Hunt continued to check the computer read-outs without a word. Kehoe raised his hand for silence, "Please everyone, I need a word alone with Agent Hunt, if you could just step into the other room and give us a moment," he motioned. After a few whispers the guards and doctors quietly moved into next sound proof glass room. Agent Hunt still didn't look away from his computer as Kehoe walked up to the console and turned looking at the group watching for a chance to read their lips. "Farewell dear friends," they read as Kehoe pressed the button securing the air-locks on the doors. Panic and despair engulfed them as the ceiling opened to the moon's deadly atmosphere. Hunt remained undaunted as bodies floated into space.

When a cry is heard across the land the same can be said of the universe. The mystery of life that is truly misunderstood is that everything and everyone intertwine; pain and death reverberate throughout the universe. Zenani's plea echoed among the stars. The cry came sweeping down the mountains and valleys of Zion, through the tranquil land, home of all souls at journeys anew. The wild, serene gardens seemed to sway with the burden of death's whisper. Balimar, lost in his daily meditation, only faintly felt the stir around him. The weeping willows danced as if caught by a sudden breeze. The beasts in the garden began to quiet and seek shelter. Even Balimar's familiar, a great saber toothed tiger, began to prowl restlessly at the foot of the stone stairs where Balimar now pled in silence for his wife, daughter and his homeland. Such upheaval in this lovely, wild place was unusual. Serenity was the only refuge he had since Zenani had been left on Earth and Kasha had returned wounded gravely within and without. She had become a shell of her former self, taking on all the blame and guilt for the loss of her only child. Balimar had tried without end or success to reach her inside the cocoon she had made for herself. She had gone into a catatonic state in order to keep her mind linked to Zenani. God only knew the pain this brought her to commune daily with a child she could not save. His only hope was to return for Zenani and now that time drew near. The passage would open soon and he would be able to restore his wife's spirit and bring his daughter home. He repeated his desires for help and strength as the voice of his daughter shook him where he stood. A great shadow soared above him and he knew where the dactyl was headed. Kasha had summoned the prehistoric bird to carry her to her sacrifice. He knew as well as she that Zenani was in great peril and that to live she must receive the life force from one of them. He shouted and startled all the animals into flight including the huge tiger. He ran for his chariot and blazed toward the Keep. The dactyl took flight as Balimar neared the castle. He could see his beloved riding on the back of the winged lizard. He tried to link with her telepathically, but she resisted him. He pleaded once more as he had in Serenity. He could not face time eternal without Kasha at his side. He needed her, especially now that Zenani was in danger. He could not lose them both, forever, not after all this time. In an instant his chariot raced faster towards the summit of the volcano that would surely be Kasha's grave if he failed. He was so close when he heard the dactyl scream and saw Kasha dive from the beasts' back toward the gaping volcano. "Nooooo! My beloved," he wailed as he doubled his effort, straining himself beyond his limit to reach her. He caught her and the chariot tipped precariously with the impact. Kasha struggled against his embrace and the tortured look on her haggard, tear-strewn face broke his heart. He held her tightly until her strength was gone. "My love, you cannot lose faith. I need you. We will trust that the Unspoken One will be awakened before all hope is gone. I felt her calling us. I know she is weak. There is time, a little, but it is all we need. The passageway is open. I can feel it. We will leave now." For Kasha there were no words, only tears of blue. Balimar landed the chariot in the open field beside his Sun cruiser, carrying Kasha through the gathered faithful holding his beloved close to heart. The ships of the Ancient Ones hovered by the thousands ready to retrieve their princess.

Troy knew when he saw the dim pulse of the blood star in his hand that something was dreadfully wrong. Kehoe's files spilled everything about the murder of his parents and the capture of the alien princess. He knew now that all these years it was she in his thoughts and dreams, warning him of dangers and somehow making him feel loved when there was no one in his life. It was her light that had glowed in his life but now that light was almost gone. When the Mantarays finally broke the asteroid field the bright stars filled him with hope. "All stations this is Blue team leader, what's your status, over?" he asked. After his squadron answered, Katie came on the vid-com, "Troy, I'm getting adverse reading from the neutron balls, something is going on and after seeing those files there's no way Kehoe will let us make it back to Earth alive. What are going to do?" Troy knew what she was saying was true but he also knew the kids and Zenani were in grave danger with each passing moment. "You're right but just maybe we can use the chaos with the aliens to our advantage. Right now those kids are probably dying because I delivered them to that monster, so it's my responsibility to try to get them out." The radio frequency disrupted with disagreements, "No way, Jose', we're all in this together" said the chorus. "If only we could get a message to General Solomon, if he saw these files they would be up here in a heartbeat, but with Kehoe jamming all our satellite transmissions there's no way." Lou popped his fingers trying to remember, "Hey I've got it!

What if we used a Russian satellite?" "So where will we be getting one of those?" Katie sighed. "Alex, our Science Officer, all of us aren't from South Central if you haven't noticed. My man, just happens to be a Black Russian, he patches through and chats with his buds all the time." Troy was feeling it now as he shouted, "Yes, it's on now! Katie get with Alex and send everything we've got and even if it don't get through with all the spying we do on each other they're bound to intercept it anyway. All stations prepare to jump, Lou let's swing wide and give Dr Frankenstein a chance to greet his guests and bust him in the chops with a little surprise of our own." The Mantarays and XL-500s' surged making their jump as Katie watched in astonishment as the neutron images disappeared from her screen, "My God, a whole sector gone, our studies of the previous reflexes wasn't this big." "That's because they only snuck in one ship. This time I've got a feeling they're bringing along the kitchen sink," Lou laughed. "Lou's got a point, it's the girl they want. If Earth is to avoid a bloodbath we've got to save them before it's too late," said Troy.

The alert was sounded on the moon base as Kehoe scrambled his reserves, "Well at least the advance warning system worked as we wanted, have we heard anything from Commander Randall?" Agent Hunt studied the large screen showing their deployment, "Not yet, knowing Randall he won't let a single ship escape and that asteroid field looks pretty tricky." Kehoe laughed, "So true, and are our little friends still alive?" "The life support is holding well but with the girl it's hard to say," he studied the monitor. " No matter, strange fruit is bountiful on earth and with the princess as bait the Unspoken One will be next." Here was proof of the hidden secrets of the pharaohs. Now he understood why they sought these people, but there was so much more. Even with battle at hand he couldn't take his eyes away from the ancient text. He had learned that modern translations only scratched the surface of what was written. His world travels had opened his eyes to things unknown to many, speaking over twenty different languages and knowing more of these distant places than the natives, reading and writing the tongues long forgotten. To him, extremes were lived. The words of a mountain man translated by a scholar are misinterpreted as much as the slang of today's youth. "All this time, this story has been before us and when a chosen few did figure the secrets, they acted. Tribal chiefs, kings, pharaohs all ruled the world. Now it's my time to master the universe," he thought. "Agent Hunt, I'm going to the command center. If we can stop the aliens at Mars those fools on Earth won't have a clue about the prize we have."

Troy's plan to give the XL-500s better concealment by surrounding them with the Mantarays had worked so far, the signatures they gave were small enough to go unnoticed with all the activity going on. They prepared to come out of the hyper-jump as they approached the moon's orbit, "Alright team, there's a perimeter of laser cannons around the moon base that we have to knock out, so we'll set down about five miles out. Once the teams reach the objective, branch out and set the charges. We blow the entrances at the same time so we can be on them before they know what hit them. Katie when we give the signal come in hot, the underground laser we'll have to eliminate on the inside," Troy briefed. Katie cleared her throat, "Excuse me, let's backup to the underground planet killer. Come in hot, hello? How bout we blow the laser then give the damn signal!" she demanded "That's why this woman is my soulmate, cause she keeps it real," laughed Lou. "I'm not laughing! Read my lips, do not call me until you blow the laser. Your butt will be sitting here eating moon pies waiting on a ride," she huffed blocking his attempt to kiss her. Troy ran footage of the base layout he got from Kehoe's files. "OK, you heard the lady we've got to nix the laser. Keep it low going in and use the shadows to avoid detection. Let's set it down and good luck," he said. The surface came up fast as Lou eased the craft down where Troy had plotted. Quickly the teams flowed out taking up the defensive until the Mantarays touched down and their pilots slid out. "1,3,6 flank left, 2,4,5 go right, ten mikes to plug your bugs in five more we blow the dam, move out," he barked. Silently the manta-suits hissed lifting the men into flying positions, within seconds they dispersed in different directions to their assigned targets. In the distance the night light glittered on the metallic lasers as Lou and Troy flew up to one, each removed a digital pulse bomb from his belt and slapped them against the metal. Time was already ticking down, the small dark figures flew from object to object until all targets were complete and then set their sights on the main compound. Troy took a high approach on the two guards and dropped in boot to face on them while Lou trimmed door with his remaining bombs. The clock showed thirty seconds as they took cover and with a quick wave everyone knelt down removing weapons and activating wrist lasers. KABOOM! BOOM! BOOM! The dust balls rose with flashes of fire flying from the entrance. They rushed in with pulse lasers blazing. Troy was actually glad to see Kehoe's troops taking guard, there was no way of knowing which way this conflict was going but there was no need for innocents to die. The blown airlocks sucked the oxygen from those not prepared while others moved clumsily in the old standard suits. Lou zoomed low firing from the hip, "Man I feel like one of those superheroes," he blasted away. "Who Superman?" "Naw brother, Shaft!" he laughed. Troy's elite soldiers laid down discipline firepower zigzagging about the complex hitting their marks. The explosions rocked the foundation as Kehoe fought to stay in his seat. "Come in Hunt! What the hell is going on?" he shouted. Agent Hunt scanned the security cameras, "It's Bishop, but this time I'll finish him myself," he huffed. "Well see that you do, I've got aliens barking through this black hole like the hounds of hell," he screamed. Guts and body parts floated past as the fight came closer to Agent Hunt, he could already see his men in fast retreat. "Get out there and kill them," he yelled at his last line of defense. He now stood alone in the medical ward watching the fierce battle. So close was the action that Troy flew delivering pulse punches which were just as lethal as his laser cannons. The power of the blood star burned life into his hand the closer he got to the princess, "Just hang on, I'm coming," he thought. Lou and Troy finally reached the entrance of the lab resting their backs to the wall, "You ready? I'm going left, go!" A quick explosion erupted and blew them both head over heels, "What the hell was that?" Lou yelled as he wrenched in pain. Troy moaned, "Try a dump truck! What kind of laser packs a punch like that?" They could hear Agent Hunt's voice blaring past the pain in their aching eardrums. "Oh, so the Bishop boy has returned. Such a pity what happened to your parents that dreadful night. How jolly it's been to watch you all these years, having not a clue of the web that lay before you. Come out, come out, wherever you are," blasting the instruments about them. "I'm sure you're wondering what this little beauty is that I have. Well thanks to your, shall we say forgotten ancestors, a gift I lifted from your Dad in Africa. Who, just like you, didn't have any idea what he was dealing with. I know you have seen the files, your people! Your people have always been the harvest for the world. Look at it as the gift, all this from your princess and those blabbing kids. LOOK!" Troy leaned and peered around the console seeing Hunt injecting himself, then blasting a hole in the floor when Lou moved to get around him. In the rear of lab he could see the medipods, "What kind of cannon is that?" Troy brushed some rubble off his head, "I don't know. It looks like some kind of staff." The light disintegrated all it blasted as Hunt twirled from the sweet elixir, "Kehoe never knew about this little treasure I kept for myself, I was there the day your father crashed from that mountain. "Omed" he whispered in his daze as I pried it from his grip. I knew only the empire Kehoe had at his disposal could unravel the mysteries of the Ancient Ones. Now, the blood of ancient ones courses through my veins and with the Scepter of Omed, I can't be stopped. So come on out Bishop or my next blast will be to the head of your beloved princess." Troy stood slowly to face the youthful Hunt against Lou's protests. "Don't do this man, that's a crazy man with a smoking stick. Come on brother we can take him." Troy shook his head as if there were no other options, "Naw, their lives are non-negotiable," as he stepped forward. This was the face he remembered from so long ago, from the shadows of his nightmares, through the tears of a frighten dazed child. He saw also the face of the child in the woman lying next to him, looking out the window of the van, lost but extending hope. How beautiful she was! Frozen in time with her spirit reaching out touching his very soul, I remember all, he thought. The cool night breeze that eased her flight that first night, his little heart fluttering with its schoolboy's crush at love's first sight. Closer he came to the only thing in his life that mattered, someone he'd not seen but had loved his whole life, for this being, this woman, he would gladly give his own life. It was this fiend that turned his world upside down, stole the lives of so many good people. In his hand ached the bloodstar with each step up the platform, as did his heart seeing the faint moisture on the glass of the medipods. Troy bent slowly through the fairy dust that surrounded Zenani and kissed her ever so gently. He couldn't figure what made him do it, only that he didn't want to lose her now. Before he could stand, WHAM! Agent Hunt's sweeping blow with the scepter crackled with lightning hurling him across the room into a heap. "Hell naw, I know you didn't just blindside my boy like that," Lou came up firing. Hunt turned and blasted without a care taking out half the room blowing Lou back outside to the hallway. Agent Hunt drifted over to Troy's limp body and lifted him by the collar, "I'm not finished with you yet Boy Wonder. How do you like your hero now, princess?" WHACK! A strike more deadly than the first sent him back across the room. Hunt, with one leap, sailed through the air and stood over him again. He laughed and lifted him once more, "This is why they left this planet because they were weak like you and the pharaohs took what they wanted, their blood." SLAP! Another blow came, so hard it knocked him back on the platform below Zenani. Troy lay outstretched below his love trying to muster the strength to continue the fight. Troy watched the bloodstar growing dim in his hand as a teardrop from Zenani fell into his palm. Dust flew as Hunt's boots landed at his head, "No more games boy, now you die." Troy felt the fire in his hand as Agent Hunt yanked him to his feet. He struck Hunt with no remorse, his open hand pierced his chest like a hot knife cutting butter and he yanked, hard. In the door he saw Lou struggling to stand, "Give Katie the signal," Troy shouted. Hunt's eyes widened when Troy held up his bloody heart, with a dying effort he still tried to choke Troy. "But I'm immortal," he choked. "Oh yeah," said Troy as he crushed the heart and watched Agent Hunt crumble like a sack of potatoes. Lou limped as he led in the soldiers, "Quickly, let's get them out!" Troy lifted Zenani into his arms and grabbed the Scepter as he followed them out of battle torn lab. He didn't think much about the explosions and sparks flying, he was just glad they were all alive. At the entrance they could see Katie soaring in with the XL-500's and waited for the dust storm to subside. Lou guided Tina's medipod himself as they began the long walk to the ship. The XL-500's could only land safely a thousand meters away from the complex, about half way they saw the cargo bay opening. Lou waved at Katie sitting in the cockpit, "Lou is everyone okay?" she asked.

"They're in bad shape. The kid's are hanging on by life support." Suddenly they could see the ground rumbling beneath the XL-500's and for a second they stopped in flight. They heard a loud grinding noise and saw the ground of the crater open. They tried to pick up the pace. They saw Katie waving, "Hurry up, guys! Please tell me that that's not what I think it is?" Troy flew up to Lou, "Here take Zenani and get out of here, I have some unfinished business." Before they could start loading the medipods, the demonic cannon stood erect aiming directly at them. Troy made out a face in the glass dome control room, Kehoe. He stopped and hovered placing himself in the middle as the last medipod loaded. Proudly Troy held out the scepter, "It's over, Kehoe. You've got what you wanted so now let the children go, this is between you and I." Kehoe didn't bother to ponder the idea, "I overheard your and Hunt's little chat, such a shame you can't find good help these days. There's no honor amongst thieves. Omed's scepter belongs to me. You know nothing of it's powers or what you're dealing with. Your deaths will all be in vain. By the way, your little message got through. Do you really think they would believe some dead black renegade astronauts over me? How quickly you have forgotten your American history, my boy. Troy turned to the ship, "Did you get all that?" "Yes Troy, they should be getting the delay transmission about now," Katie answered. Troy turned back to Kehoe, "You see Kehoe, it is a fact that people don't like to be made fools out of either, so we're even." Troy saw the anger in his face as he propelled the laser's reactors to fire, "Fool, you don't even know how to use the scepter so you all die!" The shrieking pitch the laser made before it destroyed the asteroid when he was on the dark side of the moon was one he would never forget. Out of nowhere, a soft hand touched his on the scepter igniting his bloodstar, Zenani. Without a spoken word their minds linked, "Trust in thy glory, my prince. You are the

Unspoken One." Together they raised the Scepter of Omed as Kehoe fired his laser. A bright light momentarily blinded all near or far. A large field of blue shielded the two that hung in the heavens, then released it's own fury of fire melting the laser with Kehoe screaming in the inferno.

Lou and Katie joined the cheers of the crew watching the pair drift slowly to the ground in a warm embrace. Seeing pieces of the laser crash to the ground, Troy and Zenani both felt their nightmare was over but the warm tingle in their palms said something all together different. As Troy and Zenani joined the ship the cheers quieted as everyone looked at the children in the medipods. "Troy there's a chance we can save them." Katie said. Lou just sighed, "I don't see how, if we take them off the life support they will surely die." "What do you mean?" Troy asked. Katie looked at Zenani, "Zion, take them back to Zion. It's their only chance, on that world they could heal." They watched Zenani fill the compartment with the warmth of her blue light. "Who told you that?" Lou asked. "She did, before leaving the ship. It's a place of healing, where their spirits could soar. She touched me and I could see it just as plain as day, the garden of life. Lou you said yourself they wouldn't survive." "Not on our world honey," he whispered as he held Katie. She pled with Lou, "But Zion is their home," she whispered. The light faded as Zenani turned. Troy asked her, "Is this true?" She slowly nodded, "It is, they bear the gift that shines with the light of Zion, if they aren't taken soon their souls shall return later." Troy felt the truth in her words and turned to Lou. "It's your call my friend, what she says is true." Lou sadly touched Tina's pod, "I would do anything to have her well again. Let's contact the Cape, the families should have the final word." Katie kissed his cheek and went up the deck to call back to the Cape. Lou held his head down in shame at the thought of what was happening to the children. "I feel as though we let them down, all the signs were there. We were supposed to protect them but instead we put them on a platter and fed them to a madman." "My brother, even those with the best intentions can be misled," Troy said. "It would have been an entirely different outcome if we hadn't come this far. We were the chosen." Katie came up on the net, "Hey you guys, I got General Solomon on the push and he should be here any minute. All the families have been contacted and we should have the word soon. We have some visitors." Troy glanced at the screen then to Zenani, "It's the Ancient Ones alright, looks like they have Kehoe's defense team in tow with some kind of beam. Zenani looked into the heavens and linked with Troy, "We have always come in peace, it is not the way of Balimar to destroy what we have vowed to protect. The power we serve is much greater than any man or woman, only time will tell if wounds will heal between Earth and our people." Katie entered with a smile from ear to ear, "Look, the general has arrived, maybe with the right people we can start to mend some fences." "What a sight to see!" Troy thought, the cavalry arriving after the battle, just like in the movies. Still it was a good sign, watching the Earth spacecrafts on one side and the Ancient Ones on the other. The face of General Solomon came on the vid-com with greetings, "Commander Bishop, all the families and the World Counsel have been briefed and brought up to speed on the crimes committed by Arthur Kehoe not only against humanity but also our gracious neighbors. There is much the world has been in the dark about and it is our hope for lasting peace with the Ancient Ones. The families have humbly consented to allow the assistance of our friends in this time of need." There was no response directly from the Sun cruiser as it landed near the site. It lowered a platform revealing the magnificent Balimar with Kasha at his side. The soldiers of his bronze guard in their darkness moved like the night as they began collecting the medipods. Mother and daughter came together at last in the middle of the barren plain in such an embrace that a tear of blue came down the cold dark face of Balimar. He embraced Zenani and held high his bloodstar as Kasha joined her husband and daughter. Troy turned to Lou and Katie and called for one last group hug and freely they cried. "I guess this is my cue, you know I will take care of Tina and the kids. When they're better and your little balls start to beep, you'll know we're coming home. Thanks guys for all your love and support, just help the world understand what we already know. I think I am going to enjoy this love thing." He smiled as Zenani took his hand. Troy stepped onto the platform as it began to close, swirling in a mist of blue, four bloodstars could be seen…SWOOSH they went across the heavens.

B. A. Floyd

ABOUT THE AUTHOR

B.A. Floyd enters the literary world with this debut novel, *Anemia*. The author has traveled extensively and finally settled in the last frontier, Alaska. *Anemia* involved four years of research, writing, and inspiration for B.A. Floyd. Although never before published, the author has written several pieces that may soon be on bookshelves for fans to enjoy. *Anemia* is the first of many adventures for the author and the reading public.

www.ingramcontent.com/pod-product-compliance
Lightning Source LLC
Chambersburg PA
CBHW030253290526
45785CB00001B/68